The American Quarter Horse

Also by Steven D. Price

The American Quarter Horse

An Introduction to Selection, Care,
and Enjoyment

Steven D. Price

THE LYONS PRESS

AQHA MISSION

To record and preserve the pedigrees of the American Quarter Horse while maintaining the integrity of the breed;

To provide beneficial services for its members which enhance and encourage American Quarter Horse ownership and participation;

To generate growth of AQHA membership via the marketing, promotion, advertising, and publicity of the American Quarter Horse.

Printed in the United States of America

10 9 8 7 6 5 4 3 2

Designed by Joel Friedlander, Marin Bookworks
Photographs courtesy of AQHA

Library of Congress Cataloging-in-Publication Data
Price, Steven D.
    The American quarter horse / Steven D. Price.
        p. cm.
    Includes index.
    ISBN 1-55821-643-X
    1. Quarter horse. I. Title.
SF293.Q3P75 1999
636.1′33—dc21   98-19132
                                                                              CIP

Contents

A Message from the American Quarter Horse Association

American Quarter Horse Association members and owners continually tell us that information and education are essential to fully enjoying their horses. While AQHA publishes many reference materials, this book marks a notable step in the Association's education and communication efforts.

For most of us, becoming involved with horses is a significant decision. Chances are you would never make a decision about any comparable hobby, business, or purchase without doing your homework. This book is an important source of information that can benefit people exploring the wonderful world of horses for the first time. It also is an important reference tool for owners who want a solid guide to responsible horse care and a variety of equestrian activities.

We all know friends, neighbors, co-workers, and family members who express an interest in becoming involved with horses, and it is so important they receive encouragement and advice to get started in the right direction. I encourage every veteran horse owner to welcome these newcomers and present them with a copy of this book. You can be especially important in assisting a family that has a child interested in horses.

Throughout the 1990s, the AQHA Executive Committee has made communication a high priority, and we owe a special thank-you to the committee members for their support of this publishing initiative. Serving on the AQHA Executive Committee during the life of this project were J. D. Blondin, Jerry Windham, Ken Smith, Mike Perkins, Ginger Hyland, and Don Burt. We owe special thanks to Don Burt, author of several books including *Winning with the American Quarter Horse,* for writing the introduction. His insight into the world of horses encompasses nearly every breed of horse in North America.

Researching, writing, and publishing this book would not have been possible without the experience and knowledge of Steven D. Price. With dedication and patience, Steve kept the project moving forward. Whenever we were unsure of the next step, his guidance was like that of a reassuring hand starting a colt.

American Quarter Horse Association employees also contributed to this book, sharing professional and personal advice on horse care and enjoyment. Employees from the Marketing Services, Publications, Racing and Show Departments, and the American Quarter Horse Heritage Center & Museum played major roles in refining the book, reviewing the manuscript, and selecting the illustrations.

AQHA is fortunate to have good working relationships with a stable full of corporate sponsors and several other associations in the equine industry. I thank all those that contributed photographs to make this book more enjoyable and informative.

In closing, let me say that while I am excited about the broad areas covered by *The American Quarter Horse: An Introduction to Selection, Care, and Enjoyment*, this book is by no means a complete guide to the world of American Quarter Horses. I encourage you to utilize the resources listed in the book to expand your knowledge. There are countless organizations, resources, and people available to help you and your horse.

On behalf of the American Quarter Horse Association and my own horse, Larks Smooth Move, I wish you a truly rewarding experience.

Good reading and good riding.

—Bill Brewer
AQHA Executive Vice President

Foreword

It's been said that "the history of mankind was written on horseback," and no better example can be found than in the American Quarter Horse's contribution to our culture. Exploring the background of the American Quarter Horse and its role in America's heritage will increase your appreciation of not only the breed but horses in general.

This book will give you an insight into the various kinds of riding and driving activities that will allow you to enjoy the versatility of the American Quarter Horse. If you are just getting acquainted with horses, it will answer your basic questions. What do horses eat? Where and how could I keep one? What happens if he gets sick? What equipment do I need? What do I wear? In what events can I participate?

It will teach you how to care for and work with horses and their equipment. This knowledge, along with how to develop a support team, such as other horse owners, veterinarians, farriers, feed and tack dealers, and professional horsemen, will help guide you through your relationship with horses.

The best teacher of all, however, is the horse himself. When you become a student of the horse, you'll discover the animal will tell you everything, if you care to pay attention. The basic areas of communication are the eyes and ears along with body language (yours and the horse's). This volume will teach you how to *see,* and not just look at a horse. There is no magic secret to the horse, it simply takes knowledge, time, and desire to fully appreciate the merits of this animal.

The horse only thinks in one place at a time and his basic instincts are fear (trust), mating (companionship), and hunger (food). Understanding his responses will greatly increase the effectiveness and pleasure you will derive from your horse. A horse doesn't think like a person, but a person can learn to think like a horse.

One of the greatest pleasures the horse industry extends is the opportunity to share knowledge. This book will show you how to take full advantage of the American Quarter Horse Association's resources and networks, especially on state and local levels. AQHA is a service organization, in business to help its members enjoy their horses to the fullest.

Today, the modern horse is nearly wholly dependent on mankind for his every need. The horse has an extraordinary ability to adapt himself to his environment and circumstances. He displays not only a great versatility but a willingness to submit to human domination. Where the horse was once a necessity, he is now more of a luxury.

This book presents issues and situations that those just being introduced to horses will encounter. It's not intended to be a complete guide or how-to-ride manual, because no book can cover everything. Inexperienced horse owners need to rely on their support team of experts, especially where health and safety are concerned. I hope this publication increases your interest, understanding, and participation in the exciting world of the American Quarter Horse.

—Don Burt
Past President of the American Quarter
Horse Association and author of *Showing
the American Quarter Horse*

Acknowledgments

This book happened because Don Treadway, AQHA's Senior Director of Marketing Services, agreed that a book publishing program was an idea worth pursuing. "We'll get it done someday," he kept telling me. "Just keep after me." That I did, and for several years, until Don gave me the go-ahead. I'm grateful for his initial enthusiasm and continuing support.

I also appreciate the support of the AQHA Executive Committees of 1996, 1997, and 1998.

Members of the AQHA marketing services and other departments provided invaluable advice and other assistance. Special thanks go to James May, Director of Curatorial Services of the American Quarter Horse Heritage Center & Museum and to Lesli Groves, then editor of *The Quarter Horse Journal* and now editor of *America's Horse.*

Leslie Baker, former AQHA National Publicist, was far more than a "point person" on the project. Her consulting and editorial contributions were above and beyond the call of duty; they are evident throughout the book.

The reputation of The Lyons Press for caring about books and authors is richly deserved. Lilly Golden edited the manuscript with spirit and skill, even when the project's gestation period exceeded that of her new daughter, Isabel.

At another time and place, I edited a book by Don Burt, a highly respected leader of the horse industry. We've ridden a few other trails together, so the fact that he wrote the foreword to this book is especially meaningful.

Finally, and on another personal note, I learned to ride at a summer camp where my teachers included a number of good American Quarter Horses. Although I cannot claim unswerving fidelity (I've ridden many breeds and types over the years), my affection has never wavered. In that spirit, this book is dedicated to all the American Quarter Horses that have enriched our lives.

—Steven D. Price

The American Quarter Horse and AQHA: A Brief History

Historians cite the twenty stallions and mares brought on Christopher Columbus's second voyage as the first horses to be introduced to North America. Anthropologists, however, point out that horses had been here a long time before 1493; the prehistoric ancestors of what we recognize as horses left this continent millions of years ago. Migrating across a land bridge between North America and Asia (the site of present-day Alaska), some stayed in northern Asian and European areas, where they descended into the heavy "cold-blooded" breeds, while others that headed south toward Persia and Arabia developed into the lighter and smaller "hot-blooded" breeds.

It was those hot-blooded types that came with the Spanish explorers. It is fitting that Hernando Cortez, whose horsepowered expedition did so much to stake out Spain's claim in Mexico, also was the first large ranch owner on the North American continent. In that way, horses and ranch work became associated from the very earliest days.

Even though the horses that Cortez brought and their descendants were of Arab* blood, the ones more prized by the vaquero ranchers were those with the ability to gallop in short bursts of speed and to anticipate and react to every move a cow might make.

The seventeenth-century descendants of the Spanish conquistadors' horses lived in three distinct areas and led very different lives. Some herded cattle on the vast ranches of Mexico, an area that in the colonial era included Texas and southern California. Others were appropriated by Native American tribes, most notably in the 1680s by the Comanche and Kiowa, who used them for transportation and in warfare.** The third category escaped all form of human possession, living on their own as wild mustangs. But wherever any of these horses lived, no matter who owned or rode them, the animals were prized for their great stamina, an ability to travel at all speeds for hours on end and over some of North America's most rugged country.

Meanwhile, another equine importation was happening to the north. Seventeen English horses and mares were shipped to the Virginia colony of Jamestown in 1611, and three years later another herd followed. This second group was of Spanish blood, captured in Nova Scotia from French forces that in turn had acquired them in the West Indies.

---

*Not to be confused with the Arabian, as we now define that breed.

**The Pueblo Revolt in New Mexico provided most of the animals: The Pueblo tribe rose against the Spanish, who in their rush to leave the region abandoned their horse herds. The Pueblos traded most of the horses to other tribes, which led to the rapid spread of horses throughout the West.

Even farther north, thirteen horses were brought to the Massachusetts Bay Colony in 1629. Their tasks included pulling plows and transporting produce and people (given the Puritan views on the subject, using horses for sport was quite out of the question). The horses also were used as commodities in commerce with other parts of the continent: Spanish horses were taken in trade for New England manufactured goods, then traded back for molasses.

The influx of horses continued in almost geometric progression. From two hundred horses halfway through the seventeenth century, the number grew to ten thousand in only twenty years' time. Many were Hobbies,* a mid-size muscular type that originated in Ireland; indeed, the wild ponies that inhabit the Connemara area in the west of Ireland show many of the same features. The Hobbie's short back and powerful hindquarters produced a comfortable walk and jog-trot (or pace, the more valued gait in this preposting era), and bursts of speed at the gallop. Both in conformation and in bold and courageous temperament, the Hobbie was an early and important forebear of the Quarter Horse type.

Although Puritans took a dim view of racing, eighteenth-century colonists in Virginia and the Carolinas showed no such reluctance. Their preference was for "short racing," their term for sprints at distances of about a quarter mile. There were several reasons why. Without any permanent racetracks, the contests had to be held on available cleared flat land. That meant roads, few of which had flat and wide stretches much longer than one-fourth of a mile. Moreover, these colonists used their horses for farming and driving as well as for sport, and in all weather, so owners were reluctant to have their animals use up all their energy when there was more serious work to be done afterward.

The term "short racing" implies the existence of a longer alternative. Virginia's tidewater planters, whose social and cultural ties to the British aristocracy did not end when they crossed the Atlantic, tried to duplicate the three- and four-mile contests patronized by nobility and landed gentry at such English racecourses as Newmarket and Epsom. And that required Thoroughbreds.

Toward the end of the seventeenth century, three British noblemen traveling in North Africa independently came across stallions that struck their fancy. Imported to England and bred to native mares, the Darley Arabian, the Byerly Turk, and the Godolphin Arabian became the foundation sires of the Thoroughbred breed (even today, every Thoroughbred can trace its ancestry

---

*The name survives as "hobby horse."

back to at least one of these stallions). Their progeny grew into horses that were larger than Hobbies and other native types and capable of running for far longer distances.

Starting in about 1730, Thoroughbred stallions began to arrive in the North American English colonies. The first, a son of the Darley Arabian named Buelle Rock, was bred the following year to a mare sent from Spain to Maryland. However, with few if any pure Thoroughbred mares to be mated with, he and other Thoroughbred studs were bred to native mares descended from such breeds as Arabians, Barbs, Turks, and Andalucians. The result was known familiarly as CAQRH, or the Celebrated American Quarter Running Horse.

Janus, a grandson of the Godolphin Arabian foaled in 1746, was imported to Virginia ten years later. Prolific and prepotent, Janus was described in an 1833 account based on more contemporary views "as if he had been of a different species. Janus had great bone and muscle; round, very compact, large quarters, and was very swift; all of which desirable qualities he imparted so perfectly to his progeny that many of them remain in the stock at this remote

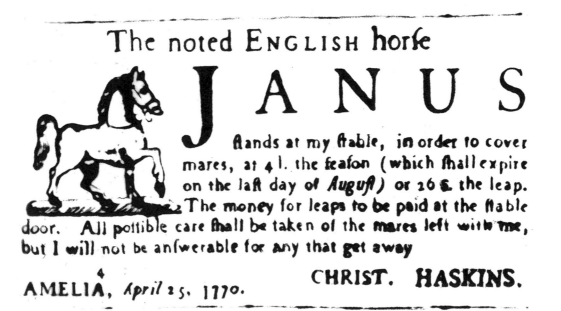

Janus was renowned for his powerful conformation and for his prepotency—the ability to pass on his unique qualities to many generations of offspring. He was still standing at stud in North Carolina when he was twenty-seven years old, covering mares that produced sons and daughters with startling speed. Advertisement from the Virginia Gazette, *1773. (Virginia State Library and Archives)*

period, and great speed and muscular form are still found in many horses whose pedigrees reach him. . . . Nearly all of his immediate descendants were 'swift quarter Nags.' . . . He was the sire of an immense number of short distance racers, brood mares and stallions." Although Janus did not found the Quarter Horse breed, his ability to pass his fine qualities on to his offspring made him the greatest imported sire of Quarter Horses.

Another legacy from these Thoroughbreds took the form of physical refinement and stamina that were soon reflected in the next generations of Celebrated Quarter Running Horses.

While the long-limbed, elegant Thoroughbred remained popular along the Eastern seaboard following the Revolutionary War, the Quarter-Mile Runner was the choice of the pioneers. Their sturdy strength was perfectly suited to the needs of settlers who crossed the Appalachians into the Midwest and Southwest, and when there was leisure time for friendly competition, the horses' speed over short distances was equally prized.

Several horses had great influence on the development of the Quarter Horse during this period. One in particular was Sir Archy, sired by an imported Thoroughbred stallion named Diomed. Among Sir Archy's sons was Copper Bottom, brought to Texas in 1839 by Sam Houston.

Steel Dust, another Quarter Horse brought to Texas before the Mexican War, became legendary over the next decade for both his racing prowess and his breeding ability. Said to have stood about 15 hands high, Steel Dust was described as a shorter, more compact version of a Thoroughbred.

He was also described as the fastest horse in Texas, as the following account will testify. The contest in question took place in McKinney, Texas, on Sunday, September 5, 1856. It was a match race between Steel Dust, who was then twelve years old, and a 16-hand Thoroughbred-type named Monmouth. The distance was one-half mile, something of a compromise between Steel Dust's normal quarter-mile route and the mile that Monmouth favored. The riders were Tom MacKnight on Steel Dust and Bob Randolph on the other horse. Both men rode bareback. According to an eyewitness:

"There were not over five thousand people in Collins County, but I believe twice that many were present . . . and everybody had a bet up. We could see the starting point through the trees and saw Jim [J. W. Throckmorton, later governor of the state] wave his black hat to start them off.

"They came down the hill neck and neck and disappeared from sight in Williams Craw. People yelled, shouted, and women and boys started to climb trees to get a view of the horses—but before they got up, the racers came over the rise.

"Big Monmouth was taking gigantic strides but the little mousy horse was making two jumps to old Monmouth's one. They were not long strides, but he was making them faster.

"Steel Dust was on the left with [MacKnight] lying squat down on his back. Bob [Randolph] was thrashing Monmouth, but I could not see that [MacKnight] was doing anything to Steel Dust. Before we could think, they were at the finish line, Steel Dust three lengths in front. Steel Dust turned sharp off the track and plowed to a stop. Old Monmouth kept right on and ran into a thicket, sweeping Bob off his back and disappearing from view, crashing off down in the woods."

A third renowned runner, Shiloh, was bred to a Steel Dust daughter to produce a colt named Billy. As the reputation of Billy and other good horses spread across the frontier, people began to refer to the type less as Quarter Running Horses than as "Steeldusts." Their abilities went beyond racing: Their lightning bursts of speed enabled them to pursue and stay up with cattle, while their agility, responsiveness, and innate "cow sense" combined to make them ideal for cutting, roping, and other ranch work. And qualities that didn't come from their Eastern forebears were added through crosses with Mexican vaquero horses and wild mustangs. If America is described as a "melting pot," no better example can be found than in the way equine "immigrant" stock blended to form the Western ranch horse.

An excellent view of the role of ranch horses comes from historian Jim Pfluger:*

Spring roundup was the most important activity on the open range more than a century ago and that importance has not changed much today. The cowman learned of his herd's condition and its increase since the previous fall's work. This was harvest time in cow country.

The roundup required special preparation including getting the horses in condition after a winter with limited work. Before the open

---

*This section is excerpted from Pfluger's introduction to *Texas Cowboys* by David R. Stoecklein, Stoecklein Publishing, © 1997 and used by permission.

ranges were fenced, roundup crews from several ranches could be out for months working hundreds of square miles. A rider may have six or more horses and he was responsible for their conditioning, training and care. Continued abuse of his string could lose a hand his job. No one, not even the wagon boss, could ride one of his "hosses" without permission. If the boss took a horse from the rider's string, it was the same as telling him he was fired.

Jack Thorp, in his book *Pardner of the Wind,* tells the story of a ranch owner whose eastern friend was coming to visit and wanted the friend to ride one of his cowboy's horses. The cowboy agreed by replying, "Sure, cut him out. While you're at it, cut out the whole mount—an' make out my pay check."

When a new hand was assigned his string, he was not told anything about the character of his horses. He was considered a good enough hand to learn about his horses on his own. Each cowboy worked the cavvy-broke (broke to ride) horses in his string. The bronc buster topped out the unbroke colts and fillies brought in from the range.

Good cow outfits had horses with cow sense, that ability to anticipate what a cow would do in any situation and not be intimidated by a bull on the prod or "mama cow" looking after her new-born calf. There was a pecking order among cowboys in an outfit, the best riders, if not allowed to choose, were assigned the best horses—the wagon boss got first choice. The experienced hands got the best cutting horses and the top ropers had the steadiest rope horses in their strings. The horses in a cowboy's string determined his value to the outfit.

Nearly all hands received at least one or two "green broke" broncs and were expected to continue training them to be useful to the outfit. According to some old hands, it took several years, perhaps six or more, for a horse to be a top roper or cutter.

As the grass "greened up" with the warm breath of spring, the chuck wagons, with the remudas following, rolled out from the ranches. Another spring roundup was beginning.

Circle horses, those younger, stronger horses without special skills, were the first to be called into action at a roundup. "Telling off the riders" by the roundup captain assigned the riders over the perimeter of a gather. They were to drive cattle to a holding point for sorting and branding. It was hard work, requiring a thorough inspection into every canyon and arroyo, behind every hill and in each mott. The size of the area may require the cowboys and their horses to be out most of the day. It was necessary that all cattle be driven to a designated point. Therefore, the circle horses required stamina or "bottom" for their day's work.

The cowboy's work was only beginning when the cattle reached the holding point. Each rider changed his saddle to a fresh horse. Depending upon the cowboy's skills and his assignment, a cutting horse or roping horse might be needed. For the younger hand, who will not get the chance to cut or rope, his mount may be a herd horse that will not spook easily among the dust and noise while he keeps the herd close or the cuts separated. It also was a good time to work a green horse, giving it experience of working close to the herd. Most likely, all except the wagon boss and top hand took a turn at flanking and branding, the less desirable work that required cowboys to dismount.

Ranch horses respected the "catch rope" and the roundup's rope corrals. All were taught to "work easy" around cattle and tolerate a rope thrown by their riders. The rope, a simple extension of the cowboy, was essential to cattle work. Two cowboys heading and heeling on trained horses could easily doctor a 600-pound steer. However, according to John H. Culley in *Cattle, Horses & Men of the Western Range,* horses were trained to be "tetchy about the rope around their legs and tail. It made them leery about stepping into the slack of the lariat when roping . . ." It also kept the horses from "crowding up" against the rope corral.

Horses' abilities were as varied as those of the cowboys who rode them. Its natural disposition plus its training determined whether a horse became a top roping or cutting horse or a favored night-herding or river-crossing horse. Cutting horses, for example, were considered a second set of brains for a rider at a roundup and were the source of pride among their owners. One such horse said to be a natural cutter was Powderhorn, a sorrel owned by world champion cowboy Bob Crosby. According to witnesses, Bob would draw a brand in the sand for Powderhorn and the horse would cut out the cattle wearing that brand.

Good ranch horses never lose their instinctive "cow." There is a story told by Jack Culley in his book *Cattle, Horses & Men* of a horse he sells to a "nester" who recently moved into the area. It was a steady cow horse showing some cutting ability. Culley, riding by the farmer's place some months later, stopped to visit. Asked if he still had the horse he bought, the farmer replied, "O, yes, we wouldn't part with Ruby. The only thing is that we don't have enough work for him here, so every once in a while he rounds up the milk cows down in the pasture on his own hook and brings 'em up and puts 'em in the corral in the middle of the afternoon."

Most horses did not distinguish themselves beyond their careers as ranch horses. However, some horses gained fame beyond their own outfits. One of the best known cutting horses in West Texas was a bay gelding called Hub. Foaled in 1876 on the Keechi Range near Jacksboro, Hub was trained as a cutting horse by Sam Graves, a hand for the 8 Ranch in King County. Hub gained a reputation as the best cutting horse on the ranch. So the story goes, Hub even won bets for his owner by cutting steers from the herd with his bridle removed.

In 1898, a cowboy reunion and rodeo was held in Haskell. In addition to the horse races and other events, a cutting contest was scheduled. A $150 prize was to be awarded to the horse that cut out the most cows within five minutes. At the age of 22 and retired to the pasture, Hub with Graves aboard won the contest by cutting out eight head, beating much younger horses. Later that day, Hub performed a second time, cutting two more steers without his bridle.

But sometimes, a horse's intelligence was more than the cowboy considered possible. In *Pardner of the Wind*, Thorp told the story of two horses, top rope horses in their day but getting on in age:

When a big steer, or a cow, or bull was roped, the roping horse kept his head to the animal and the rope tight, not only because that was what he was taught to do, but also because anything else was likely to result in his getting snarled up in the rope and thrown. The strain came just behind the horse's shoulders, and at this point he was apt to get tender and sore. Also, holding heavy cattle was hard on the front legs. Some old rope horses were cute enough to be mighty careful not to run within roping distance of a heavy animal. I once knew two rope horses that grew up together and were pals, and in their prime they were top roping horses. But as they got older, while they would always make a great show of willingness to overtake a steer, they would never carry the rider quite close enough for a throw. One spring, come roundup time, these two old-timers were not to be found at all. Don't tell me they didn't know! For, within a week after the crew left for the lower end of the range and the roundup, the two old bums showed up all right at the home watering. The same thing happened the two following years, and the head man told the foreman to let them have their liberty, for they had earned it—both were more than eighteen years old.

Ranch owners continually evaluated both their cattle and their horses and "bred up" their stock. Cowmen had their own ideas of what combinations of breeds worked best for the demands of their horses. Conformation of the horses varied somewhat but all hands wanted a horse stout enough to handle a 1,000-pound steer, the speed to sprint after a "bunch quitter" bolting from the herd and the ability to "turn on a dime." According to several contemporary accounts, cowmen and cowboys preferred dark, solid-colored horses; paints and palominos were rarely seen on the ranch.

W. B. Mitchell, who ranched near Marfa, Texas, described his saddle band of the 1880s as mainly Quarter Horses mixed with Spanish blood to provide the best cow horses. According to Mitchell, the typical cow horse weighed from 950 to 1150 and stood 14.3 to 15.2 hands high. This was the result of breeding up from shorter and lighter Spanish or mustang horses.

The Bell Ranch of northeastern New Mexico continued to upgrade its ranch horses by importing Texas stallions. John Culley, in his classic *Cattle, Horses & Men,* recalled that ". . . we replaced the Thoroughbreds with some useful range bred studs from the JA ranch in Texas." The JA was Charles Goodnight and John Adair's legendary ranch in the Texas Panhandle. Culley noted that "The semi-legendary Steeldust or Quarter horse, appearing to be more a type than a family or breed, was a byword throughout the range . . ."

Texas cow horses, nearly always from a Quarter Horse blood line, were exported to virtually every Western state for cattle ranching prior to World War II. It is estimated that nearly one million horses were taken from Texas. As shown in the 1890 census, Texas nearly equaled the number of horses in the 11 Far West states of the Great Basin and Pacific coast. However, in only twenty years, the greater number of horses would be in the central and northern Great Plains states and west into the Inter-Mountain region. As Texas ranges were fenced, fewer horses were needed compared to the demands of relatively open ranges farther north.

Will James, always an admirer of good cow horses through his art and his stories of cowboy life on the northern plains, once noted in his book *Horses I've Known,* "Some of our best cowhorses was from the south, Steel-dust and Comets, the first strain of our American horse brought over from Spain, and the breed kept alive and carefully strained from that stock by the first cattlemen of Texas."

Throughout the last century and into this one, men who recognized the value of Steel Dust and Billy types bred or bought horses with their bloodlines: Coke Blake and his horse Cold Deck; Dan Casement and his Concho Colonel; Ott Adams and his Little Joe and Joe Moore; George Clegg and Old Sorrel, the foundation sire of the King Ranch's Quarter Horses; William Anson and his Jim Ned of the "Billy" line; Samuel Watkins and his Butt Cut, Peter McCue, and Dan Tucker; and Coke T. Roberts and his Old Fred.

The fame and versatility of these horses were legendary. J. A. Estes, editor of *The Blood Horse,* the weekly Thoroughbred magazine, was moved to pen the follow-

Pedigree of

Dan Tucker,

The famous racing stallion now owned and kept by Thos. Trammell, Sweetwater, Texas.

Dan Tucker was sired by Barney Owens. 1st dam, Butt Cut, by Jack Traveller, he by Steel Dust, out of Queen, who was sired by Pilgrim, by Lexington. 2nd dam, June Bug, by Harry Bluff the sire of Steel Dust. 3rd Dam, Munch Meg, by Snow Ball. 4th Dam, Monkey, by Boanerges.

Jack Traveller was sired by old Steel Dust. Dam, Queen, by Pilgrim, by Lexington. Harry Bluff is Whip and Timoleon stock, and was sired by Short Whip, out of Big Nance, a thoroughbred mare. Barney Owens was sired by Cold Deck, and out of the Overton mare. Cold Deck was by Billy Boy, he by Shiloh, and out of a Steel Dust mare. Cold Deck's dam was Dolly Coker, by Old Rondo.

For further information in regard to this famous breed of racers, address.

Thos. Trammell.   Sweetwater, Texas.

Quarter Horse stallion-at-stud advertisements such as this one circa 1890 extolling Dan Tucker's pedigree were vital records for establishing the breed registry. Steel Dust played prominently into Dan Tucker's pedigree. (AQHF Robert M. Denhardt Collection)

The forefathers of many outstanding racing Quarter Horses came into their own around the turn of the century. This stallion foaled in the 1880s was of the Cold Deck lineage. (AQHF Robert M. Denhardt Collection)

ing verses in honor of Peter McCue, who had been registered as a Thorough-bred to be eligible for major track races:

> "Ain't you never heard what Peter done?
> Run the quarter-mile in twenty-one
> And he run it backwards in twenty flat;
> Why, stranger, where have you been at?"
>> "What else could he do,
>> This Peter McCue?"
> "He could gallop the range with tireless legs,
> He could build a fire and scramble the eggs;
> Though he never learned to subtract or divide,
> He was mighty good when he multiplied."
>> "But tell me who
>> Was Peter McCue?"
> "Well, he come out of Illinois,
> Bred up there by the Watkins boys,
> Called a Thoroughbred—that's for the sucker,
> Of course he was got by Old Dan Tucker."

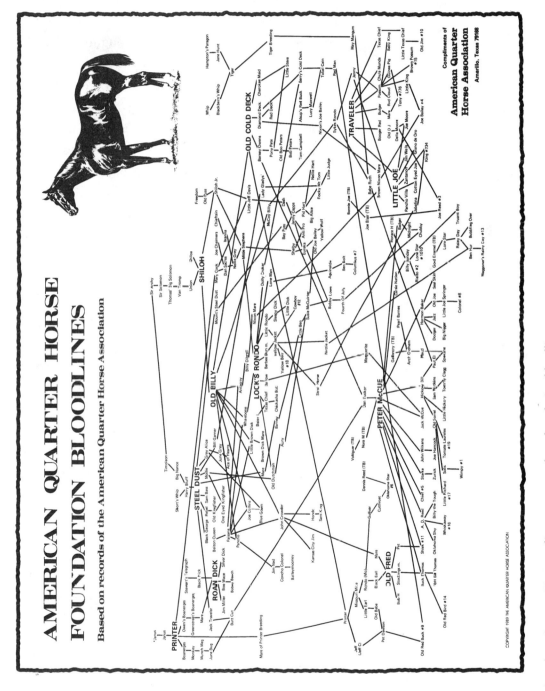

AMERICAN QUARTER HORSE
FOUNDATION BLOODLINES

Based on records of the American Quarter Horse Association

Compliments of

American Quarter Horse Association

Amarillo, Texas 79168

COPYRIGHT 1980 THE AMERICAN QUARTER HORSE ASSOCIATION

American Quarter Horse pedigrees trace to these foundation bloodlines. (AQHA)

A prominent early breeder of Quarter Horses, William Anson played an important role in documenting breed characteristics and pedigrees. (AQHF Robert M. Denhardt Collection)

Some of the men who kept and carried the flame not only practiced, they preached. Anson and Casement wrote articles throughout the 1910s and '20s that discussed the "Steeldusts" as breedable types. According to "Uncle Billy" Anson, an Englishman who spent most of his adult life in Texas and had a contract with the British government to supply cavalry mounts, "The immense breast and chest, enormous forearm, loin and thighs and the heavy layers of muscle are not found in any other breed in the world in the same proportion. The desire for speed at short distances developed this type in distinction to that of the Thoroughbred, even as a [human] hundred-yard champion is generally thickset and heavily muscled in comparison to the miler."

It was, however, a scholar named Robert M. Denhardt whose writings had the greatest impact. During the 1930s and '40s, Denhardt collected material on the history of the Quarter Horse type, especially its physical characteristics. An article in a 1939 issue of *Western Horseman* titled "The Quarter Horse, Then and Now" proved to be a particularly important catalyst that helped the breed* develop an all-important registry.

---

*What defines a breed? Geneticists say a breed is a group of similar animals within a species that humans have developed and maintained. Sportsmen, however, require a registry or stud book as an essential method of maintaining quality control.

This 1908 Quarter Horse show in the Fort Worth, Texas, Stockyards Coliseum is proof of the Quarter Horse's popularity more than thirty years before the official breed registry was formed and the name "American Quarter Horse" was adopted. (AQHF Robert M. Denhardt Collection)

The Birth of AQHA

Denhardt went on to convene a meeting in Fort Worth in March of the following year. Its purpose was to organize a breed registry and open a stud book. In addition to the idea of issuing stock subscriptions to finance the organization, Denhardt suggested specifications to establish conformation standards. The specifications (paraphrased here) deserve to be set forth, because they give a comprehensive summary of the features that were prized in the descendants of Steel Dust and Billy.

The head: short and broad; little fox ears; wide-set, kind eyes; large sensitive nostrils; well-developed jaw. The neck: medium-length; slightly arched, full neck that blends into the shoulders; the head joins the neck at nearly a forty-five-degree angle. Shoulders: medium height but sharp withers and deep sloping shoulders for a good saddle back. Chest and forelegs: deep broad chest;

15

In 1937, Bob Denhardt began in earnest to develop evidence and enthusiasm for an American Quarter Horse registry. His tireless research, persuasive writing, and energetic promotion are recognized as having laid the groundwork for the foundation of AQHA in 1940. He served as the organization's first secretary. (AQHF Collection)

great heart girth; wide-set forelegs; smooth joints; very short cannons; medium-length pasterns; powerfully muscled forearms. Back and barrel: close-coupled, short back with deep well-sprung ribs. Rear quarters: broad, deep, and heavy; full down to the hock. When viewed from the rear, great even width from top of thigh to bottom of stifle and gaskin. Wide, deep, and straight hocks. Bones, legs, and feet: flat, clean, and flinty bones; a well-rounded, roomy foot with an especially deep open heel. Stance: at ease with legs well under the horse, giving him the ability to move quickly in any direction. Action: very collected; the horse turns or stops with noticeable ease and balance, with hocks always well under him.

In short, these characteristics described the "bulldog" type of horse known as the Quarter Horse.

 The AQHA Timeline

1940s

1940:

- The organization that Denhardt proposed took the name of the American Quarter Horse Association (the name "American Quarter Horse" replaced "Quarter Horse" as reference to the breed and its history as a breed indigenous to America). Horses to be registered would have to meet both bloodline and performance standards, the latter calling for running one-quarter of a mile in 23 seconds or "satisfy the Association that [he] was capable of Quarter Horse performance under ranch conditions."

- First AQHA-sanctioned horse show.

1941:

- Wimpy, owned by the King Ranch, was Grand Champion at the Southwestern Exposition and Fat Stock Show in Fort Worth. That title earned him the honor of receiving registration number 1 in the stud book. The next eighteen horses also were designated as foundation sires.

- Because the criteria for registration involved subjective standards, J. H. "Jim" Minnick did fieldwork, inspecting candidates with regard to their ranch horse skills.

1945:

- The American Quarter Racing Association was founded to serve the needs of American Quarter Horse owners who were not interested in ranch horses. A registry for racing purposes, its functions included proper identification of runners.

Rillito Park in southern Arizona was one of the first modern tracks to feature American Quarter Horse racing. (AQHF Robert M. Denhardt Collection)

1946:

- AQHA moved from Fort Worth to Amarillo, Texas.

1948:

- First issue of *The Quarter Horse Journal,* the official publication of AQHA.

1949:

- The American Quarter Racing Association and a third group, the National Quarter Horse Breeders Association, merged with AQHA.

1950s

1950 THROUGH 1957:

The drought that covered the Southwest meant that residents of that region had less time and money to devote to their pleasure and work horses. As a result, racing gained a chance to grow, while interest in American Quarter Horses spread to other parts of the country.

1952:

- New AQHA headquarters were built in Amarillo.

- Horses that had won a certain number of points at horse shows and races were designated as Champions. The first eight that were so named had won points in racing, halter, cutting, and reining, thus representing the classic American Quarter Horse versatility as well as superior performance and conformation.

1955:

- Go Man Go was named World Champion Quarter Running Horse (he was also World Champion in 1956 and 1957). The horse's successes focused widespread public interest on the sport.

1958:

- The "educational mission" program produced the first series of films, pamphlets, and judging clinics.

1959:

- The first All American Futurity was won by Galobar.

1960s

1960:

- Committees dealing with Public Information and Education, Youth Activities, Equine Research, and Finance were inaugurated, together with junior horse show classes and a speakers bureau.

1962:

- After decades of discussions, AQHA decided to register all foals of horses registered as Permanent, Tentative, or National without inspection. Horses that had been registered in the Appendix registry could advance to the main registry, while the new Appendix was open only to horses with Thoroughbred and American Quarter Horse blood.

1964:

- Membership exceeded 30,000 for the first time.

1966:

- The first convention held east of the Mississippi took place in Cincinnati, Ohio.
- Membership reached 37,000 with more than 54,000 horses registered (the total registration reached 500,000).
- Creation of the designation "AQHA Supreme Champion" for horses that achieved distinction in three different fields: halter, performance working events, and racing.

1967:

- The first All-American Quarter Horse Congress was held in Columbus, Ohio.

1968:

- Registered American Quarter Horses recognized in thirty-eight international countries.

1970s

1 9 7 0 :

- Creation of American Junior Quarter Horse Association as an outgrowth of youth activities programs.

- The "excessive white markings" rule passed (the rule was later challenged in court and subsequently sustained on appeal).

1 9 7 2 :

- Election of Bud Ferber of New Jersey, the first president from east of the Mississippi.

1 9 7 4 :

- The first World Championship Quarter Horse Show, held in Louisville, Kentucky; 692 horses represented forty states and five Canadian provinces.

- The one millionth registration took place (the certificate was not assigned to any specific horse, but was reserved by AQHA, the first breed organization to have registered that number of horses).

- Membership passed the 75,000 mark.

1 9 7 5 :

- The nonprofit American Quarter Horse Foundation was established.

1 9 7 7 :

- The Youth Scholarship Program was established.

1 9 7 8 :

- More than 119,000 new registration and more than 200,000 transfers were recorded.

- The first AQHA Superhorse was named: Vickie Lee Pine, owned by Howard Pitzer.

1979:

- The amateur horse show division, distinct from existing adult and youth divisions, was proposed.

1980s

1980:

- The Youth AQHA Performance Champion Program was inaugurated, honoring those who earned at least 50 points in youth performance classes.

1982:

- Ernest Browning and Robert M. Denhardt selected as first inductees in the American Quarter Horse Hall of Fame.

1983:

- The two millionth horse, a filly named Two Million owned by the King Ranch, was registered on August 18.
- Membership surpassed 140,000.

1984:

- New headquarters along I-40 in Amarillo.

1986:

- Incentive Fund rewarded owners with cash awards based on their horses' performance in AQHA shows.
- Television series, *America's Horse*, developed.
- Formation of Racing Council under AQHA guidelines and bylaws.

1988:

- New Novice Program attracted more than 47,000 youth and amateur entries.
- *The Quarter Racing Journal*, a new monthly specialty magazine, was launched.

1989:

• Groundbreaking ceremonies for American Quarter Horse Heritage Center & Museum, including the American Quarter Horse Hall of Fame.

1990s

1990:

• AQHA celebrated its fiftieth anniversary with a festival and convention in its birth city, Fort Worth, Texas.

• AQHA clearly defined its mission statement, expanding beyond its duties as a registry to focus attention on membership services.

Since 1991, the American Quarter Horse Heritage Center & Museum in Amarillo, Texas, has showcased the history and modern activities of the American Quarter Horse breed. (AQHF by Wyatt McSpadden)

The American Quarter Horse and the chuck wagon are enduring symbols of cattle drives in the American West. This historical chuck wagon is on display at the American Quarter Horse Heritage Center & Museum in Amarillo, Texas. (AQHF by Wyatt McSpadden)

1991:

- AQHA established new Horseback Riding Program to provide awards and recognition to members who enjoy spending time riding or driving their American Quarter Horses.

- The Phillips Ranch registered Three Million Cash, a granddaughter of Dash for Cash, and the three millionth American Quarter Horse registered.

- The American Quarter Horse Heritage Center & Museum opened to the public in July.

- AQHA sponsored the equestrian competition at the 1991 Special Olympics World Games in Minnesota, providing volunteers and horses.

1992:

- AQHA installed new multimillion-dollar computer records system, providing faster, more accurate service.

The sprinter's speed that led to the creation of the American Quarter Horse breed still attracts owners and fans. Visitors at the American Quarter Horse Heritage Center & Museum in Amarillo, Texas, can get a jockey's-eye view in historical starting gates used in the most famous American Quarter Horse race, the All American Futurity. (AQHF by Wyatt McSpadden)

- The American Junior Quarter Horse Association World Championship Show relocated to Fort Worth, Texas, after eighteen years in Tulsa, Oklahoma.

- Registration numbers climbed, reversing an eight-year decline brought about by economic conditions that affected the entire horse industry.

- An innovative racing incentive program called The American Quarter Horse Racing Challenge was conceived, offering a new series of regional races and a season-ending championship day.

- AQHA World Championship Show offered a record $1 million in cash and prizes for its record 3,112 entries.

1993:

- The American Quarter Horse Association of Professional Horsemen was formed, providing a strong relationship between AQHA and industry professionals.

- The first AQHA Best Remuda Award was presented to the Haythorn Land and Cattle Company of Arthur, Nebraska. The award signaled a new milestone in recognizing an important segment of American Quarter Horse history, past, present, and future.

- The Racing Challenge debuted.

1994:

- MBNA America™ became a title sponsor of the Racing Challenge.

- The American Quarter Horse Foundation introduced a new Historical Marker Program to acknowledge horses, people, and events significant to the breed's history.

Known for its versatility, the American Quarter Horse breed is enjoyed around the world in nearly every equestrian discipline. (AQHF mural by Robert Lapsley)

1 9 9 5 :

- DNA genetic testing replaced blood-typing as the required method of verifying a horse's parentage.

- Under AQHA's sponsorship, nearly 150 American Quarter Horse owners volunteered their horses and time for the 1995 Special Olympics World Summer Games in Connecticut.

- The American Junior Quarter Horse Association began the STAR Program to cultivate leadership, knowledge, and horsemanship among young horse lovers.

- AQHA joined the masses with a home page on the Internet.

- The American Quarter Horse Foundation announced a new development initiative to raise substantial new monies for equine research, youth and racing scholarships, and educational outreach, including the American Quarter Horse Heritage Center & Museum.

- AQHA officially recognized affiliates across the United States and Canada, providing a stronger link to its grassroots through these associations of American Quarter Horse owners.

1 9 9 6 :

- The record at the classic American Quarter Horse racing distance was shattered by Evening Snow. The gelding broke the 21-second barrier, becoming the first horse of any breed to travel 440 yards in :20.94.

- The youth organization previously known as the American Junior Quarter Horse Association adopted a new name—American Quarter Horse Youth Association (AQHYA)—to more clearly reflect the organization and its members.

- American Quarter Horses entertained at the Olympic Summer Games held in Atlanta, Georgia, exposing an international audience to the breed's athleticism and versatility.

- The AQHA World Championship Show celebrated twenty years in Oklahoma City with a record 3,437 entries and $1.4 million in cash and prizes.

1997:

- AQHA Legacy Awards were presented honoring those who bred American Quarter Horses for fifty or more consecutive years.

- Ride '97, a new national trail ride series, welcomed horses of all breeds and riders of any discipline to ride across the country.

- A new Breeder Referral Program increased AQHA's ability to link prospective American Quarter Horse owners with established breeders.

1998:

- The success of Ride '97 leads to a commitment for Ride '98, and the trail-blazing series went international with rides in Canada, Europe, and South America.

- AQHA and the National Reining Horse Association worked closely with the United States Equestrian Team to add reining as the sixth discipline in which the USET fields teams for international competition.

- The MBNA America Quarter Horse Racing Challenge headed into its sixth year with a $2.5 million series of forty-five races run in ten regions across the United States and Canada.

- *America's Horse,* a bi-monthly magazine, was launched.

The American Quarter Horse Association continues to be the largest equine breed registry in the world. As of 1998, 3.6 million American Quarter Horses have been entered in the registry as AQHA continues its function as the official record-keeping and regulating arm of the American Quarter Horse industry.

In 1997, AQHA recorded the registration of 110,714 American Quarter Horses in addition to 193,953 transfers of ownership.

As the nerve center for the industry, AQHA maintains current statistics on American Quarter Horse ownership in each state and countries worldwide.

The Association plans and conducts the annual convention for AQHA members; the annual AQHYA World Championship Show and the AQHA World Championship Show held in November in Oklahoma City; and the MBNA America Quarter Horse Racing Challenge Championships and Racing Conference, also held each November.

Serving nearly 325,000 worldwide members and the more than one million people who own and enjoy American Quarter Horses through a Board of Directors and a five-member Executive Committee, the Association has expanded through the years to meet the new demands and responsibilities of a rapidly changing industry and the American Quarter Horse breed.

The departments within AQHA record transactions of ownership of all American Quarter Horses; process show and race results of approved events; catalog performance and produce data on all American Quarter Horses; maintain Association funds; and organize and release information about the American Quarter Horse industry of interest to owners and the general public.

FOR FURTHER INFORMATION

The monthly magazines *The Quarter Horse Journal* and *The Quarter Racing Journal* report on AQHA current events as well as other developments throughout the American Quarter Horse world.

For more complete accounts of the development of the breed and AQHA, *They Rode Good Horses: The First Fifty Years of the American Quarter Horse Association* by Don Hedgpeth (published by AQHA) covers the Association up to 1990.

The Colonial Quarter Race Horse by Alexander Mackay-Smith (published by Colonial Quarter Horse Publication) is a scholarly account of the early years of America's racing history.

AQHA offers the following videos:

On the Fifth Day. Tracing horses from prehistoric time to the beginning of the American Quarter Horse breed in the New World. Also available in Spanish. 28 minutes.

The Horse & Society. Host Pat Mahoney explores the relationship between man and horse throughout the centuries in this documentary originally produced for public television. Details the key roles of horses in the development of civilization. 59 minutes.

All in a Day's Ride. The cowboy's life is presented in scenes from the Pitchfork Ranch in Guthrie, Texas, the JC Ranch in Wyoming, and the Texas Cowboy Reunion at Stamford, Texas. Cowboys talk about the American Quarter Horse as a valuable working cow horse on America's ranches. 25 minutes.

From the Beginning. The formation of the American Quarter Horse Association in 1940 is recalled by two founders, Robert Denhardt and J. Ernest

Browning. Also included is the first motion picture footage of American Quarter Horses, taken between 1940 and 1942, which includes Wimpy, King P-234, Little Joe Jr., and other foundation sires. 24 minutes.

AQHA at a Glance. An inside look at the workings of AQHA headquarters. Learn how the largest horse association in the world provides member programs and maintains the integrity of the American Quarter Horse. 19 minutes.

The American Quarter Horse: You'll Always Remember the Ride. Entertaining overview of the many talents of American Quarter Horses. Highlights AQHA events, including shows, races, and AQHA-sponsored programs. 10 minutes.

Inside the American Quarter Horse Heritage Center & Museum. A brief tour of the museum dedicated to the American Quarter Horse. Learn about the interactive displays and exhibits, including the Hall of Fame. 5 minutes.

AQHYA: Check This Out! Catch the excitement of AQHA's youth organization and learn what the American Quarter Horse Youth Association is all about. 9 minutes.

II

Getting Started with Your American Quarter Horse

Horse Ownership: Preliminary Considerations

You've been taking lessons for a while now, and your instructor says you're well on your way to becoming a competent rider. That's music to your ears, because riding isn't just a passing fancy; you hope to stay involved with horses for the rest of your life. But as much as you enjoy lessons from a knowledgeable neighbor or at the local stable, you've also gotten to the point where you feel there's something lacking in your life and in your backyard: an American Quarter Horse of your own.

Before you start scouring the countryside for that horse, however, you must take the time to consider certain fundamental and essential issues. Both "fundamental" and "essential" are the right words, because there's no way to overemphasize the fact that owning a horse is a substantial undertaking. To borrow a phrase from certain wedding ceremonies (not such a far-fetched source, since you'd be taking on a new family member), the decision to acquire a horse is not to be lightly or unadvisedly entered into.

Ownership involves responsibilities, and substantial ones at that. Horses aren't goldfish or dogs or cats: You don't keep them in a bowl on a table or exercise them by walking them around the block twice a day or leave them for a weekend with a bowl of dry food. Horses require a considerable amount of dedication and resources, and that begins with someone to care for them.

The Human Factor

Let's start by listing the qualifications for the job that you are thinking about applying for, that of primary caregiver.

The time demands are significant. Each and every day will call for morning and evening feedings, plus such other chores as cleaning, grooming, and exercising. The schedule takes precedence over the weather or your mood or things you'd rather be doing.

And that's just the very basic routine. In addition is periodic "administration" work, like ordering feed, getting the horse ready for a visit from the veterinarian or farrier, and making repairs on the barn, pasture, and other facilities. On top of that are unforeseeable but inevitable events, such as the time that must be spent tending to a sick horse.

Not only will you need a great deal of dedication and an equally large sense of responsibility, you'll need access to capable assistance. Everyone takes a business trip or vacation or otherwise leaves home now and then, and no one is spared the occasional medical ailment that confines you to the house, if not to bed.

Accordingly, every horse owner needs a backup resource in the form of a another person who can look after the animal when you cannot. That person might be a member of your immediate family, a neighbor, or someone from a stable in your area. Not just any person will do, of course; you need someone who's physically capable, reliable, and knowledgeable. That last criterion is important, since most emergency situations that require a background in horse care are just as likely to happen while you're away as when you're around to call for help.

Whether you're at home or away, ready access to a knowledgeable horse-man is a very big plus. Unless and until you feel confident that a cut, sore, bump, or awkward step doesn't require a vet's attention, you'll be both emotionally and financially better off consulting with someone who is thoroughly familiar with horse care. And in the best of all worlds, that person will never object to coming over, even after any number of "false alarms."

The Right Land

Keeping a horse at home requires a substantial amount of land. Since land use is governed by local zoning regulations, determining whether you can legally maintain a horse on your property is the next step. Don't assume anything. The previous owner of your house may have had a horse, but he could have been violating zoning ordinances that local officials may suddenly decide to enforce—against you. Your next-door neighbor may have a horse, but there may be different zoning regulations on each side of the property line.

As you'll discover when you start checking, zoning is seldom a straight "yes" or "no" situation. More often it's a "yes, but . . .", with the "but"applying to the minimum amount of land per horse, the distance between a barn and property lines, and the manner of manure disposal. There also may be restrictions or outright prohibitions of barns, paddocks, and riding arenas, not to mention easements or other limitations on access to riding trails.

Assuming that zoning is not a problem, you are now faced with the question of how much land you will need. The "one acre per horse" rule of thumb that we often read or hear about isn't entirely accurate. It fails to take into account the beating that a small paddock or pasture takes from even one horse's normal grazing and movement. The grass is gone in no time, and the bare soil becomes mud. The more land you have, the more easily and effectively you can rotate between a place for the horse and areas left to regenerate.

Pastureland must be not only available, but also suitable for horse keeping. The ideal is reasonably level grassland that can be enclosed. It should also have either a pond or stream of drinkable water or access to a pipe or hose to fill a watering trough.

The foliage, which should be free from poisonous weeds and trees, should consist of a variety of forage suitable to your horse's nutritional requirements. Most varieties of grass are acceptable, although one variety of hay grass, tall fescue, often contains a fungus that can cause severe reproductive problems in mares. If you're planning to own a broodmare, have the pasture tested to determine whether it contains this strain. If so, reseed with fungus-free varieties.

Then, too, you'll want someplace to ride. Although a ring or corral is useful for general exercise and specialized forms of training like reining or jumping, horses benefit as much from a change of scenery as humans do. That's why ease of access to a field or trail must be factored into the "can-I-own-a-horse?" equation.

Finances

What does owning a horse cost? You'll get as many answers as the number of people you ask. Among the elements are the purchase price, the facility in which the horse is kept, basic management and upkeep requirements (for example, hoof care by a farrier), and what the horse is used for. Liability insurance also may be necessary, particularly if friends or neighbors will be riding on your property. Beyond these fixed costs are the unexpected and unpredictable but inevitable medical expenses that all domestic creatures seem to incur.

Even the cost of keeping a horse at home has no definitive universal bottom line. Do you have you a "latchkey" barn and paddock that your horse can move right in to, must you build from scratch, or can you refurbish a preexisting facility?

No matter how much you spend to acquire the animal, the purchase price is just the tip of the financial iceberg. Ongoing expenses include goods or services from feed dealers, farriers, and veterinarians, but even these costs vary according to where you live.

Competing in horse shows or taking part in other equestrian activities will require specialized tack for the horse and apparel for you, as well as the expense of training and getting to and from the competition.

That's why the safest and wisest answer to "what does it cost to keep a horse at home?" is to suggest you ask a friend or neighbor who already has a horse and—this part is crucial—uses it for the same purpose for which you will use yours. Make a list as he or she itemizes expenses, then translate the information into a budget of your own, always bearing in mind that budgets are seldom written in stone.

Alternatives to Backyard Horse Keeping

All is not lost if zoning restrictions, insufficient or unsuitable land, or financial limitations prevent you from keeping a horse at home. There are alternatives, of which the most popular one is boarding.

Locating a stable where you can board a horse of your own may require looking no farther than the place where you now ride. You know the management, the staff, and the facilities, and because you continue to ride there, all obviously meet with your approval.

But perhaps the stable is full, or you want a level of instruction or activity that the place does not offer, or the board fees are more than you care to spend. In such cases, you must look elsewhere.

Assess a new barn in terms of certain basic questions. Does the place have the type of activity in which you're interested: Western or English showing, dressage, barrel racing, or team penning, for example? Is there a resident trainer (or a staff person) in case you plan to continue taking lessons? Do other trainers conduct clinics there? Is there ample ring space to accommodate you at the times when you'll want to ride (a covered arena is a blessing on cold or rainy days)?

Is your horse likely to be happy there, too? To answer that question, investigate whether the stalls are ample and clean. Is there sufficient turnout paddock and pasture space? Does the place give the impression of being a clean, safe, and functional facility where the staff genuinely appears to like working with horses?

The answers to these questions come only through observation and inquiry. Spend time at the stable and watch what goes on. Talk to staff members and boarders, and then see whether a local vet, farrier, feed dealer, and/or tack-shop proprietor can confirm your impressions. After all, you wouldn't entrust your child to a nursery school without thoroughly doing your homework; your new horse deserves no less.

As to finances, boarding charges are based on the services to be provided. "Full board" means just what the words indicate: All necessary services, including feeding, stall and horse cleaning, and turnout exercise, are done by the barn's staff. "Rough board" describes a less expensive arrangement of just feeding and watering; additional services such as stall cleaning, grooming, and paddock turnout time are either done by the horse's owner or provided by the stable at additional cost. Because every stable seems to have its own idea of what constitutes the two kinds of board, it's wise to ask the manager to itemize the services and any extra charges.

Leasing

You say you want a horse, but you can't keep it at home? Or perhaps you can't afford to buy a horse or otherwise don't wish or don't feel ready to own one. Leasing a horse from a stable fills that need. Similar to leasing an automobile, the arrangement gives you exclusive use of the animal. You're charged for the board fee, as well as farrier and vet expenses. If the animal needs long-term medical attention, you pay those bills, too (and you usually pay for the use of another horse while yours convalesces).

Most stables that offer this arrangement do so on a relatively long-term basis, usually for a minimum of six months. Some barns also make half leases of the same horse available to two people whose schedules don't conflict; the stable's manager is in charge of making sure the horse has sufficient rest time between uses.

Co-Ownership

Co-ownership is a more permanent two-party arrangement than co-leasing. The horse can live at a boarding stable or in someone's backyard.

With regard to the latter, you may have the necessary land, while someone else has a bit more extra time and money. Or you may have the property, while someone else already owns a horse that needs to move to a new home. Whatever each person might have to offer, the net result is satisfaction of all the requirements for owning and keeping a horse.

Co-ownership can be an ideal solution, but before making any commitment, make sure that you and your partner are completely in sync. A written partnership agreement spelling out which of you does what and when in the way of riding, stable chores, and other pleasures and responsibilities is essential. So are provisions that cover everyone's financial obligations. The document should cover every possible situation, both good times and bad, especially how to handle the possibility that one or both of you wants out of the partnership.

Remember that it's the "oh, that'll never happen" and the "oh, we'll worry about that later" scenarios that lead to bruised feelings, blunt confrontations, and even lawsuits. To be on the safe side, ask an experienced horse owner to look over the agreement. Invest in the services of a lawyer if a professional viewpoint will make both parties feel more comfortable. Such expertise can go a long way toward heading off any problems that may arise down the road.

Working for Board

One way to keep your horse at another person's facility is by bartering your services. In exchange for part or full board for the animal, you'll be responsible for such chores as feeding, mucking stalls, grooming, and taking care of turnouts for a number of horses at the stable.

When the work is done in exchange for lessons for the rider and training for the horse, as well as for the horse's board, the worker is commonly known as a working student. Many well-known riders and trainers have gone this route on their way to success in the horse business.

Another alternative is a paying job as a groom or in the office of a professional stable, with all or part of your salary going toward your horse's board or for a lease on a horse that's owned by the barn.

That is to say, with a bit of ingenuity and lots of hard work, the opportunity to have a horse to ride is within reach of almost everyone.

FOR FURTHER INFORMATION

AQHA offers the following videos on the benefits of owning an American Quarter Horse:

America's Horse. An entertaining, in-depth look at the American Quarter Horse and why he is America's favorite horse. From breeding farms in Florida to a roundup in Texas, from showing in North Carolina to chariot racing in Idaho, and from rodeos to trail rides, *America's Horse* features the American Quarter Horse in a variety of settings. 28 minutes.

The American Quarter Horse: You'll Always Remember the Ride. Entertaining overview of the many talents of American Quarter Horses. Highlights AQHA events including shows, races, and AQHA-sponsored programs. 10 minutes.

The following videos provide an overview of what owning a horse involves:

Horse Sense. Judge, trainer, and college equine professor Dr. Jim Heird provides sensible safety, grooming, and halter-breaking tips for the novice horse enthusiast. Basic clipping, bedding, and trailer-loading techniques also are covered. Excellent for 4-H and FFA clubs. 26 minutes.

Horse Sense, the Second Year. Breaking and training techniques for two-year-old horses in preparation for advanced training for all performance events are given by trainer Don Dodge with the assistance of Mike Kevil. Methods and philosophy used from the first saddling through ninety days of riding are presented. 26 minutes.

Horse Sense III, the Rider. The basics of riding a horse are covered by Dr. David Whitaker, college equine specialist. Points highlighted include attire, saddles, bits, ground safety, saddling and bridling, mounting, dismounting, basic riding positions, and gaits. An excellent introduction to the fun sport of horseback riding. 33 minutes.

Stabling: Setting Up Your Facility

Once you decide to keep a horse at home, the urge to rush out and start shopping can become overwhelming. First things first, however, beginning with the preparation of where the horse will live, work, and play.

The most basic maintenance arrangement is field-keeping, known in some parts of the country as pasture-keeping or as just plain "pasturing."

The minimum requirement is several acres of land. As we noted in the previous section, although zoning regulations often prescribe a minimum of one acre per horse, any animal that's restricted to a single acre will quickly clean it of all vegetation. Depending on the season and climate, that formerly lush field turns into a grassless desert or a rice paddy that neither human nor animal will find appealing.

Any prospective pasture should be as well drained and rock-free as the terrain allows. Plentiful grass also is essential. Horses are by nature grazers, and

The elasticity of high-tensile polymer fencing deflects and absorbs impact instead of cracking or splintering. (The Quarter Hourse Journal)

being confined to land with nothing to nibble on makes them anxious and irritable or bored. There can't be any poisonous foliage. If you have any doubts or questions about existing vegetation, a knowledgeable neighbor or your county's agricultural extension agent are sources of information.

Fruit trees can also be a problem when harvest season deposits loads of bellyache-producing apples or other windfall "treats" on the ground. The wilted leaves of other attractive trees, such as red maple, peach, cherry, and plum, can prove toxic.

Drinkable water is essential. The alternative to a stream or pond that provides a constant source of clean water is a trough fed by a hose or pipe (any permanent underground pipes should be installed below the frost line). In those parts of the country where deep freezes are a part of winter, someone will have to break holes in a frozen pond or tote buckets of ice-free water.

Fencing keeps the horse where you want him (actually, it keeps him from where you don't want him). Sturdy wooden post-and-rails treated with

Slip boards are an alternative to post-and-rail fencing. Wood fencing is a good choice because of its visibility and sturdiness. (The Quarter Hourse Journal)

weatherproofing are long-lasting and relatively maintenance-free. Steel or polyvinyl chloride (PVC) plastic are popular alternatives. Posts need to be at least four feet above the ground and set eight to ten feet apart. At least one-third of the post should be sunk into the ground; embedding it in a concrete foundation gives additional strength.

The railing is always nailed, screwed, or bolted to the pasture side of the post. That's so the posts can provide support when a horse leans against the fencing—and he *will* lean.

Electric fencing is another alternative. The system requires a power source and a transformer to produce an amount of current for a cautionary shock when the horse touches the wire. Animals soon learn to respect the boundary, while humans sooner or later remember to shut off the power before handling the wire. Electric fencing must be routinely checked to make sure a fallen branch or other object hasn't grounded or otherwise short-circuited the system.

Although barbed wire has a long history of enclosing livestock, it's a poor choice for horses. Unlike cattle, horses that become entangled will struggle to free themselves. The serious injuries that can result are easily avoided by another choice of fencing.

A lake or pond as part of the boundary is often an appealing possibility, but there can be drawbacks. Horses can swim, and they've been known to walk across frozen ponds in winter. All-around fencing prevents that possibility.

Any sort of fencing requires at least one gate. Tubular steel or sturdy wire is an alternative to wood. A minimum width of twelve to fifteen feet lets a horse and the person leading him pass through together safely and comfortably. A pickup truck or tractor can get through, too, a benefit when delivering heavy items or removing manure from the field.

Positioning the bottom of the gate a few feet off the ground is practical, especially when snowdrifts immobilize anything that's lower. A gatepost that a closed gate can rest against absorbs the weight of a leaning horse. That's important because horses tend to spend a fair amount of time hanging around—and against—gates, especially around feeding time.

Sturdy hinges and an equally strong latch, or a length of chain and metal snap, will keep the gate closed and the horse inside. Some owners use both for the simple reason that when it comes to finding ways to escape, horses are as clever as the Great Houdini.

Even in a pasture with trees that serve as windbreaks, your horse will be grateful for additional shelter against winter snows, summer sun, and year-round rain. The shed needn't be fancy, just sturdy. A three-sided design works nicely. An open front facing south shields its occupant from chilly north winds, while a sloping roof with a wide overhang lets rain and melted snow run off.

A second shed outside the field can store feed, hay, and grooming essentials. If you plan to keep saddles and bridles there, too, choose an enclosed building with a door that has a sturdy lock—tack is a frequent target of thieves.

A possible downside to field-keeping a single horse is that many horses don't do well living alone, and living outside full-time seems to heighten their unhappiness. In addition to losing weight, they become restless and bored, which leads to such bad habits as cribbing, pacing, and sometimes a case of psychosomatic (but no less dangerous) colic. That's why, all other things being equal, if you're planning on field-keeping, buying a horse that's already accustomed to solo outdoor life would be a wise choice. Otherwise, the companionship of a second horse, perhaps a retired senior citizen, or a burro or goat is likely to work. Or you can divide the animal's time between field living and an indoor stall.

Another disadvantage to field-keeping is that pastured horses get dirtier faster than horses that live inside. They also grow longer coats during autumn and winter. As a result, their owners learn to devote lots of time and elbow grease in the curry-wash-and-rub department. And since long hair retains moisture longer than short hair, cooling out a horse after hard exercise takes longer.

Nevertheless, many horses thrive in field-keeping situations. And so do their owners.

Barns

The many good reasons for having a barn start with the benefits of a shelter from severe weather. Equally welcome is the convenience of having grooming, feeding, and other necessary horse-keeping items under the same roof as the horse. Having a stall in which to keep your horse, as opposed to having to spend time catching him and then bringing him in from a field, has its charms, too. It certainly does in bad weather.

Many criteria that pertain to pastures also apply to a barn's location. You'll want it on well-drained land that provides access to drinkable water. Accessibility by vehicles also is important, unless toting sacks of feed and bedding and bales of hay over a distance is your idea of a good time.

Barn design leaves much to individual taste and budget. Books and magazine articles provide inspiration and instruction; ask a tack-shop clerk or librarian to recommend reference sources.

Inspecting the facilities of horse-keeping neighbors is another good way to learn; you can often profit from their planning mistakes. Companies that manufacture and install prefabricated barns advertise in magazines, and their representatives will be happy to consult with you about your specific needs.

Even though you may now feel certain that one horse is the most you'll ever own, people have been known to change their minds. A two-stall barn is not appreciably more expensive than one with just a single stall. Bags of bedding, wheelbarrows, and other large items can always be stored in the spare stall, and besides, you never know when your horse will have a sleepover barn-mate. If you don't want a multistall facility now, an option is a design that allows for easy additions should you ever wish to expand.

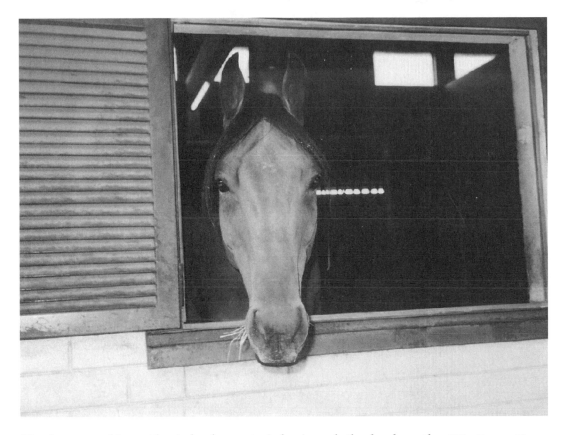

The shutters on this outside window keep out wind, rain, and other harsh weather. (The Quarter Horse Journal)

A door that faces the south or west protects the interior from cold and wet northern winds. Other external architectural considerations include a roof that slopes away from the building's door and is covered with shingles, fiberglass, or metal. More than one window permits cross-ventilation, while a vented cupola on the roof allows rising warm air to escape. As for a solid foundation, poured concrete is a popular choice.

The inside ceiling should be at least fifteen feet high for the sake of safety. Similarly, light fixtures must be installed in places where a rearing horse will not bump into bulbs or fixtures.

The flooring should be level, waterproof, and nonskid or at least skid-resistant. In that regard, although concrete is suitable for foundations, it's not the best choice for a stall floor: It's slippery when dry and even more so when wet. Moreover, concrete is hard on a horse's feet, and although rubber matting helps, deep bedding is troublesome and expensive.

Wood floorboards are easier on feet, but wood retains moisture and is slow to dry out. Bare earth (soil or dirt) is preferable in that regard, but pawing hooves create ruts and holes that must be filled in. Clay gets high marks for absorbing moisture and is easy on feet and legs, but it also needs frequent attention. Sand dries out feet and becomes hard when wet and packed. The bottom line: Many horse keepers find that a combination of earth or clay and rubber matting works satisfactorily.

Rubber matting has benefits from a health and stable-management viewpoint, too. It prevents urine moisture from seeping into flooring, which means a drier stall with less foul odor and less likelihood of thrush. The rubber layer also reduces wear and tear of soil or clay flooring caused by horses' pawing. Because a single sheet of wall-to-wall matting to cover an entire stall would be difficult to manage, matting is sold in smaller pieces, with the better ones having interlocking edges that ensure a tight fit.

No horse deserves cramped quarters. A box stall for an average-size American Quarter Horse should be at least twelve feet square. Whenever possible,

Stall bars let a horse see out into the barn—and let people look into the stall. (AQHA photo by Wyatt McSpadden)

stalls should be on the side of the building that's away from prevailing winds so windows can be kept open for ventilation as often as possible.

Metal grilling on the top half of the inside stall wall and door lets a horse look out, and you can have a good view inside, too. A door that isn't the sliding variety should open outward.

Stall furnishings begin with a feed bin or manger bolted to the wall about four feet off the floor. A device that automatically fills and replenishes water may seem convenient, but because a horse's refusal of water is a sign of distress, many horsemen prefer to provide water by hand so they can monitor the intake. In that case, they hang two heavy-duty rubber buckets from hooks on the wall, then carry or hose in refills.

Like everyone else, horse owners always end up with more items than they intend to have. With this in mind, don't stint on the size of a tack room. Nor should you cut corners on its utilities and furnishings. You'll need electricity for a ceiling light and for one or two outlets for appliances. A sink with hot and cold running water plus an outside hot and cold spigot for a hose to wash the horse are convenient as well as useful. An intercom with your house or an extension telephone is invaluable in case of emergencies.

Dampness is an archenemy of leather. To keep your tack room as dry as possible, invest in a dehumidifier if you live in a damp climate.

Since security for your tack is a constant consideration, the door needs strong hinges and a good solid lock. Similarly, windows should be secured when no one is around, or else barred or made too small for even a tiny person to crawl through.

One or more saddle racks can be mounted on the wall at a convenient height. Portable folding metal racks for cleaning as well as storage are an alternative. Bridle racks on the wall should have rounded tops so that the leather retains its shape.

You'll want ample shelving and cabinets for grooming and tack-cleaning equipment. A lock on any cabinet in which veterinary medication and supplies are kept is a sound safety feature.

Two fire extinguishers in working order (the second as a backup) should be prominently displayed.

Tack and accessories take up lots of room, so it is best to designate a separate room to store feed and bedding. The room needs to be dry and well ventilated, with a rodent-proof cement or solid wood floor. A door on the outside of the building needs to be horse-resistant, too; horses are not only good at getting out of places, they're good at getting into them, especially when the reward is feed.

Even though you feel certain that raccoons, field mice, or squirrels can't get into the storage room, grain, pellets, and other feed belong in covered metal bins or in heavy-duty plastic cans.

Hay and straw come in large, heavy, and dusty bales. Since you're likely to have substantial amounts on hand at a time, the barn's attic can be used as a hayloft if it was designed as such. Otherwise, a separate room or even a shed can serve as a storage area for large quantities of hay and bedding. Whichever you choose, the area must be dry and well ventilated to prevent spoilage and spontaneous combustion fires.

A WORD ABOUT PREEXISTING BUILDINGS

Even though there may already be a barn on your property, you must still assess its value in terms of all the elements that apply to a new structure. Neglect through disuse is likely to have taken its toll: The foundation may have cracked, beams supporting the walls may have rotted, or the attic hayloft is now an accident waiting to happen. Such a state of disrepair requires weighing the expense of refurbishing the barn against the often cheaper cost of pulling it down and starting from scratch either on the same site or in another, better place.

The same critical approach applies to a building that's never housed livestock, like a garage or woodshed. Even if you're planning to do the refurbishing work yourself, the advice of an architect, contractor, or carpenter is worth seeking if you're less than thoroughly knowledgeable about such matters.

Speaking of garages, exhaust fumes are as unpleasant and lethal to horses as they are to humans. Moral: Don't even begin to think about adding a stall on to your garage so you can house a car and a horse under the same roof.

Manure Pit

No matter where he lives, a healthy horse will produce about ten pounds of manure a day. In addition, muck- and urine-soaked bedding needs to be stored someplace before there's enough to haul away. The refuse attracts insects and emits an odor that not everyone enjoys inhaling, so determining where to build your manure pit begins with first checking your local zoning and health restrictions. Some communities take a dim view of liquid equine waste leaching into the soil and mixing with groundwater, and if that's the case, your first choice of location may need to be altered to accommodate those concerns. A cement base and/or sides for the pit also may be required.

In the best of all worlds, the pit will be close enough to your barn to be handy, yet far enough away from it (as well as from wherever humans live) not to be a nuisance. The site should also be accessible to vehicles that will cart away the refuse to a landfill site, a mushroom farm, or wherever you plan to dispose of the waste.

Arena or Riding Ring

Just as a horse owner can get along without a barn, not everyone needs an enclosed space to ride in. However, if you plan to do specialized training and don't have easy access to someone else's arena, you'll want one of your own.

The arena needn't be fancy. Any expanse of level, well-drained, rock-free land will work. Although the exact size will depend on available land and the kind of work you'll do, a minimum of approximately one hundred feet by seventy-five feet makes a useful general-purpose ring.

Fencing confines the horse and helps keep his attention focused on his work. Four-foot-high post-and-board similar to pasture fencing works well. (Exceptions are the very low boards that enclose dressage arenas and the heavy-duty metal pipes for arenas in which cattle will be worked.)

Many rings don't have gates as such. Instead there is a section where the top and bottom rails can be slid out of their brackets for a horse to pass through. At some point, the arena will need leveling (riding along the rail plows a trench), so whether the fence has a gate or not, its opening should be wide enough so a tractor can drag the surface.

Unless the soil composition is naturally rich in sand, you might want to lay down approximately one foot of it. Even after normal work mixes it into the soil, sand-rich footing helps the surface dry faster after a rain. Sand also will cushion against impact that leads to sore feet, tendon and joint strains, and other causes of lameness. That's especially important if you and your horse will be involved in jumping, cutting, reining, or roping. On the other hand, footing that's too deep will strain tendons, so once again, if you're in doubt, ask an expert.

Selecting Your American Quarter Horse

The Right Horse for You

Once you've decided that you can have a horse, you're now faced with a question that's as challenging as it is important: Of all the available American Quarter Horses in the world, which one will be the right one for you?

The answer begins with a series of preliminary decisions. They concern color and markings, gender, age, size, temperament, conformation,* and level of training or performance. Pedigrees are important to consider, too, but only if you're interested in breeding or taking part in certain activities.

COLOR

Color is one subject we can deal with in a straightforward and definitive way.

American Quarter Horses come in thirteen registrable colors, all clearly set forth in the *AQHA Official Handbook of Rules and Regulations.*

- **bay:** ranging from tan through red to reddish brown, with a black mane and tail and usually black on the lower legs.

- **black:** true black, without any light areas; the mane and tail are also black.

- **brown:** a body color of brown or black with light areas at the muzzle, eyes, flank, and inside upper legs; the mane and tail are black.

- **sorrel:** a reddish or copper-red body color; the mane and tail are usually the same color as the body, although they may be flaxen.

- **chestnut:** dark red or brownish red coat, mane, and tail (the terms "sorrel" and "chestnut" are sometimes used interchangeably, with the former more frequently applied to Western horses and the latter in English-style riding).

- **dun:** yellowish or gold body, with black or brown mane and tail; a dorsal stripe and usually zebra stripes on the legs and a transverse stripe over the withers.

---

*We'll get to the very important factor of conformation when we start looking at a prospective purchase.

- **red dun:** a form of dun with a yellowish or flesh-colored body color; a mane and tail that are red or reddish, flaxen, white, or mixed; a red or reddish dorsal stripe; and usually red or reddish zebra stripes on the legs and a transverse stripe over the withers.

- **grullo:** a smoky or mouse-colored body color (not a mixture of black and white hairs, but each hair mouse-colored) with black mane and tail; usually a black dorsal stripe and black on the lower legs.

- **buckskin:** a dark yellow or gold coat with a black mane, lower legs, and tail; no dorsal stripe.

- **palomino:** a golden yellow coat with white mane and tail.

- **gray:** a mixture of white with any other-colored hairs. Gray horses are often born solid-colored or almost solid-colored and grow lighter with age as more white hairs appear. A dapple gray has darker spots on his coat.

- **red roan:** a more or less uniform mixture of white with red hairs on a large portion of the body, but usually darker on the head and lower legs. A red roan can have a red, black, or flaxen mane and/or tail.

- **blue roan:** a coat composed of white and black hairs, with black mane, legs, and tail.

American Quarter Horses are further distinguished by white markings, the most common of which are:

FACIAL

- **snip:** a marking between the nostrils.
- **star:** any marking on the forehead.
- **strip:** a narrow vertical marking anywhere between the forehead and nostrils.
- **blaze:** a vertical marking that extends the length of the face.
- **bald face:** a very broad blaze, including one that can surround the eyes and/or muzzle.

LEGS

- **coronet:** a narrow marking around the coronet above a hoof.
- **pastern:** a marking that covers an entire pastern (there can also be a self-explanatory "half pastern").

- **sock:** a marking that extends from the coronet halfway to the knee or hock.

- **stocking:** an extended sock that reaches the knee or hock.

To distinguish American Quarter Horse from other breeds whose coats contain white markings, AQHA has addressed the question of how much white is too much in different ways for breeding and for nonbreeding stock.

With regard to breeding stock, there cannot be white above a line around each leg at the center of the knees or the point of hock, or (roughly) beyond a line from the center of the base of each ear to the cheeks and back beneath the head. However, there may be a single area of white beyond the above parameters that can be completely covered by a one-inch-diameter disk.

Geldings, spayed mares, and mares whose owners declare them to be nonbreeding stock have been allowed greater latitude. In these cases, white markings can extend farther up the legs and around most of the head. In all cases, AQHA is the ultimate arbiter of whether a horse can or cannot be registered.

How relevant is a horse's color to your choice of animal? Although equestrian lore includes cautionary sayings like, "Horses that are gray won't earn their hay" or "Four white socks and snip on his nose? Knock him on the head and feed him to the crows," the short answer is that color is just a matter of taste. Some horsemen dislike horses of particular colors or markings because of bad experiences with similar horses, but even they would admit they're being superstitious.

You'll see many bay, sorrel, and chestnut American Quarter Horses, but that's only because nature—and selective breeding—produce more in those colors than in others. As for markings, some people like a horse with lots of "chrome" (as white markings are sometimes called), while others would rather have less white. Again, it's strictly a matter of personal taste. Ultimately, although we all have favorite equine colors or markings, when it comes down to choosing a horse, as cowboys say, "a good horse is *any* color."

GENDER

Unless you're planning to go into the breeding game, a stallion will more than likely prove to be an unwise choice. The very masculine characteristics that make them so eye-catching can make them difficult to ride and even more difficult to handle. They're seldom good candidates for home-keeping, especially by less-than-experienced handlers.

Mares can prove a corresponding handful when they come into season, but they tend to be far easier than stallions to manage from the saddle or on the ground.

Geldings often are regarded as wise choices for first-time owners. With temptations of romance out of the picture, these horses usually have the steadiest temperaments.

AGE

Like puppies and kittens, young horses are adorable and fun to have around. But you're in the market for a worker, not a pet, and colts and fillies need training and seasoning before they become safe and responsive saddle horses. That's the reason why first-time owners are better off steering away from horses below the age of five.

At the other end of the age spectrum, old horses have drawbacks, too. They are prone to infirmities that come with age, such as irreversible bone and joint deterioration. The passage of time will bring other problems, too, so just when you and your old buddy have worked out a useful relationship, you'll find to your regret that it's time to retire him and look for a replacement.

Once again, the right answer for your situation depends on what you plan to do with the horse, but anywhere from age seven or eight to fourteen or fifteen is a realistic range. Even here, the higher end of the scale is often a wiser choice when it comes to finding a steady, solid citizen. Another benefit for newcomers to ownership is that older horses tend to be easier keepers (even if they've had years to perfect escape-artist strategies).

SIZE

The American Quarter Horse is historically a compact breed, ranging only a hand (four inches) or so above or below 15 hands. Crossbreeds, such as American Quarter Horse–Thoroughbred mixes, can be taller, but generally not much more. That means you won't have a very great range of height within which to choose.

Nevertheless, height alone is not the only measure of matching a horse and rider. As you will have discovered from personal experiences and observation, horses comes in different body types: long-legged or short-legged, and wide-barreled or slab-sided. Then, too, we humans come in different sizes and shapes. A large person on a small horse would present as awkward a picture as a tiny youngster on a 16-hand or taller horse would. That's why proportion is a factor in the selection process.

TEMPERAMENT

Like size, a horse's temperament becomes most relevant when you're examining individual animals, but at this point it's something else you'll want to add to your list of considerations. Although often a function of gender and age, temperament is also a mark of specific personalities. You won't want a stubborn steed that you're likely to go to war with on a daily basis. On the contrary, just as you'll want a horse with the physical ability to perform the jobs he'll be asked to do, you'll want one with a trainable and cooperative mind.*

Be sure to mention disposition when you start your search. Nobody will ever fault you for saying that you prefer a quiet and cooperative horse; as the expression goes, you don't want a horse that just goes in a snaffle—you want a horse that *stops* in a snaffle, too.

LEVEL OF TRAINING

Are you interested in barrel racing? Team penning? Hunt seat equitation? Trail riding? What you plan to do and when you hope to do it will in large part determine the right horse. If you're a relative newcomer to a particular sport, chances are you'll benefit from a horse that's "been there, done that" and can show you the ropes. Recognizing that fact will save you time and energy, since you can confine your search to the most likely places.

If, however, all you want is a nice ol' guy for pleasure riding and maybe a little something else, your range is considerably wider.

Now let's start looking.

The Role of the Expert or Adviser

Before you set out on your quest, please realize that the search should not be a solo venture. You'll need help in the form of expert assistance.

"Expert" or "adviser" in this case means someone who has sufficient knowledge about what constitutes a good horse. Professionals, such as trainers, can serve as agents for prospective buyers by locating, evaluating, and negotiating a purchase. You can find one of these consultants through a free service that

---

*Choosing an American Quarter Horse will put you ahead of the game in this department, because historically they've been bred as much for this kind of disposition as for their physical characteristics.

AQHA provides. You also may be fortunate enough to have a qualified adviser in your riding instructor, the manager of the public or private stable where you ride, or a friend or neighbor who has successfully kept a horse under the same circumstances that you plan to.* "Successfully" is a key word here. A history of crises or outright disasters is evidence that the horse keeper lacks the essential knowledge, and possibly the good sense, to be much good to you, even by negative example.

Equally important is a thorough understanding of what will be the "right" horse for you. Almost anyone can help you buy a horse, but you're not in the market for any horse. That's why your adviser must be impartial and have your best interests at heart. He or she must be able to

The assistance of a knowledgeable adviser is vital at every step of the selection process. (AQHA photo by Wyatt McSpadden)

say "no" just as easily, if not more so, than "yes," because restraining your enthusiasm—usually for the first horse you see—may be the hardest part of the job.

Even before you and your adviser think about looking for a prospect, he or she can perform a very valuable service in helping you learn what to look for. As we've said earlier in this book, you're not operating in a vacuum. You don't (or shouldn't) wake up one morning and decide it's such a lovely day, you think you'll buy a horse. You most likely know a horse or two and perhaps many more. Take advantage of your adviser's expertise by looking at one you know,

---

*Look for an expert who also will be able to advise you on more mundane matters, such as where to buy feed and hay and where to dispose of manure.

perhaps a horse the expert owns or one that you've been riding. Make this your trial run. Try to forget you know the animal very well; instead, make the effort to look at him as if you're seeing the horse for the very first time.

As you walk around the horse to form a general impression of his conformation (or physical characteristics), bear in mind that no horse qualifies as "perfectly conformed." There's simply no such animal. Every horse has at least one "hole," some sort of flaw in his conformation that's less than perfection itself. That's why horsemen evaluate not only in terms of how many good points a horse might have, but how few undesirable ones.

Among the questions you and your adviser should discuss are: Is the horse's back relatively short with well-defined withers that are level with the rump? Does the shoulder slope at the same approximately forty-five-degree

The horse in this painting by Orren Mizer embodies the ideal American Quarter Horse conformation. (AQHA)

The AMERICAN QUARTER HORSE

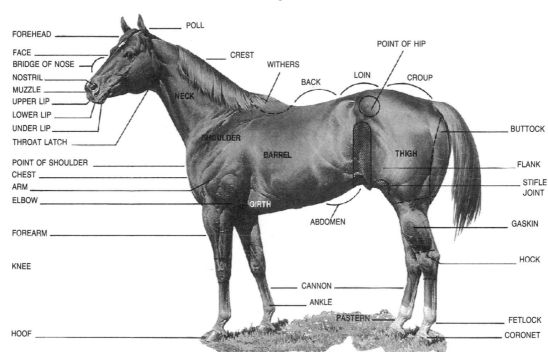

FOREHEAD
POLL
FACE
CREST
BRIDGE OF NOSE
WITHERS
NOSTRIL
MUZZLE
UPPER LIP
NECK
LOWER LIP
UNDER LIP
THROAT LATCH
SHOULDER
POINT OF SHOULDER
BARREL
CHEST
ARM
ELBOW
GIRTH
FOREARM
ABDOMEN
KNEE

POINT OF HIP
LOIN
BACK
CROUP
BUTTOCK
THIGH
FLANK
STIFLE JOINT
GASKIN
HOCK

CANNON
ANKLE
PASTERN
FETLOCK
HOOF
CORONET

The parts of the horse.

angle as the pasterns? Are the chest and the girth deep and wide? Is his neck set on right, not in an upside-down ewe-necked fashion? Are his ears set apart and are they small without being "piggy"? Are his nostrils large enough to allow generous intake of air? Are his eyes set wide apart for maximum vision ahead and to the sides and rear?

A well-conformed horse is more than the sum of his parts. Accordingly, the overall impression should be one of balanced symmetry. Do all the parts come together in a pleasing proportion, not as though the animal had been assembled from leftover parts?

Specifically, symmetry means that those parts of which there are more than one should match. One foreleg should not be thicker or thinner than the other. The hind legs should match, too. As for feet, one shouldn't be larger or rounder than its mate.

When viewed from the rear, hind-leg muscles should be equally developed; otherwise, the horse may be using one side more than the other.

Similarly, more wear on one side of a hoof is a clue that the horse is bearing more weight on that side. If the horse is wearing one or more corrective shoes, ask your adviser the reason why. Keep an eye out for contracted heels, dropped soles, and/or the telltale parallel rings in the hoof that indicate a history of founder.

Very few legs, especially those of an older horse, don't have some sort of bumps and scars. Run your hand down each leg and see for yourself. Try to keep in mind that a scar from an old puncture wound is just a blemish that most likely will not affect a horse's usability. On the other hand, a bump from a spavin or splint indicates a problem that might affect the animal's soundness.

Among foreleg lumps of which you should become aware are sidebone, or bony, protuberances on a coronet band; ringbone in the pastern joint; and splints on the sides of a foreleg between the cannon and splint bones.*

A serious hind-leg problem is bone spavin, a bony growth at the front of the hock that is often a degenerative condition that results in incurable lameness.

Touching a horse's back is another way to tell a great deal about his soundness. Press firmly along the spine. A sound animal will dip his back, while one with problems will tense in front of his croup. You won't learn all you need to know by examining one horse, or even several, in this way, but it's a good start, especially with your adviser's guidance.

Locating a Horse

The first place to look might be no farther than the stable where you're taking lessons or hiring horses for pleasure rides. That can be a real advantage: The people there, especially your instructor, know your abilities and requirements. If there's no horse in the barn that's right for you, the manager or trainer can ask around. Another avenue is to contact an American Quarter Horse breeder; AQHA offers free referrals to established individuals. Breeders normally have a large selection of horses on hand, representing an array of ages, dispositions, and training levels.

You can learn about horses for sale the same way many people learn about available jobs. That's by networking, the equivalent of dropping a pebble in a pond and watching the ripples expand in ever-widening circles. On every level, the horse world is a big "web." Trainers and grooms routinely go to shows where they see many horses. Even when they don't, they spend time with their

---

*For more information about conformation points, see the material taken from the AQHA publication *A Guide to Buying American Quarter Horses* in the appendix of this book. Another useful booklet is Dr. Marvin Beeman's authoritative *Conformation: The Relationship of Form to Function;* an understanding of the points that Dr. Beeman makes is an essential step in any horseman's education.

counterparts at other stables. Farriers and veterinarians go from barn to barn, where they hear about everything. Horse owners go to feed dealers and tack shops. Everyone talks, especially when the subject is horses that are for sale.

Advertisements for horses appear all over the place. Tack shops and feed dealerships have bulletin boards. Local *Pennysaver*-type circulars and general-interest newspapers (look under "Livestock") have classified sections. You probably won't learn more than "Quarter Horse, sorrel, 15.2, 10 yrs, quiet, easy keeper" but it may be enough to follow up on.

Good places for prospective first-time owners to look include racetracks and horse shows. (AQHA photo by Wyatt McSpadden)

Ads in regional and national equestrian magazines, including but not limited to *The Quarter Horse Journal* and *The Quarter Racing Journal*, contain not only advertisements but articles that give the names and backgrounds of breeders, trainers, and dealers in your part of the country. Although you may be somewhat reluctant to approach "big names" about wanting a horse that will never win a national title, those aren't the only animals that such people know about. A case in point involved someone who was looking for nothing fancier than a trail horse. He brought up the subject to a noted trainer he happened to meet at a horse show. That's how a lovely older Western pleasure show horse that the trainer's daughter had outgrown found a new home and a new career.

Speaking of competition settings, another fertile ground for locating horses is at rodeos, where contestants may have horses they're looking to retire. You won't find out unless and until you speak up and ask. If the person you approach can't help you, he or she may know someone who can. That's what networking is all about.

American Quarter Horse racetracks are yet another place. Although security can be a barrier to being admitted to the backside area, getting in is not impossible. A veterinarian or farrier who has clients at the track may help you find a trainer who has a racehorse that's suffering only from a case of the "slows," or a lead pony horse that's for sale. It's entirely possible that the trainer may know an outrider, or lead-pony rider, who's looking to sell a horse or whose sister-in-law is moving to a city and can't take her barrel racing horse with her. You won't know until you make the initial inquiry, and those network "ripples" widen faster than you might think.

Other places have horses for sale on a seasonal basis. Summer camps and dude ranches seldom want to keep most, if not any, of their animals over the winter, so check with them toward the end of their season. Conversely, stables where high school and college rodeo and horse show association members ride may have an overabundance of horses that aren't earning their oats when school is let out for the summer.

Another option to explore is the world of horse sales. Many well-regarded breeding and sales operations hold periodic auctions, complete with detailed catalogs and presale inspection periods during which horses can be tried. You'll learn dates and locations through announcements and advertisements in regional and national horse publications and at American Quarter Horse shows.

The sale catalog is indispensable. First of all, it contains the rules of bidding and payment procedures by which anyone making a bid is deemed to be bound. It also lists the names and addresses of sellers, including those you might want to telephone in advance of the sale to learn more about horses that caught your eye during the presale inspection period.

Local livestock auctions are geographically widespread and offer horses of many types. However, you should understand that there are different types of sales and not all may be the best place to purchase the kind of horse a first-time owner is looking for. Then, too, auctions can be intimidating, fast-paced proceedings that allow little opportunity or space to try out an animal in which you're interested.

Trying Out the Prospect

You've focused on your requirements, secured the help of a professional expert or another person to serve as your adviser (a neighbor, say, who has owned American Quarter Horses all her life), and "networked" a list of prospects. As is frequently the case, it was your adviser who heard from her farrier about the first horse you'll look at, a twelve-year-old bay registered American Quarter Horse. The only other details the farrier could pass along were that the owner, who is going off to college, showed the horse in Western pleasure and horsemanship classes, and when the horse wasn't being trained or in competition, the owner's mother and grandfather took him out on trail rides.

Sounds promising, you agree, so you phone to make an appointment. "Ask them to leave the horse in his pasture," your adviser told you, and you remember to make that request.

The owner and her parents are waiting for you and your adviser at the door to their barn. You look inside and notice a tidy, workman-like atmosphere. That's a good sign, because people who maintain clean, organized stabling facilities tend to devote the same amount of care to their animals.

Cribbing, or sucking air into the lungs, is a bad habit often caused by boredom. (The Quarter Horse Journal)

With the owner's permission, your adviser takes a closer look at the horse's stall for any signs of kick marks or teeth marks. The former are clues of an unhappy or sour horse, the latter of a stable vice called cribbing, where a horse clamps his teeth on to the feed manger or window ledge and then sucks air into his lungs. Cribbing isn't the worst habit a horse can have (a strap buckled tight around his neck will discourage him), but it can be a factor in making your determination. And that's the object of this inspection period: to gather as much information about your prospect as you can.

As you follow the owner out to the pasture, you understand why your adviser wanted the horse left there. Among the questions you'll ask yourself are: Is the horse eager to see his owner? Does he walk right up to the person, or is catching him a chore? Does he readily accept a halter? Does he lead easily, or does he show reluctance or outright stubbornness by lagging behind? Does he charge out of the pasture, dragging his handler by the lead shank?

You can begin to check the horse's conformation and way of moving as he walks up to the barn. Use the information found in this book's appendix and the points your adviser shared while you two were examining that earlier "trial run" prospect.

A good attitude is especially important in a pleasure horse. Accordingly, pay attention to the horse's temperament. Does he seem kind, the sort of good guy you'd be happy to ride and work around? Does he carry his ears pricked forward in a pleasant and alert, nonaggressive position? Similarly, do his eyes radiate kindness as well as an interest in what's going on around him?

First impressions also are valuable when it comes to watching the horse move. Even while being led at the walk, does the horse move well from the shoulder in a loose, athletic manner? Does his head move at every stride in an unrestricted fashion? When viewed from the front and rear, do his legs move straight forward and back without "paddling" in or out?

Other evidence of temperament will become evident as you watch the horse being groomed. Does he stand quietly on cross-ties or while tied to a spot near the barn door? Without confusing any playfulness with outright bad manners, see how he accepts being handled. Does he pin his ears and nip or otherwise object to having his coat, mane, and tail brushed and feet picked out? Or does he stand quietly and even relish the attention?

Once the horse is groomed, but before he's been tacked, is when your adviser will inspect his coat, looking for clean, problem-free hair. She'll also be on the lookout for evidence of spur marks (evidence that the horse may need aggressive encouragement), girth galls, or scars.

Running a hand down the animal's legs is how to look for any indication of tenderness, swellings, bumps, or splints. If your adviser finds any, she'll ask the owner for explanations and other relevant information.

Examining the horse's mouth not only checks the condition of his teeth, but also confirms his age. In this case, an indentation called the Galwayne's groove appears in the upper incisors at age ten and moves farther down the tooth with each passing year. At age fourteen or fifteen the groove should be about halfway down the tooth. Another indication is the change of shape of the front (nipper) incisors' top surface: at age fifteen they have turned from round to triangular.

While inspecting the head area, your adviser will also focus on eyes and ears. A horse that doesn't respond normally to visual or audible stimuli, such as waving a hand in a nonthreatening fashion or quietly clucking from behind, may have some degree of vision or hearing impairment or loss. Other more obvious clues to problems are fluid discharge from or crud around the eyes, tilting the head (as if to escape internal auditory nerve pressure), or tenderness around the ears.

As you and your adviser watch the owner tack up, notice whether the horse is headshy about the bridle. Does he readily accept the bit, or is getting it into his mouth like root-canal work? How does he behave while the blanket or pad and the saddle go on, especially when the cinch or girth is tightened: Does he stand quietly, or does he try to bite or kick?

If you've liked what you've seen so far, you can't wait to climb aboard and try the horse. But not so fast—that's not the way the procedure goes. Someone of the owner's choosing, in this case the young lady herself, always gets on first. It's a matter of safety, in case the horse misbehaves. It's also a matter of perspective, because you'll have a much better view of how the horse moves when you're down on the ground.

So you and your adviser and the owner's parents troop over to the corral to watch the owner put her horse though his paces. She starts by asking for nothing more complicated than the basic walk, jog (or trot), and lope (or canter) in both directions. Questions that you'll ask yourself here begin with whether the horse has a regular and rhythmic four-beat walk, two-beat jog, and three-beat lope. Does he move calmly, straight, and forward? Does he make smooth transitions between the gaits? Does he halt easily and squarely? Does he back in a straight line with any resistance? Does he change directions without any steering problems? Does he make smooth and even bends around his turns? How are his turns on the forehand and on the haunches? If the horse is asked to step over a cross-rail or another low obstacle or to move off the rider's leg while she opens a gate, does he do so with no hesitation?

Much as you may like how the horse goes for his owner, remember that your job is to be critical. Keep your eyes open for any resistance, evasions, or other "holes" in the horse's performance. A horse that does something funny with his usual rider on his back is more apt to do it with you.

The owner then may be likely to move on to such advanced work as flying lead changes and a spin or two. A horse that's trained in the hunter-jumper disciplines would be asked to trot, then canter over one or more low jumps. If the horse is a barrel racer and there are barrels in the ring, or if he's a roping or team penning horse and there are practice cattle handy, this is the time for a demonstration.

Let's say that you and your adviser still like what you've seen. The owner dismounts, you step aboard, pick up the reins . . . Now what?

Begin the trial ride by asking the horse to perform the basic gaits.
(AQHA photo by Wyatt McSpadden)

Put simply, ride the horse to the best of your ability without trying to impress anyone. The people watching aren't horse-show judges, they're concerned owners who just permitted a stranger (that's you) to get on their horse.

The key word as you put the horse through his paces is "critical," in the sense of "fault-finding." The owner, who knows her horse, has a vested interest in downplaying or disguising any shortcomings the animal may have. That's not dishonesty; it's salesmanship. Therefore, it's your job to look for any such faults in the horse's athletic ability, training, and soundness.

Start at the beginning, as if the owner hadn't ridden the horse. Before you mount, loosen and then retighten the cinch or girth: Does the horse lay his ears back or turn to nip? Is he easy to mount or does he move away from you? Does his back react as you settle in to the saddle by humping ("coldback"), or do his hindquarters droop from the additional pressure? Does the horse move off your leg cues easily (he's just been ridden, so he should be tuned in to a rider's leg)?

Is his walk four-beat and comfortably paced without any "jigging"?

Pay special attention to the jog (or trot), which is the best gait to assess a horse's way of going. A sound horse keeps his head steady; a major tip-off to any problem is an excessively bobbing head, since a horse will raise his head as a lame foreleg strikes the ground and drop it as a hind leg hits. Is his trot equally comfortable and a good two-beat gait?

As you jog a fifty-foot- to sixty-foot-diameter circle, listen for any irregularity in that two-beat footfall. As you decrease the circle's size to ten or fifteen feet, the horse will be forced to put additional weight on his inside legs and their joints while his outside legs take larger steps. That's when any problems are likely to become evident; you'll both hear and feel any variations in the jog's rhythm.

Then change direction, not by halting and turning, but by staying at the jog as if going through the center of a figure eight. There should be no change in the sound or feel of rhythm or regularity during the change of direction or in the new direction. Although many horses have one direction they prefer, you certainly shouldn't feel you're now riding a different animal.

Just as humans are right- or left-handed, many horses have their favorite lead. That's something to remember when you ask for the lope (or canter). Nevertheless, you shouldn't have to struggle to achieve one lead or the other. While you're in that gait, listen and feel for a regular three-beat rhythm. Also listen for any sounds of labored or raspy breathing that could indicate an unsoundness known as "roaring."

Transitions between gaits will bring out many hind-leg weaknesses. Even a horse that's very heavy on his forehand will need to support himself behind, so your adviser will want to see you move from jog to halt, lope to walk, and all other combinations.

Your trial ride should last just as long as necessary, and no longer. The owner and her parents have better things to do than watch you ride the hair off their horse. Nor is it fair to tire out a horse under any circumstances, particularly if other prospective buyers are due later in the day.

You dismount (listening for any signs of wheezing or labored breathing—the "detective work" isn't over yet), hand the reins to the horse's owner, and you and your adviser walk off a little way.

"What do you think?" the adviser wants to know.

What's to prevent you from replying "I'll take him!"? Once again, the answer is, "That depends."

Although you may feel in your heart of hearts that the horse is the right one for you, the kind of unbridled enthusiasm that leads to reaching for your checkbook may be premature. Nowhere is it written that you must buy the first horse you look at. If you have a list of other prospects to see, what's the harm in looking at them, too? What if there's another horse you'll like just as much, or perhaps even more, than the one you just saw? The answer is, you won't know until you look.

Here's where your adviser will be of great value. Everyone who's spent time around horses has seen a prospective owner fall in love with the first horse he or she looks at. That's why you've got to listen to your adviser's kind but firm "hold your horses!"

There's a strategic reason, too. Appearing overeager works against an opportunity to negotiate a lower price. Saying you want to think about it is an accepted reaction, as is admitting that you have other horses to look at. Of course, the seller is likely to reply that her fine critter may be sold out from under you, and maybe that's true. Should you take the chance? Ask your adviser.

If you're truly interested in this horse and your adviser concurs, ask the owner whether you can take the animal home on trial. A week or ten days is more than enough to see how he works out at your place, since it may take a few days until he grows accustomed to the change of scenery. The owner may be reluctant to entrust her good animal to a first-time horse keeper, but the promise of supervision by your adviser may persuade her.

The Purchase

Whether it's the first horse you see or another one, at some point you'll find the horse that's right for you. The price will be subject to negotiation, an acceptable and accepted practice—that's why it's called horse tradin'. But rather than conclude the deal with no more than a handshake as money changes hands, consider the value of a sales contract.

As with co-leases or other types of transactions, written agreements that spell out all the terms reduce the chance of misunderstandings. They also can provide procedures to resolve disputes that may arise. The agreement needn't be more complicated than any other sales contract, but it should contain the following provisions:

- The horse is identified as specifically as possible, especially by his AQHA registration number if one exists.

- The seller warrants that he or she has the right to pass unrestricted ownership of the animal. The seller further warrants that any AQHA registration papers are valid.

- The amount and manner of payment are spelled out. Whether the entire sum will be paid at once or over time, or whether after a veterinarian's examination, and whether any down payment is refundable are all questions that need to be addressed.

Many, if not most, first-owner horses are sold "as is," and that's how the phrase appears in sales contracts. Its rough translation is "you're buying only what *you* think you're buying." In that way, the seller makes no guarantees about the horse's abilities or physical condition. However, "as is" doesn't let the seller entirely off the hook. One implied warranty ("implied" means that it's imposed by law) in any sale is that the item is suitable for the purposes the buyer says he wants it for. So if you tell the seller what you want in a horse and he says or does nothing that would lead you to believe the horse won't fit your requirements, even a written "as is" provision in which the seller disclaims all warranties won't stand if you later claim an intentional misrepresentation.

Vague? Complex? That's the law, or rather, it may be the law, because some legal provisions that govern commercial transactions vary from state to state. Any questions about what a contract should or should not contain are best answered by a professional. In this case, that's a lawyer.

VETERINARY EXAM

Even with a trial period, you don't want to commit yourself until a veterinarian has conducted a prepurchase examination. You, not the seller, select the vet, but not just any one. Veterinarians specialize, and the small-animal doctor who looks after Rover or Kitty may not have the large-animal expertise required for equine practice (but he or she may be able to recommend a colleague). Your adviser is far more likely to know an equine vet, or you can use the person your riding lessons stable uses.*

A prepurchase examination by a veterinarian of the buyer's choosing is an essential part of the selection process. (Bayer Corporation)

Like your adviser, the vet should be able to assess the horse in the context of your capabilities and the animal's intended use. For example, one that might not pass as a high-performance cutting or roping competitor could be perfectly acceptable as a pleasure riding mount.

Vets seldom say, "Buy this horse." More times than not they make their recommendations in terms of pros and cons, with an emphasis on the latter. They'll itemize all the actual and potential problems their examination reveals. Then, and again with the assistance of your adviser, it's up to you to make your decision.

Vets also are reluctant to comment with respect to whether horses are worth their specific asking prices; such diplomacy keeps customers. And with further regard to money matters, how much you'll spend for the prepurchase

---

*You can also use the locator service provided by the American Association of Equine Practitioners by phoning (800)GET-ADVM.

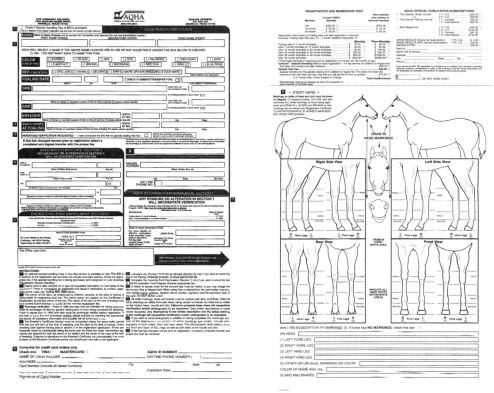

Registration application

exam will depend on what you want done: X rays, blood workups, and ultrasound all cost more.

Registration

Registering a horse with AQHA is insurance to protect your investment. Registration takes little time or money, yet it greatly improves a horse's sale value.

AQHA offers two registration possibilities. The "AQHA Numbered" section comprises the largest portion and consists of horses whose parents were both numbered American Quarter Horses. A second type of registration is "Appendix."* These are horses that have one numbered American Quarter Horse parent and one Thoroughbred parent as recognized by that breed's registry, The Jockey Club. Additionally, foals that have one numbered American Quarter Horse parent and one Appendix-registered parent also are eligible for registration in the Appendix section.

*An Appendix horse may advance to the AQHA Numbered Registry by fulfilling Register of Merit requirements and by meeting physical standards as outlined in the *AQHA Official Handbook,* copies of which are available from AQHA.

Certificate of registration

Transfer report

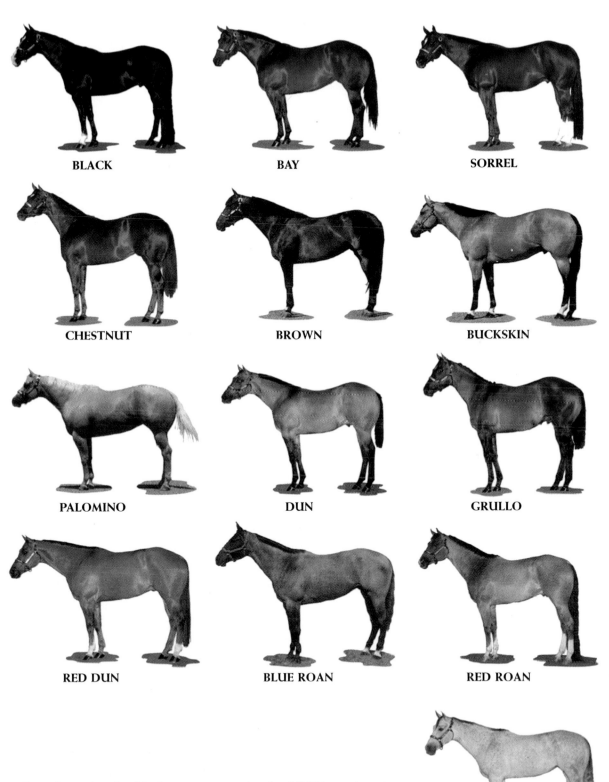

BLACK

BAY

SORREL

CHESTNUT

BROWN

BUCKSKIN

PALOMINO

DUN

GRULLO

RED DUN

BLUE ROAN

RED ROAN

GRAY

In order to be elegible for registration by the AQHA, an American Quarter Horse must be one of these thirteen recognized colors. As an example of recognized markings, the sorrel has stockings on his hind legs and a star on his forehead.

Rugged Lark became one of the most famous American Quarter Horses to perform in the spotlight. He was recognized in 1996 with the AQHA Silver Spur Award for his contributions as an ambassador and entertainer.

Modern racetracks are a far cry from dashes along colonial country roads, but the goal remains the same: to reach top speed as quickly as possible, then to cross the finish line first.

In October 1996, Evening Snow became the first horse of any breed to break the 21-second barrier from a closed starting gate. The gelding covered the classic American Quarter Horse distance of 440 yards in :20.94 and traveling in excess of 54 miles per hour.

A cutting horse does all the work, giving the rider little to do but enjoy "the best seat in the house."

Calf roping is another AQHA horse show event that traces its roots back to actual ranch work.

Few bonds in life are stronger than the one between an owner and his or her American Quarter Horse.

Each registered American Quarter Horse has a registration certificate, whether regular or appendixed. Among the benefits of having one is that only horses with valid up-to-date registrations are eligible to compete in AQHA-approved events. A certificate should be checked carefully at the time of purchase to make certain the animal in question is indeed a registered American Quarter Horse.

To maintain current ownership records, AQHA requires notification or an official transfer whenever a horse changes owners. Notification must be sent to AQHA on a transfer of ownership form, which must be completed by both the seller and the buyer, along with the horse's registration certificate and proper transfer fee. Once AQHA records the transfer of ownership, the horse's registration certificate is mailed to the new owner.

If the seller or sale company does not provide a registration certificate and a properly completed AQHA transfer of ownership form (seller's information), you should have no obligation to complete the purchase. Also, if a horse's registration certificate does not list the owner as the person who is selling the horse, you should not purchase the horse until the seller has updated the ownership record with AQHA.

If the horse has changed owners several times and transfers of ownership were not recorded with AQHA, you can seek AQHA assistance in updating the horse's ownership record. However, it's best to investigate this process before you commit to buying the horse.

In summary, once you've selected a particular American Quarter Horse, but before any money changes hands, check the registration certificate both to ensure the seller is the current owner listed and to ensure that the document describes the horse according to his age, hair color, and markings (such as the white hair patterns on the head and legs, brands, and scars). Watch as the seller completes the transfer of ownership form to ensure its accuracy.

Registration eligibility requirements and information about any registered American Quarter Horse can be obtained by calling AQHA.

FOR FURTHER INFORMATION

AQHA offers the following videos on the subject of choosing an American Quarter Horse:

Survival of the Fittest. Dr. Marvin Beeman, noted equine veterinarian, discusses
   American Quarter Horse conformation and the relationship of form to

function. Suitable for beginners and experienced horsemen. Also available in Spanish. Two parts. 26 minutes each.

Form to Function: The Importance of Conformation. The effect of a horse's conformation on his ability to perform is illustrated. Suitable for beginning and experienced horsemen interested in knowing why an ideally conformed horse is most often found in the winner's circle. 11 minutes.

III

Caring for
Your American
Quarter Horse

Nutrition and Feeding

The expression "eats like a horse" describes people who can gorge themselves on great quantities of food and then come back for more. In reality, it doesn't work that way with horses—any horse that behaved like that would become sick as a dog.

For such big, strong animals, horses have a remarkably delicate digestive system. The system responds well to a good diet and a regular schedule, but a horse that becomes upset by what he eats or by physical or temperamental stress will respond with a variety of ailments, such as colic or founder.* That's why creating and maintaining a healthy feeding routine is the single most important favor you can do for your horse.

Another reason experienced horsemen pay close attention to their animals' eating patterns is that any break in routine means their horses are telling them that something is wrong. Most serious is a horse that goes "off his feed," completely rejecting anything that's offered. That's a red flag that a visit from the veterinarian is needed as soon as possible.

The Equine Digestive System

Understanding how the equine digestive system works will put the subject in perspective.

The system begins in the mouth, where chewed food becomes mixed with saliva. The liquefied food passes through the five-foot-long esophagus into the stomach.

Given a full-grown horse's size, his stomach has a relatively small capacity: just two to four gallons (or only about 10 percent of that of a cow). Not much digestion occurs in the stomach, through which it takes almost twenty-four hours for food to pass.

The longest segment of the digestive system is the small intestine, which accounts for some 70 percent of the system's one hundred feet. It's here that most nutrients are absorbed. The food then enters the large intestine through the cecum, a "holding tank" with a capacity of some ten gallons where bacteria break down what was once hay and other roughage into cellulose and glucose.

---

*But not by regurgitating—horses are incapable of vomiting.

The food then forms into feces in the large and small colons and is eliminated through the rectum.

A healthy horse makes manure approximately every three hours. The quantity and condition of the droppings indicate how well the animal's digestive system is working; they are, in fact, indications of the overall way the horse is being maintained. For example, the presence of undigested grain is evidence the horse isn't chewing his food properly, which should prompt his owner (or a veterinarian) to check the state of his teeth. Droppings that are very soft indicate a diet of too much green grass or hay or pasturage that has a high legume content; loose stools are also a sign of stress and fatigue from overwork. Hard manure is a tip-off to a diet that contains dry hay, too much grass hay, or too little water.*

A water pail set on the ground can be easily knocked over, so a permanent solid trough is far more effective. (The Quarter Horse Journal)

Water

If we define a nutrient as a substance that's essential to sustain a living creature by providing energy and growth, water must head the list. Half of a horse's body weight comes from water, of which a loss of even 20 percent can prove fatal. The average full-grown horse needs a daily minimum of eight to ten gallons, increased by such factors as weather with high temperatures

---

*In the event of hard stools or constipation, a bran mash will act as a laxative. As an example of preventive care, many horsemen routinely feed their horses a mash every week, a subject about which your veterinarian is the best judge. Typically, the mash is a mixture of bran and oats in a 2:1 to 4:1 ratio mixed with enough hot water to make a firm but not runny consistency. The mash is then fed when cool.

and low humidity, a dry, high-fiber diet (most notably hay), and/or strenuous activity.

Water must be available at all times, whether from a stream or pond, from a trough in the pasture, or from buckets or an automatic fountain in the stall. Since horses will drink less when their water is dirty or stagnant, keeping troughs and buckets clean is an important stable chore. They need periodic scourings to remove all traces of feed and hay particles, algae, and any other foreign substance.

Horses won't consider snow or ice to be a source of water, so winter chores must include clearing off any frozen pond or trough as often as necessary.

Feed

The nutritional requirements of horses consist of proteins, carbohydrates, fats, minerals, and vitamins.

Proteins account for 20 percent of a horse's body weight. They are essential for growth and tissue repair. Sources include legume grasses and hay, as well as grain.

Carbohydrates are the energy-creating "fuel" portion of the diet.

Fats supply energy and body heat. Oats and corn are important sources.

Such minerals as salt and calcium are essential for strong bones and steady, solid growth.

Grass and Hay

Unlike the carnivorous predators that hunted them, equines in the wild never had to work hard to find food. It was always as close as the grass at their feet.

Horses left alone at pasture spend most of their waking hours grazing. That's what eons of evolution have programmed them to do. This constant intake of grass provides a steady supply of nutrients. Almost as important in modern times, grazing provides the animals with something to keep them busy, and that in turn keeps them emotionally content.

Domesticated horses rely on fresh or dried grass that we call "hay" for anywhere from half to all of their nutritional needs. That takes a substantial amount: Horses at work require a minimum of 1 percent of their body weight in grass or hay each day, which works out to ten to fifteen pounds for a full-grown American Quarter Horse.

HAY

All horses, even those that are pasture-kept, require hay for the roughage that moves food through their system (the fiber also stimulates saliva production). Determining which type to feed depends on availability, as well as any special nutritional needs.

Hay comes in two categories: legumes and grasses.

Legumes produce nitrogen and are higher in protein and calcium than grasses. Alfalfa is a popular and widely available nutritious choice.

There are several things of which owners of horses that feed on alfalfa need be aware. First, an alfalfa diet causes horses to excrete excess nitrogen in the form of urea; the animals increase their water consumption and, therefore, urinate more frequently. That in itself doesn't signify a kidney problem.

Alfalfa attracts an insect known as the blister beetle, whose body contains a potentially fatal toxin that damages a horse's intestinal lining. Alfalfa hay grown in parts of the country inhabited by these beetles must be examined for any that were crushed during harvesting and baling (dealers in these regions typically certify hay that is blister beetle–free).

Leading the list of other popular legumes is red clover. It contains about two-thirds the digestible protein of alfalfa, but it has a higher total of digestible nutrients and therefore provides slightly more energy. However, red clover is more prone to mold than alfalfa.

Another legume called lespedeza tends to retain higher quantities of dust.

Hay grasses, which are richer in carbohydrates than legumes, can be divided according to the climate where they grow. Cool-season grasses include timothy, the most prevalent and popular hay grass. Other types are brome and red-top (known in some parts of the country as red-tip). Among popular warm-season varieties are Kentucky bluegrass, Bermuda grass, Johnson grass, and bahia grass.

Because legume hays are generally too rich to be fed by themselves, most horsemen add hay grasses to make a mixed hay; for example, alfalfa and brome or clover and timothy. The blend is usually produced from several varieties growing together in the hay field, not from being mixing after harvest.

The cereal grasses, such as oats, barley, and wheat, need be mentioned only briefly. These hays are lower in calcium than legume and grass hays, and their nitrate levels (for which they should be tested) can be too high for safe consumption. Silage fed to cattle is unacceptable for horses, whose digestive system is much more sensitive than that of cows. Because silage is too wet for horses, it is almost certain to produce colic.

The quality of both legume and grass hay depends on when it was cut, cured (another word for aged), and baled. Young, immature plants can be identified by small stems and many leaves and an absence of visible flowers or seed heads. They are highest in protein and other energy-producing nutrients, but lower in cellulose fiber. Conversely, as a plant ages, its fiber content increases while its nutritional value declines.

The best hay, which is known as "first-cut," is harvested before the grass goes to seed.

The quality of hay depends on postharvest factors, too. Hay that is baled while wet is likely to form mold, much like the mildew that comes from storing wet clothing; the mold can cause colic as well as heaves. Hay that is too dusty can produce asthma and heaves, while hay that was baled after it dried out will have lost its optimum nutritional value.

Learning how to recognize top-quality hay is a matter of using your senses, just the way we judge any other kind of food. Good hay feels tender, neither brittle nor soggy; first-cut hay is soft because it comes from young tender plants. Good hay smells sweet, and it's free from dust, mold, and insect carcasses. On the other hand, moldy hay has that unmistakable odor of musty clothing that comes out of old trunks or suitcases. Dusty hay is also easy to recognize. Although a certain amount of soil is bound to remain in baled hay (and dusty hay can always be wet down before feeding), keep in mind that if you're buying by weight, it's hay you want to pay for, not the soil in which it was grown.

Grass hay plants have their seeds in their heads, while the seeds of legumes are in the flowers (clover is a common example). Rub a head or flower and see whether it falls to pieces easily. If it does, if there's no resistance, it's "gone to seed" and has less nutritional value than younger plants. If more than half the grass in a bale is in that condition, it's not top-quality hay.

With regard to color, look for green. Shades of brown are a sign of bleaching by the sun or exposure to rain, both of which cause a loss of nutrients to some degree. A bale with faded hay on the outside is acceptable if the interior is a darker green; the pale outside indicates only that the bale was exposed to light.

When you sample baled hay, don't inspect just the outside of the bale. Ask to have a bale cut open or use a sampling gadget that bores through to a bale's core. As we've learned, a bale with a moist center isn't acceptable. In addition

A bale of hay breaks into slices called "flakes." (AQHA photo by Wyatt McSpadden)

to its poor nutrition, it might set itself on fire from spontaneous combustion. Instead, you want hay that's dry throughout the bale.*

The experience of lifting bales will teach you what one should feel like. Any bale that seems heavier than normal could contain a substantial amount of moist hay.

There shouldn't be a significant presence of weeds, such as thistles and other broadleafs. Weeds lessen a hay's nutritional value, so why accept junk food when you're paying for a better meal? Weeds also tend to retain moisture and thus promote mold growth faster than pure hay grass.

Buying hay—in fact, all your feed—from a reputable dealer is sound advice. Your expert adviser, veterinarian, or a professional horseman can point you in the right direction. If you choose not to use a dealer, ask a county extension agent or university agricultural service to analyze the pasturage in terms of suitability and nutritional content before you buy hay from a nearby farm or before cutting and curing any grass on your own property.

---

*Even after you've learned what to look for, don't feel self-conscious about inspecting hay. While you're looking, remember that examining more than one bale is considered a professional approach.

Most hay is sold in bales, usually in a rectangular shape that can weigh anywhere between forty and one hundred pounds. These bales are the easiest to handle and store. They also come apart easily into "flakes," slices or chunks, that measure approximately eight inches across. Several flakes usually take care of a morning or evening feeding.

Larger units of hay, such as the circular bales that weigh upward of two hundred pounds, are more suitable for multihorse facilities. It generally requires special equipment to move them and large ring feeders to prevent waste.

Alfalfa cubes are an alternative to baled hay. Weighing twenty to thirty pounds per cubic foot, they contain less waste than baled hay and are easily handled and stored. However, cubes are more expensive than baled hay.

Pelleted hay is composed of grass that has been ground and compressed into pellets that weigh some forty pounds per cubic foot. The drawback is that they don't provide enough colic-suppressing roughage or stimulate saliva production. Nor do pellets afford horses the activity that comes from grazing: Stabled horses tend to wolf down the pellets, then spend the rest of their time being bored. That's why owners who feed pellets supplement them with baled hay.

Hay should be stored under a roof, out of the rain and snow. Haylofts above barns are designed for that purpose, providing a dry and well-ventilated environment. Since moisture is the enemy, hay must rest on a dry surface. Concrete tends to absorb and retain dampness, so the bales belong on wooden pallets instead of a concrete floor.

How much hay to buy at one time depends on your horse's requirements (which your veterinarian can help you determine) and your storage facility's capacity. Buying as much as you can store at one time makes a certain amount of sense, since buying in bulk usually results in a better rate. Don't worry about any loss of quality: Good hay can be stored indoors for up to two years without losing much more than 20 percent of its nutritional value.

Horse owners with limited feed needs and equally limited storage space might investigate buying in to a larger supply, such as from a nearby horse dealer or trainer. Or a group of "backyard" owners might form a co-op arrangement if a member of the group has a large storage area.

As for the cost of hay, the universal response of "it depends" once again applies. Prices fluctuate according to the time of year, the yield of that year's crop (like other agricultural produce, hay quality and quantity vary from year to year), the quality of the hay you're buying, and the transportation distance from the source of the hay.

GRAIN

Horses survive very nicely in the wild on grass alone. But feral animals don't do any work, so they need a limited energy supply. Working horses need more energy, which comes in the form of grain.

Grain not only provides more energy than grass or hay, it supplies it more efficiently: Horses digest 70 percent of the grain they eat, as opposed to about 50 percent of the hay. Grain is also an important source of phosphorus, an essential mineral.

Leading the list of feed grains are oats, the standard by which all other feeds are judged. Oats are an excellent source of protein and phosphorus. They're easy to digest, too: When eaten, they form a loose mass in the horse's stomach.

Although wheat in itself isn't a good grain for horses, its outer coating, which is known as bran, is rich in phosphorus and niacin. Bran is bulky and a mild laxative, and it mixes well with oats.

Corn is low in protein compared with other grains, so it makes a good choice for horses that are fed protein-rich legume

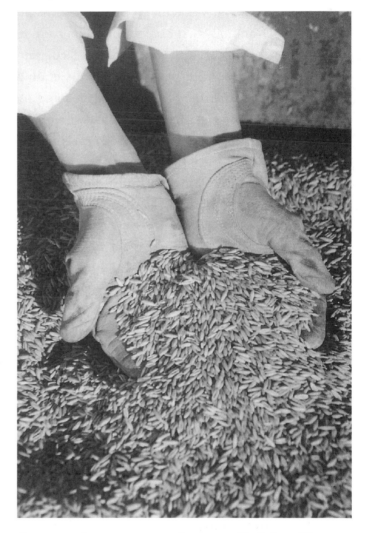

Oats are an important source of energy and body heat. They are a main ingredient of sweet feed. (*The Quarter Horse Journal*/Richard Chamberlain)

hay and/or are turned out in pastures full of clover. Corn is full of calories, and since calories turn to fat when they are not burned up, corn-fed horses tend to feel the summer heat faster than horses on other feeds.

Barley, which is high in protein, is full of energy. However, its hull is too tough for horses to chew, so barley must first be ground up; the cost of that process makes barley relatively expensive.

Although beet pulp isn't a true grain, it's an alternative feed for horses that cannot or should not eat grain, especially for animals that need to gain weight. Composed of crushed beets, the feed must be thoroughly soaked for at least eight to ten hours; it cannot be stored in a saturated state, since it will spoil. Soaking is essential: Beet pulp that is not completely saturated absorbs water from the horse's stomach, with a colic-producing result.

There's no way to harvest feed grain and avoid picking up soil, leaves, and other foreign matter. That's why grain must be cleaned by filtration through mesh netting before it is bagged and sold. When shopping for oats, look for dust-free kernels. Open a few whole shells (you can't do that with corn or barley) and see whether the kernels inside fill the entire shell. Full shells mean you're getting full value.

The terms "crimped" and "rolled" both refer to the process of crushing hulls to make the entire feed more digestible. Some horses bolt their grain so eagerly they don't bother to chew, while others, especially older animals with tooth problems, are unable to chew. Like ground barley, crimped or rolled oats or corn are easier for your horse to digest, but processing costs passed along to the consumer may be difficult for you to absorb.

Commercial feed is a practical alternative to grain. Premixed with supplements added, it's popular with owners of one or two horses and limited space. Another advantage is that everything is well distributed throughout the sack, so thorough mixing already has been taken care of.

This type of feed comes in two kinds. Sweet feed is so called because of the presence of molasses, a very tasty addition that holds the other ingredients together. Pelleted feed is composed of ingredients that are compressed; each pellet is an all-in-one tiny energy capsule.

As for ingredients, you'll find grain products; plant protein products such as cottonseed, peanuts, or soybeans; processed grain by-products (often beer brewery leftovers); alfalfa meal; cane or beet molasses if sweet feed; plant clipping forage for protein and fiber; roughage such as corncobs and grain hulls; and vitamins and minerals.

The package label will tell you the minimum percentages of nutrients. As a general rule, experts recommend a minimum of 10 percent protein, 3 percent fat, and 5 to 20 percent fiber. About 10 percent is moisture, and the rest is energy-producing carbohydrates.

The price of sweet or pelleted feed is generally competitive with grains. That's because the manufacturer purchases the ingredients in far greater bulk than an individual or a group could, and the savings are passed along to consumers.

Which grain or feed to use depends on the type of feed, the size and age of your horse, and the amount of work the animal does. Again, your vet is the best source of information. As he or she will remind you, caloric density is determined by weight, the reason why you should feed by weight and not by volume. Even with the same type of grain, the size of kernels can vary, so relying on how much fits in a scoop or a coffee can isn't an accurate guide. Instead, weigh the amount of grain that fills a scoop or can, then use the server accordingly.

Use a can to measure feed if you wish, but the amount you feed your horse should be based on the weight of the can's contents, not the volume. (The Quarter Horse Journal)

VITAMINS AND MINERALS

A well-balanced diet should provide all the nutrients any horse needs (whether a vitamin or mineral deficiency exists can be revealed by analyzing feed, and blood and hair samples). But just as there are times when stress or a physical ailment that you may face is helped by a vitamin or mineral supplement, so your horse may require similar additions to his feed. As the following brief survey shows, vitamins and minerals are important to equine metabolism and overall well-being, in the sense that their absence opens the door to all sorts of problems.

Vitamin A wards off infections, helps promote healthy vision and skin, and provides certain neurological benefits.

The **vitamin B complex family,** which includes thiamin (B_1) and niacin, stimulates and maintains normal appetite and growth, and it also helps to release energy from other nutrients.

Vitamin D is well known to be necessary for the absorption of calcium and phosphorus for teeth and bone growth.

Vitamin E helps maintain muscles and nerves, and it promotes healing.

With regard to minerals:

Sodium transfers nutrients to cells, promotes muscle action, prevents heat stress, and maintains water balance.

Calcium and **phosphorus** promote bone growth.

Potassium metabolizes carbohydrates and helps muscles function efficiently.

Magnesium aids neurological processes.

Iron supplies oxygen to cells, with the assistance of copper.

Zinc promotes good skin as well as proper weight maintenance.

Iodine governs the horse's thyroid functions.

Selenium supports muscle and cell activity.

These and others are found naturally in grains and grasses. They appear in commercial feed, and many horsemen routinely put them into home-mixed grain. What, then, is the value of commercial supplements* found on tack-shop shelves and in catalogs?

The answer will depend on whom you ask. Some horsemen and veterinarians swear by supplements, while others argue that giving them to horses on proper diets is superfluous at best. Something on which everyone agrees, however, is that too much of a good thing (selenium or zinc, for example) can produce toxic levels.

One final word on a supplement that everyone will appreciate: A splash of vegetable cooking oil added to your horse's feed will add a shine to his coat.

---

*You'll come across the words "chelated minerals" on some labels. Chelated minerals are attached to other substances to increase absorption, particularly in older horses.

SALT

One "supplement" that is essential for every horse is salt. A mature horse requires three ounces a day, the reason why a salt block that also has such trace minerals as potassium and calcium belongs in every stall and pasture.

In that regard, a horse sweats not only water but sodium, potassium, calcium, and other salts. Known collectively as electrolytes and sold as such, these minerals should be added to the horse's drinking water after strenuous exercise in hot weather.

First-time owners need to be aware of their horse's nutritional requirements, but they shouldn't lose sleep over whether the diet needs altering. As a practical matter, the vast majority of horses go on eating just what they did before they moved to new homes. After all, any former nutritional problem would have shown up in the animal's appearance and performance. Since your horse was healthy enough for you to buy him, the expression "if it ain't broke, don't fix it" makes sense in this regard, too. Of course, any questions on the subject should be addressed to your veterinarian.

Should any changes be indicated, however, they need to be made gradually. Switching from a legume to a grass hay, for example, takes about two weeks for a horse's system to adapt to; that's the time required to produce the type of intestinal bacteria that can digest the new substance completely.

Feeding Schedule

Now for how and when to feed.

Arrange your life so that you can feed your horse twice a day, once in the morning and again in the late afternoon. Then stick to the schedule. Horses are such creatures of habit that they become upset when meals are delayed, even if they are out in a pasture with plenty of grass. Some have been known to become so stressed that colic results. That's why feeding within the same hour each and every day is the ideal, subject to other activities (for example, taking along a grain-and-hay picnic is unnecessary if you two are out on a late-afternoon trail ride).

Hay can be fed on the ground to a horse that's outdoors. Choose a dry patch of ground (perhaps under a shed roof) away from manure. However, feeding hay off the ground leads to less waste and cleaner hay. If indoors, the hay can be placed on the floor of the stall. In either case, break up the flakes so the horse won't waste hay by flinging an entire flake around.

Feeding hay off the ground leads to less waste—and cleaner hay. (The Quarter Horse Journal)

A haynet is a more efficient method than serving hay on a stall floor, especially when a horse likes to eat his bedding. Hang the net securely and, for safety's sake, high enough so the top is never below the horse's chest even when the net is empty.

When equine allergies require hay to be fed wet, it needs to be more than just moistened. Drench the hay with a hose or soak it in a tubful of water for ten minutes or more. Your vet will show you the proper consistency.

Grain or feed belongs in a manger or feed bin bolted to the stall wall or in flat-bottomed feed tub out in a pasture. Loose buckets are easily tipped over, which spills—and wastes—the contents.

A stalled horse that looks forward to his breakfast will likely bolt down his grain, so you'll want to take the edge off his appetite by first feeding a few flakes of hay. (He won't be hungry enough to fall for that ploy in afternoon feedings, though, since he knows grain is on its way.)

Not every horse that bolts his grain needs to be fed crimped or rolled grain. A few large rocks or bricks placed in the feed bin forces him to nose around them for smaller mouthfuls at a time.

Don't take for granted that the feed you bought is still in edible condition. Sweet feed, beet pulp, and even grain can spoil, so make a sight-and-smell test part of your feeding routine.

Just as we've been cautioned to wait an hour after eating before we go swimming, the same sort of time frame applies to horses. Give your horse at least forty-five minutes to start digesting his meal before you work him. Similarly, don't feed him while he's still hot from work; wait at least a half hour after he's thoroughly cool.

As for treats, a few carrots or an apple or two are always appreciated (lumps of sugar are an acquired taste that some horses never develop). Breaking or cutting the vegetables or fruit into small pieces reduces the chance of choking. If you insist on hand-feeding, remember that teeth don't distinguish between a piece of carrot or apple and the fingers that are holding it: Present the treats on your flattened palm.

A net hung at the height of a horse's head is an efficient way to feed hay. (AQHA photo by Wyatt McSpadden)

Then, too, horses that receive frequent hand-fed goodies begin to expect them. That can lead to inquiring nips at any hands in the general vicinity of their face. Many owners and riders always place treats in feed bins, and their horses are no less grateful.

🐎 Stall Maintenance

A horse that spends any time in a stall will appreciate more than just a bare and ultimately damp floor. That's the purpose of bedding, which provides a mattress-like cushion that also absorbs the moisture that comes from the animal's waste products.

Wood shavings or sawdust are a very popular kind of bedding throughout the country. They are also commonly used for overnight stabling at competitions, where exhibitors can bring their own or purchase on site. Shavings and sawdust are also relatively inexpensive; a sawmill or lumber company in your area may be happy to let you haul away as much as you wish. If you choose to buy, both shavings and sawdust are sold commercially in bags that can be stored more easily than bales of straw.

Between the two choices, shavings don't clump up into thick clods when wet as sawdust does, nor do shavings create so much dust (a major consideration if your horse has allergies).

The most traditional, if not the most widely used, material is straw. The most prevalent variety is wheat straw, which is less dusty than oat or barley straw. Although straw drains well and has a crispness and color that many horsemen find appealing, it is less absorbent than shavings or sawdust. Then, too, many horses also find straw appetizing, with undesirable grass bellies as a result. If that's the case with your horse, he'll need to bed on something that's less palatable.

As for other choices, ground corncobs, peanut shells, and peat moss are used in certain parts of the country. So is shredded newspaper. One substance that should never be used is moldy hay, an open invitation for colic. As they can do with feed and grain, groups of owners can save money buying bedding in bulk.

There's no hard and fast rule about how much bedding to lay down in a stall, but between four and six inches is an ample depth, whether or not the stall has rubber matting. Five or six inches is appropriate to cover concrete floors. In any case, bedding must be deep enough so any horse can stand and, if he sleeps lying down, stretch out in comfort.

Mucking Out

One of the less appealing aspects of horse care is cleaning stalls, known in the trade as mucking out. Nevertheless, the chore is unavoidable, but once you get the hang of it, mucking out becomes second nature.

How often his stall needs to be cleaned depends on how much time your horse spends in it. Also relevant is how much time you spend in the barn and your personal views on cleanliness and work; reaching for the manure fork whenever you spot something that needs to be removed should become second nature, if only because you'll have lightened the load when it's time for a more concerted effort. Otherwise, mucking out once a day, usually after morning feeding, is the bare minimum.

You'll need a fine-tined manure fork, a regular three-prong pitchfork, a broom and shovel, and a wheelbarrow. The procedure begins with vacating the horse from the premises, either by turning him out in his pasture or putting him on cross-ties in the aisle. First pick up the largest pieces of droppings with the manure fork and deposit them in the wheelbarrow. The large pieces come easily, but smaller ones, especially those that the horse has stepped on, will need to be unearthed out of the bedding. In all cases, remove only the manure and leave as much of dry bedding as you can (cat owners will see the similarity to litter box maintenance).

Whether to remove wet bedding depends on how wet it is. Urine-soaked straw may have to be consigned to the manure pile via the wheelbarrow, while patches of bedding that are no more than damp can be scattered around with the pitchfork to dry. The same technique applies to wood shavings, but wet sawdust that's formed clods will have to be carted away instead of broken up and scattered. Use your judgment, bearing in mind that a wet environment invites thrush. In the course of mucking out, bedding will end up in the aisle. That's the job for the broom and shovel. Neatness counts everywhere in a barn.

If your horse lives indoors at night or otherwise spends a great deal of time in his stall, a more thorough cleaning at least once a week is necessary. The chore is called stripping the stall. After you move the horse outside and muck out his stall as you do on a daily basis, you'll push all the dry bedding to one side of the stall with the pitchfork or broom. Then remove all the wet bedding to the manure pile. Let the stall air out as long as your horse can stay outdoors; the longer, the better, even for the entire day. Then spread the dry bedding back around the stall as a base layer and top it off with fresh bedding. No matter how thick the bedding and how tight the matting fits together, the underlying flooring will become wet. Removing all the bedding and mats and scraping the dirt base every spring and autumn is another unenviable but essential part of stable management.

Your manure pile will need periodic mucking out, too, certainly long before it reaches overflowing. Horse owners who bed with straw can often make an arrangement with a local mushroom grower, who may want to cart away your horse's by-products. Otherwise, you're the one to haul the waste away to the local landfill or wherever else you're permitted to dispose of it.

Manure in pastures also should be disposed of, either removed or spread around to dry and decompose. Doing nothing about the waste exposes your horse to flies and parasites. That's why riding arenas need to be cleaned on a regular basis, too.

As always, the best way to learn about cleaning chores is by hands-on training. As long as horses have been domesticated, no human being has ever refused an offer to help muck out or strip a stall. Your expert friend, a neighbor, or any other horse owner will be as happy to let you practice as Tom Sawyer was to let his pals whitewash the fence.

Grooming

Several very important reasons underscore why taking the time and making the effort to groom your horse on a regular basis is essential. Perhaps most important is understanding why grooming has far-reaching health benefits. A horse's coat is his outer layer of skin. Daily brushing rids the coat of dirt and dried sweat that, if allowed to build up, can clog pores. That clogging encourages infection and traps toxic waste within the horse's system. Regular brushing also stimulates blood circulation and helps build and maintain good muscle tone.

Washing and brushing also focus your attention on any changes in the condition of the coat and skin. For example, dandruff or hair loss often indicates vitamin deficiencies. Then, too, working over every part of the horse's body puts you in a position to check for sores and cuts, strained muscles, or any other possible or actual medical problem. That's why, at least in the best of all worlds, horses should be groomed both before and after being exercised or turned out to romp around a pasture.

A horse that spends his days and nights in a pasture (and not a barn) should be groomed at least every other day. Although accumulated dirt and mud can act as insulation against cold winds and freezing temperatures during the winter and against insects during the summer, the potential for clogged pores and other skin ailments still exists.

There is also the matter of respect. Even though you may be the only person who will see your horse on a particular day, when he looks his best it is a reflection of your pride in and affection for him.

The well-furnished grooming kit contains the following items:

- **currycomb:** The serrated edges of this hard rubber or metal tool loosen matted dirt and scrape away excess mud.

- **dandy brush:** Its strong stiff fibers remove caked dirt, mud, and sweat.

- **body brush:** Its softer bristles massage skin while removing dirt and loose hair.

- **all-purpose brush:** Its medium-firm bristles remove light dirt.

- **finishing brush:** Its soft bristles smooth hairs flat as a final grooming step.

- **stable rubber:** Rubbing with this linen towel brings out coat shine.

- **mane comb:** The relatively wide spaces between teeth are designed for manes and forelocks.

- **sweat scraper:** This long, thin metal scoop removes excess sweat and wipes away water after bathing.

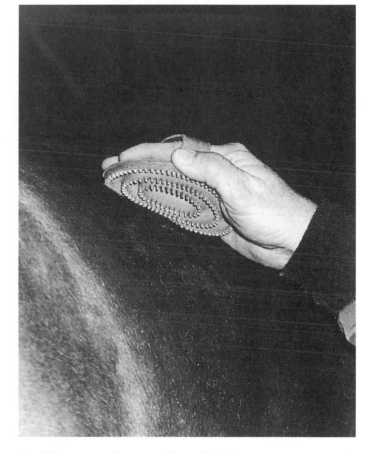

A rubber currycomb removes loose dirt. (The Quarter Horse Journal)

- **sponge:** Used to wipe eyes, the inside of ears, nostrils, and other sensitive places, such as under the tail.

- **shedding blade:** Its small metal teeth remove loose hair during the shedding season.

- **body clippers:** This scissors-style machine, with its narrow head, trims face hair, mane, and fetlocks.

- **vacuum cleaner** (optional): For removing dirt.

- **hoof pick:** This metal implement removes debris from the hoof (see page 95).

Using a dandy brush on the forelock. (AQHA photo by Wyatt McSpadden)

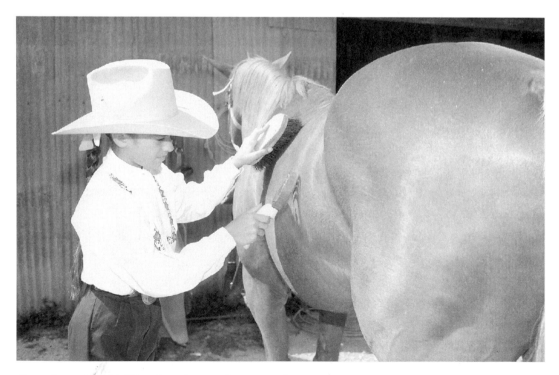

Grooming with a body brush and a metal currycomb. (AQHA photo by Wyatt McSpadden)

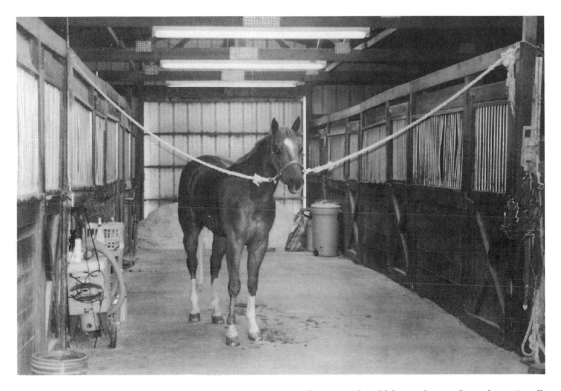

To prevent a horse from stepping over a cross-tie rope, the ropes should be no lower than the animal's head. (*The Quarter Horse Journal*)

Cross-Tying

Cross-tying your horse is preferable to securing him by just a single rope. Cross-tie ropes restrict a horse's movement forward, backward, and side-to-side so he won't be able to move very far away as you groom him. Similarly, the best place for indoor grooming is in an aisle or the barn doorway. Any space wider than about twelve feet gives a horse enough room to turn around and twist the cross-ties.

Make sure the cross-tie ropes are fastened to the walls or doorjambs no lower than the horse's head so he won't be able to step over them. Secure the snaps on the ends of the lines with twine that's strong enough to hold the horse under normal circumstances, but not so strong that the twine won't break in case the horse panics. Given the choice, a loose horse is preferable to one that injures himself in a frenzied effort to escape restraint.

Cross-tie ropes should snap to the rings on the sides of the horse's halter. The operative word is "halter," not "bridle." Attaching the cross-ties to a bit creates an accident waiting to happen: A startled horse that yanks back will severely damage his mouth.

1.

2.

3.

4.

5.

6.

7.

A step-by-step technique for tying the safety, or quick-release, knot. A tug on the loose end releases the knot. (*The Quarter Horse Journal*)

Leaving a horse cross-tied when you've finished working on him is unfair. Imagine how you'd feel if you couldn't reach a biting insect or annoying itch. Moreover, standing on cement or any other hard flooring material is uncomfortable, especially when a horse stamps in dismay at being so confined. Any horse will appreciate being put back in his stall, even if it's only for what you consider a short period of time.

Brushing

Take the law of gravity into account when you clean a horse: Do it from top to bottom and from front to back, because that's the way loose dirt falls and blows.

Start on the horse's near (the term for left) side. Using the currycomb, brush the neck, body, and upper leg hair in a circular motion to remove dried mud and caked sweat (the comb's teeth are too hard for the animal's face or below his knees and hocks). If you're using a metal comb, stroke in the direction the hair lies, never against it. Knock the dirt out of the currycomb frequently by banging it against the floor or the side of the barn.

The dandy brush sweeps away the dirt that the currycomb loosens. Use short strokes along the horse's neck, body, and legs. Unlike the currycomb, these bristles are soft enough to use all the way down to the feet.

As the name suggests, the mane comb is for the mane and forelock (but not the tail, because the comb's teeth will break the finer hairs there). Comb small sections of the tail at a time, using your fingers to remove any brambles or burrs. Then brush out carefully with the body brush.

Like horses themselves, the hair of their mane is trainable. Any part of the mane that stands up in cowlicks needs to be brushed over whenever the horse is groomed. If simple brushing, or wetting first and then brushing, doesn't make the hair lie flat, braid the offending portion into little plaits, then pull them over on the side you want; the weight of the braids will encourage the hairs to cooperate. Leave the braids for a few days, checking periodically to make sure the horse doesn't rub them out.

The bristles of a body brush are soft enough to do a horse's face and outer ears. Brush gently with one hand, using your free hand to shield the animal's eyes against blowing dust. This is also the time to wipe around the eyes and nostrils with a damp (but not a soaking wet) sponge.

Then go over the rest of the horse's coat with the body brush for any remaining traces of dirt. For a final polishing touch, wipe the coat with a clean towel.

Cleaning Hooves

There are two reasons why horsemen clean hooves in a particular order. Horses are creatures of habit, and they seem to object less to procedures that are performed the same way each and every time. Then, too, if you happen to be interrupted during the process, you're more likely to remember where you left off (admittedly a small point, but anything that saves time is welcome). Starting with the near front hoof, work your way counterclockwise back to the rear hoof, the off (or right) rear, and finally the off front hoof.

To lift a horse's leg, stand next to it facing the animal's rear. Run your hand that's closer to the horse (your left hand if the near leg) down the leg to the fetlock while leaning your shoulder against the horse's body. Say "lift" or "up" in a soothing but authoritative tone. If the horse hasn't been so trained or is being stubborn, gently pinch the tendon above the fetlock with your thumb and index finger, and lean with slightly more weight against the horse's body. You two may end up playing a waiting game, but at some point you'll win: The horse will lift his leg.

Once the leg is off the ground, support the back of the hoof in the palm of your hand that is closer to the horse (the left hand if it's the near front leg). Working the hoof pick with your other hand, scrape around the

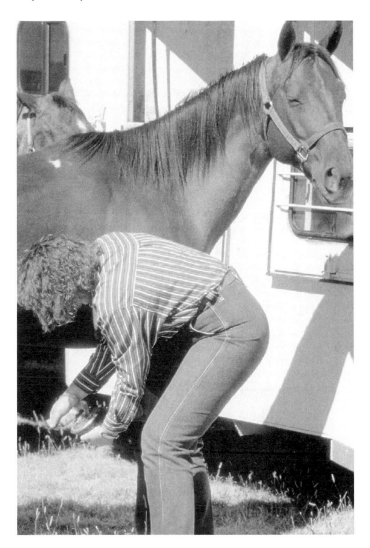

A foot should be picked out from its heel to its toe to lessen the chance of injury. (AQHA photo by Wyatt McSpadden)

inside of the horseshoe or hoof wall to remove wadded hay, bedding, small stones, or anything else that doesn't belong there. Always work the tip of the pick away from you to prevent injury to yourself.

Next, working from the heel up to the front, clean out the two clefts formed by the frog (cleaning from back to front reduces the chance of wedging anything in the heel). A healthy horse shouldn't react to your tapping the frog gently with the hoof pick, but if he does, that indication of tenderness could mean a bruise or the onset of thrush.

Cleaning a horse's feet is also an opportunity to make sure shoes are securely in place and have no missing nails. Also check to see whether hoof walls are solid, resistant, and free from cracks or chips. Don't limit your inspection to feet; check "upstairs" at the pasterns, fetlocks, and lower legs for cuts, abrasions, or anything out of the ordinary.

Hooves that are too hard for too long become brittle. Hoof dressings retard further loss of moisture, and in some instances protect susceptible hoof walls against the corrosive effect of contact with urine. If your veterinarian or farrier thinks the hooves need it, apply the dressing with a brush. Paint only around the coronet band of a horse that is shod, because dressing tends to seep into horseshoe holes and loosens shoes. If unshod, the entire hoof wall should be painted around its outside.

The last step of grooming may be the application of fly spray if your horse is afflicted with the pest. Be sure to stand upwind when you spray. Apply the spray to a cloth to wipe the horse's face and ears, taking care not to get any in his eyes.

"But," you may be thinking, "what if I honestly don't have the time to give my horse a complete grooming each and every time I ride?" The equally honest response to that question is "do the best you can." A brief brushing and sponging away sweat stains, along with picking out hooves, will suffice, just as long as such abbreviated grooming sessions don't become a habit.

Bathing

Although nothing on a hot day is more inviting than a nice long bath for your horse—especially when you can cool off, too—restrain that generous impulse. Bathing removes dirt, stains, and dried skin, but it also washes away a coat's natural protective oils. A thorough shampoo bath no more frequently than once a week is enough if you groom and sponge or hose away saddle stains on a daily basis. Even then, your horse's coat may still need a conditioner to restore its sheen.

Most horses accept insect spray as a matter of course, especially when it's accompanied by a reassuring hand. (The Quarter Horse Journal)

If you use a hose, set the taps for a gentle spray of warm water. Otherwise, fill a bucket with warm water. Spray or sponge from the horse's neck back to his tail and from top to bottom. This preliminary washing removes the top level of dirt.

Next, fill a bucket with warm water and add an antibacterial soap. Sponge around the horse's head and face, taking care not to get any soapy water in his eyes or ears. Rinse with clean water and a clean sponge. Horses are sensitive about faces, so don't linger there any longer than necessary.

Then from the neck back and in small sections at a time, work in a good lather, first one side down to the fetlocks and then the other. Thoroughly rinse away lather with warm, clean water (a hose will make the job easier). Scrape excess water with the rounded side of a sweat scraper, but go no lower than the knees and hocks.

Wash the mane and tail, soaking the hairs as completely as you can. A shampoo will bring out natural luster.

Gently dry the horse's face with a clean cotton towel, then walk him until the rest of him is just as dry. Turning a wet horse out in a pasture gives him the

A horse appreciates a hose bath, as long as the spray is kept well away from his face. (AQHA photo by Wyatt McSpadden)

golden opportunity to roll and undo all your hard work. Be aware, too, that hand-walked wet horses have been known to sink to their knees and roll the second the person at the other end of the lead shank looks the other way.

Pulling Manes and Tails

Several times a year (the exact frequency depends on how quickly the hairs grow) your horse's mane and tail may need to be "pulled," or thinned and shortened.

The first step is to back-comb a small handful of mane hair to separate individual strands. Then pull out no more than a half dozen of the longest hairs. Repeat until you've worked your way through the entire mane. Although yanking doesn't cause the horse any pain, the process is often disconcerting, so if your horse frets or otherwise shows his annoyance, feel free to stop and pick up where you left off a few hours or even a day or two later.

Although scissors or clippers aren't useful to thin a mane, they can be used to clip a "bridle path," literally a path behind the ears to accommodate the bridle.

Clipping

Once the horse is dry, he should be clipped.* You may need assistance with this job from someone familiar with horse handling and clipping. Many types of clippers are used, ranging from dog clippers found in a discount store to special horse clippers. Blades come in several sizes. The most frequently used sizes are 10s and 40s. The 10s are used for thick hair that is found in the bridle path, underneath the jaw, and on the legs. The 40s are used for fine hair that is found on the muzzle, around the eyes, and both inside and outside the ears.

When using a size 40 clipper blade, hold the clippers against the skin and start by clipping the muzzle as close as possible. Next, clip the hairs of the nostril that show when the horse is at rest. You may choose to carefully clip the eye whiskers above and below the eye, holding the eye closed and protected with your thumb. However, some horsemen do not believe it's wise to shorten these antennae, or feelers. Regardless, be careful not to clip the eyelashes.

The ears are usually the most difficult to clip and most resisted by the horse; therefore, many people save this part until last. Be cautious and careful. When restraints are needed, the most commonly used one is the twitch. Have someone help you when using a twitch. One person should hold the lead rope and twitch while the other clips the hair on the ears. Start clipping the ears by running a smooth stroke with the clippers down one edge of the ear, then do the same to the other edge. From there work to the inner part of the ear, being careful to work all hair out and away from the inner ear. The most important thing to remember is to take your time, be smooth, and make the inner ear as clean and hairless as possible.

To clip the other parts of the horse, change to size 10 clipper blades. To clip the bridle path, you must first know how long it should be. Take your horse's ear and gently lay it back along his neck. Add a thumb's length to figure out the approximate length the bridle path needs to be.

Begin clipping by pressing the clipper blades against the skin at the poll at the top of the forelock (do not clip off the forelock!). Work back toward the mane slowly, occasionally lifting the clippers to allow clipped hair to fall to the ground. The object of clipping underneath the jaw is to clean hair from that area and sculpt the line underneath the horse's head without making the

---

*This section on clipping is taken from the AQHA brochure *Your First Horse Show*. The advice particularly applies to horses in show competition; many recreational riders restrict clipping only to making the bridle path in their horses' manes.

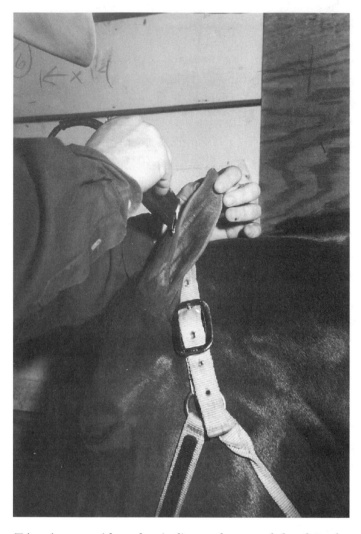

Trimming ears with an electric clipper takes a steady hand. It takes practice, too, so the guidance of an experienced instructor is the best way to learn. (The Quarter Horse Journal)

jaw appear clipped. Therefore, smooth, careful strokes with the clippers are necessary.

Start underneath the throatlatch of the horse and move the clippers in the direction of the hair to remove all long hairs from this area. Then clip from below the chin toward the throatlatch, clipping the chin area close and slowly lifting the clippers from against the skin, blending the hair from the throatlatch to the chin. Finish by clipping the hair along the jaw line, stroking either from the front to the back, or from the outer part to underneath the jaw.

To clip the legs, start by clipping the coronet in short upward strokes, being careful to remove hair from the hoofline only. Next, clip the fetlock area by removing hair from around the ergot (the tough growth of skin on the back of the fetlock). To remove any "wild" hairs on the leg that are growing long, turn the clippers over, holding the top side of the clippers in the palm of your hand, and clip in a downward stroke in the direction of the hair growth.

On white legs, clip the white hair so it is less likely to hold dirt and look dingy. Make a smooth stroke from the coronet to the point where the dark hair begins. This should be done so that, after the white hair has been clipped, the darker hair remains its natural length.

Clipping away body hair is another procedure that needs doing only several times a year. Again, the precise number of times will depend on how fast and thick your horse's coat grows (bear in mind that a horse that is kept inside, especially one that is regularly blanketed, will not grow as heavy a coat as one that lives outside).

Not all horses take kindly to clippers, and especially to the electric variety. If yours objects, try letting him become accustomed by switching the clippers on and holding them near his body; then touch them lightly against his side. When it comes to the actual clipping procedure, watching an experienced horseman do it the first few times or doing it under someone's supervision is a good way to learn.

After the body and legs are clipped, either entirely or in such patterns as "trace" or "hunter," clip and trim the fetlocks, around the ears, and under the jaw (including the whiskers).

Cleaning Sheaths

One part of your gelding's anatomy that requires periodic attention is his sheath, where dirt, mineral residue from urine, and a pasty secretion called smegma will accumulate. Cleaning prevents buildup that lead to sores and conditions that interfere with normal urination.

How often a horse needs this procedure depends on how fast the buildup accumulates. Some horses must be cleaned every month or two, while others require only an annual washing. Your veterinarian will advise you.

Since very few horses will literally stand still while their sheath is being attended to (many horses need to be tranquilized), it's a chore best left to the experienced hands of your veterinarian or another expert.

🐎 Feet and Legs

The expression "no foot, no horse" can't be overemphasized, for without sound feet that can bear and move weight, a horse simply cannot be expected to provide transportation for himself, let alone for a person on his back.

The mechanics of how a foot works underscore how its parts react in something of a chain reaction. As a horse steps down, weight is first applied to the frogs, the pair of elastic wedge-shaped "cushions." The frogs spread and push the bars of the feet outward. In turn, the bars push the heel and the rear portion of the quarters outward, too. The frog also pushes upward to the plantar cushion, which spreads and pushes the lateral cartilage outward. At the end of the step, the wall of the foot and the bars will have received the brunt of the weight.

The condition of the hoof, that hard wall that surrounds the foot, is an indication of the condition of the entire foot. It's also an indication of the care the horse has been receiving. A healthy hoof gives off a shiny, translucent gleam. Its walls have no cracks or streaks. You'll hear a solid thud (neither dull nor hollow) when you lightly tap the hoof with a hammer or hoof pick. Proper care in trimming and shoeing will keep walls from growing steeper and the heels from contracting over time.

The hoof adapts to weather. Contact with soft ground causes it to become soft, while hard, dry ground produces a hard hoof that may require moisturizing dressing.

Among other benefits of exercise, it causes blood to circulate through the foot, and that promotes hoof growth. Like the human fingernail with which it is frequently compared, the hoof itself has no nerves, which is why it can be trimmed without causing pain to the horse. And it *must* be trimmed. A hoof grows approximately three to four inches a year, and an untrimmed hoof can affect a horse's action, structural soundness, and, in extreme cases, his health.

Shoeing

Horses wear shoes for the same reason we do: Their feet need protection against hard surfaces. Because horses' feet grow at the rate they do, a farrier's* attention is necessary every six to eight weeks, and perhaps more frequently in cases of corrective shoeing (the equine equivalent of orthopedic footwear). Leaving shoes on too long will create problems, not the least of which are contracted heels.

When it's time to change shoes, the farrier first removes the worn one, then works on the foot to make sure it is trimmed and balanced. Trimming involves cutting away dead portions of the sole and cleaning the frog, as well as cutting down the wall and rasping it level. The precise shape of the hoof and foot and the horse's overall conformation and way of going will determine any variations.

Balance is especially important, because an unbalanced foot is likely to lead to stress, strains, and lameness.

---

*The word "farrier"comes from *fer,* the French word for iron, the metal of which horseshoes were once made (they're now steel as well as iron). Farriers are often known as "horseshoers" or, in some parts of the country, "blacksmiths." With regard to the latter, iron was once considered one of the so-called "black" metals (tin, by contrast, is a "white" metal). Hence, the word "blacksmith."

Just as human footwear is specialized for different activities, so the type of horseshoe your horse will wear depends on what you and he do. Shoes for trail riding are usually fitted with toe caulks, a kind of cleat for better grip. Caulks are also useful for hunters and jumpers; their shoes have holes drilled into them so caulks can be screwed in or removed as conditions warrant. Since any kind of cleat would interfere with sudden or sliding stops, horses used in cutting, roping, and reining wear flat shoes. And since weight is always a consideration among racehorses, runners are fitted with lightweight aluminum "plates."

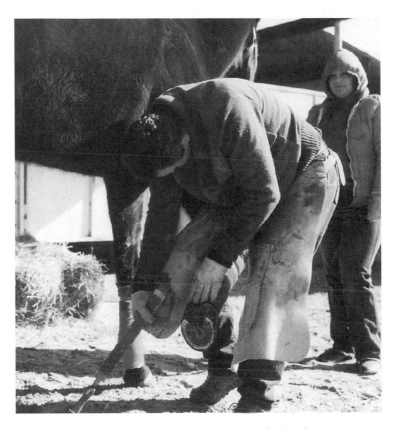

A hoof is filed with a rasp before a new shoe is nailed in place. (The Quarter Horse Journal)

If the farrier and/or vet think it advisable, your horse may be fitted with pads between his feet and shoes to protect his soles and frogs.

Shoeing is a fascinating procedure that hasn't changed very much over centuries. Although shoes come in a variety of sizes and some horses can wear them right "off the rack," most shoes need to be shaped to the specific shape of the foot. Heating the metal until it is flexible, the farrier hammers the shoe against an anvil, measuring it against the foot until it is the right size and shape. Nailing the shoe into place causes the horse no more discomfort than trimming his hoof does (or having a manicure bothers us).

Although shoeing is a job that should be left to a farrier, you'll need to learn how to remove a loose shoe. Your farrier, vet, or a very experienced expert is the person to demonstrate the process and then guide you.

You'll first use a farrier's rasp to file down the clasp, which is the overhanging piece on the toe. With a pliers-like tool called a shoe puller, carefully remove the shoe, starting at the outside heel and then the inside heel. Work forward, pulling toward the center of the foot so you don't harm the wall. Finally, rasp the hoof's edge smooth. In the case of only one or two loose nails, you can pull them out with pliers or a shoe puller. Then call the farrier.

Riding or otherwise working a horse with even one unshod foot even for a short time is a bad idea, so your farrier will need to replace the missing shoe. An alternative, however, is an Easyboot, a piece of footwear that surrounds the entire foot and is most often used as temporary protection (your farrier is the best judge of whether your horse would benefit from its use).

Whether the visit is part of a regular schedule or an emergency call, you can help your farrier—and your horse—by observing the following courtesies:

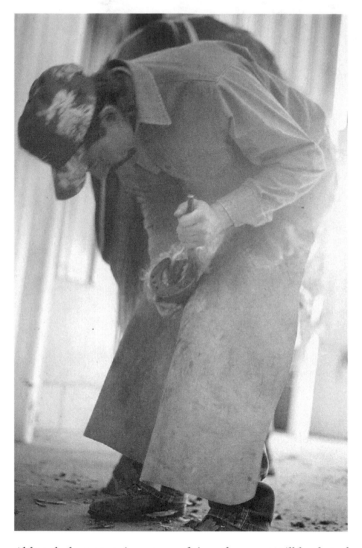

Although shoes come in a range of sizes, they must still be shaped to fit a horse's foot. (AQHA photo by Wyatt McSpadden)

• If you can't keep a scheduled appointment, inform the farrier well in advance. Few professionals are as busy as horseshoers, and anything you can do to stay on his or her good side will pay dividends.

• Your horse should be ready for shoeing in his stall with clean feet. Farriers don't have time to help owners chase and capture horses out in fields, or wait on the sidelines until the animal has been rounded up, brought in, and had his feet cleaned.

• Your farrier will appreciate a clean, level, and dry area in which to work.

• Some horses object to the shoeing process, the way some small children balk at having their hair cut. If yours is such a reluctant participant, your smith may be obliged to discipline him accordingly. That's all part of the game, so don't automatically take your animal's side.

• Discuss any special needs or upcoming activities that might affect your horse's shoeing or a future scheduled appointment. For example, if your plans include a long trail ride a week before the next scheduled visit, the farrier can decide whether your horse will need new shoes in advance of the trip. Or if you and your horse are about to try a new sport (jumping or reining, for instance), a different kind of shoe may be in order. But the farrier won't know unless and until you bring up the matter.

Boots

Boots protect a horse's feet and legs against interfering with, brushing, or otherwise banging against each other. Made of leather or new space-age synthetic material with felt, fleece, or rubber padding, boots are fastened by means of straps or Velcro.

Where or how the horse interferes with himself determines the kind of boot he needs.

Shin and ankle boots cover the ankle and cannon and are primarily used on forelegs. The rear-leg equivalents known as splint boots provide more support than protection.

Tendon and ankle boots protect and support tendons and the backs and insides of ankles. They come in open-front or wraparound styles.

Skid or sliding boots, most often seen in Western performance competitions, protect hind-leg fetlocks and pasterns against the scrapes and cuts that often come from sliding stops.

Galloping boots are worn routinely by racehorses. They cover ankles, shins, and tendons against the abrasion of racetrack surfaces.

Bell boots are designed to protect against overreaching (also known as forging) by hind feet. A horse "overreaches" when his hind foot strikes the back of a front foot. Made of heavy rubber and shaped like a bell, the boots fasten with Velcro. Quarter boots are bell boots that are shaped narrower in front and wider in the rear.

Whether your horse will benefit from any of these devices depends on his way of going, as well as the activity in which both of you take part. The best sources of advice for specific questions are your vet, farrier, or another expert.

Skid boots. (Professional's Choice)

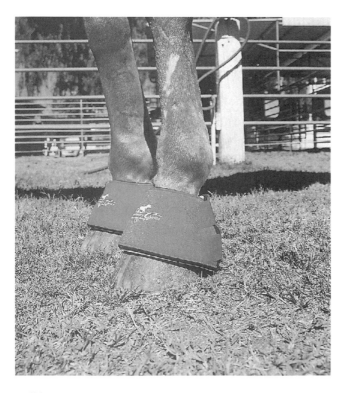

Bell boots. (Professional's Choice)

Leg Wrappings

Horses' legs are wrapped for three reasons: for support during exercise or performance; to ease stress and to avoid cuts and bruises during shipping; and as treatment for wound injuries, including post-surgical care.

Pressure is the concept that governs the proper use of bandages. The longer a horse wears a bandage, the more padding should be used and the less constricting the bandage should be.

FIGURE-EIGHT WRAP

A figure-eight wrap, which is only for support during exercise or performance, employs a reusable elastic bandage such as Vetrap. It starts at the top of the lower leg, just below the knee on front legs, and about three inches below the hock on hind legs.

In order to get and hold the tendons into the correct position, always wrap from the inside, from front to back. That translates into clockwise for off legs, and counterclockwise for near legs. Another essential technique is to stretch the elastic bandage as far as it goes, then let it come back to approximately 50 percent of its tension. Otherwise, too much compression will harm the tendons.

Work your way down the leg, wrapping with even pressure and overlapping each previous layer by three inches. When you reach the ankle, make a figure-eight pattern by wrapping up and then down. Alternate up and down until there's a diamond-shaped pattern at the front of the leg (the figure eight allows the fetlock to move naturally).

Some people use sheet cotton or gauze padding under the wrap to absorb some of the pressure of the elastic. Whether or not you do, you'll minimize potential damage to tendons by removing this type of bandage right after your horse has finished working.

POLO WRAP

A polo wrap, so called because it's routinely used in that sport, is done with heavier padded bandages. It's good for everyday exercise, especially on horses that tend to overreach, or catch their front legs with their hind feet. Polo wraps are also suitable wear for shipping.

Start about halfway down the inside of the lower leg and wrap forward (clockwise on off legs and counterclockwise on near legs). Bring the wrap around so that it is pulled front to back on the outside of the leg, which allows the tendons to remain flat against the leg. Wrap down below the fetlock, then up toward the knee. Pull firmly but not too tight. Make sure the tension is even so that no one area receives more or less pressure than any other. Secure the wrap in place to the outside of the leg.

COVER BANDAGE

This long one-piece bandage covers a great deal of leg area. As the name suggests, it's used to cover wounds and for other medical purposes. Because it doesn't support the leg, a cover bandage cannot be used for exercise, nor for that reason is it a first choice for shipping.

For extra protection during shipping, a quilted shipping wrap can be used beneath a polo wrap. (The Quarter Horse Journal)

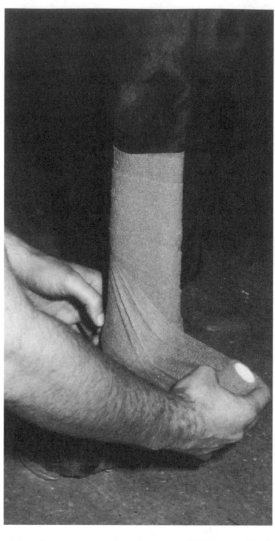

Bring the wrap around so that it is pulled front to back on the outside of the leg, which allows the tendons to remain flat against the leg. (The Quarter Horse Journal)

Start at the inside of the leg and wrap front to back (on the outside of the leg), applying firm pressure. Then secure the bandage in place with its Velcro straps.

COMBINE ROLL

This medical bandage's absorbency on one side makes it especially good for postoperative care or for other types of wounds. It can also be used as a shipping bandage.

Because a combine roll is made of thick padding, it can be pulled tight. Wrap it in smooth layers, then secure it with adhesive, over which pieces of Vetrap can be wrapped for greater security.

SHIPPING BANDAGES

Even horses that are model passengers are candidates for leg and foot bumps, bruises, and sprains during trailer trips, even of short distances. That's why experienced horsemen routinely use shipping bandages.

Starting at the lower quarter of the leg, wrap downward. Crisscross around the fetlock, down the pastern, and over the coronet band and heels. After covering the upper hoof area, wrap back up the leg to below the knee or hock.

TAIL WRAP

Although this section is about legs, any discussion of bandages should mention tail wraps.

Legs aren't the only part of the horse that can suffer during shipping. A tail wrap will keep tail hairs from being rubbed off, as well as protecting the dock against any damage. In the case of hunters and jumpers en route to a competition, a tail wrap will also prevent braids from being rubbed out.

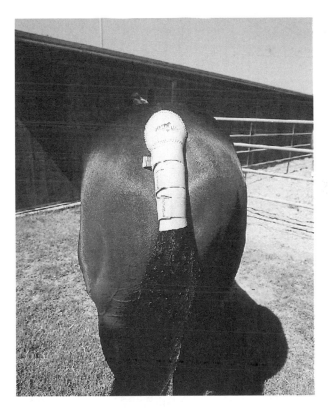

Tail wrap. (Professional's Choice)

Facing the horse's rear, drape the tail over one of your shoulders. Start wrapping as close to the top of the tail as possible. Begin on the tail's top (the hair) side; the bottom of the dock has no hair and can be easily injured.

109

Work down the tail to the end of the tailbone, overlapping each turn. To create the pressure needed to hold the bandage in place, tighten at the top of the tail so the hair there can cushion the pressure. "Roll" the wrap lightly on the underside of the dock; a bandage that's too tight there can cut off circulation. Then wrap back up, securing the finished product with strings, but tie the knot no tighter than the wrap itself.

Alternatively you can bypass the wrapping process altogether by using a neoprene tail bag—a one-piece, Velcro-closing time-saver.

The best way to learn to wrap is to watch your expert friend demonstrate the different techniques and then practice under his or her supervision. One thing you'll observe is that experienced wrappers keep the horse on cross-ties. They also crouch, rather than sit on the floor, so that if the horse cocks a foot or shows any sign of displeasure, they can move out of kicking range as fast as possible.

Vetrap, polo, and other reusable wraps should be kept clean by washing and drying, either by hand or by machine. When you roll them up again, start with the end that has the Velcro or other closing (the rule of thumb is "first wrapped, last unrolled"). Make the roll as tight as possible, too.

For information about diseases and conditions that affect hooves and feet, see pages 135–136.

For further information on foot and hoof care as a part of daily grooming, see pages 95–96.

Horse Clothing

Horses in the wild grow thick coats that serve, depending on the climate and season, as a snowsuit or a sweatsuit. Domesticated horses that are clipped and trimmed or ones whose owners want them to have a light coat don't have that luxury. They need to wear clothing.

Until relatively recently, the colder the day or night, the more blankets a horse wore. The "layered look" was very much in fashion, and some horse owners still use this technique. However, the same technology that reduced the number of layers that skiers and other cold-weather athletes now wear has been applied to equine wardrobes.

Quilted turnout blankets are very popular, and for good reason. The outer cover is water-repellent, and the polyfill insulation provides warmth without excessive weight. (Another advantage to so-called space-age fabrics is their resistance to horses' teeth, essential if your horse's idea of a good time is to turn his clothes into confetti.) A nylon inner lining doesn't chafe, while fleece insets at the withers virtually eliminate irritation from rubbing. A belt-like strap around the girth called a surcingle keeps the blanket in place. Contour shaping also contributes to a good, comfortable fit.

If winter in your part of the country doesn't call for anything as heavy as a quilted blanket, a turnout rug* with a nylon or cotton duck outer layer and a wool or fleece lining will take the chill off the day or night.

A cooler, a popular warm-weather item, is a loose lightweight blanket that covers from ears to tail. Its purpose is to prevent the horse from catching a chill after exercise; the loose fit lets the cooler stay dry in spite of contact with a wet horse.

Also widely used after exercise is the antisweat sheet, a mesh garment that traps body heat while allowing sweat to evaporate. The sheet is also used in winter under a wool cooler; the combination acts as the functional equivalent of a heavier blanket.

Some clothing keeps horses neat and clean in a showring environment. A thin nylon rain sheet is one. A cotton duck sheet is another, keeping dust off a freshly groomed horse. A fly sheet made of nylon or cotton mesh is appreciated on any buggy day, whether your animal is waiting to go into the arena or is cross-tied at home.

As a practical matter, very few horses possess all the above items, and those that do tend to be show or racehorses. A relevant question is, therefore, how many—if indeed any at all—will your horse need? The answer, as is so often the case, would be to ask your veterinarian or expert about climate-control necessities. In the case of what should go into a horse's formal horse show wardrobe, most trainers have very definite ideas on the subject.

Fitting a Blanket or Cooler

There's no such thing as one size fits all in horse clothing, and your horse's individual physique will be a factor in selecting his wardrobe. Blankets that are designed for American Quarter Horses have lots of room through the shoulders

*"Rug," an old British term for blanket, survives primarily in tack-shop catalog terminology.   **111**

A well-fitting cooler. (AQHA photo by Wyatt McSpadden)

and extra hindquarter darts. Those with two panels along the back and two at the sides are contoured for horses with rounded barrels and hindquarters.

Blankets are sized in inches, so finding one that will fit your horse begins with measuring from the center of his chest back along one side to the rear of his rump. Depending on the shrinkage factor of the particular fabric, you may be well advised to buy one size larger; blankets and sheets for show wear should be even roomier to accommodate a horse that's wearing a saddle.

The surcingle strap should buckle or snap on snugly, but without being restrictive. (Buckles seem to fasten more securely than the hook-and-eye type of closing.) Leg straps are a solution to the problem of horses that manage to twist their blankets or coolers out of position, including but not limited to the garment's hanging upside down off their bellies. The straps cross under the belly so they don't rub the horse's legs. A tail cord can be useful, too; the detachable variety can be removed and washed without having to launder the rest of the blanket. Another alternative is a blanket or sheet with longer sides than normal. Some horses that object to putting their heads through a closed-front blanket or cooler will prefer an open-front model that buckles or snaps closed.

Your horse's former owner will be the best source of information about such a preference, or your horse himself will let you know.

If the animal's existing wardrobe is in good condition, you might consider buying the blankets at the time you purchase the horse.

Cleaning

Although quilted and wool blankets can be washed at home, they're very heavy (sometimes unmanageably so) when wet, plus the horsehairs that come off will clog all but the most industrial-strength washing machine. You may decide you'd rather have blankets dry-cleaned.

Coolers are made of lighter wool that tends to stretch out of shape when wet. Block the garment dry, as you would a wool sweater, instead of letting it droop over a clothesline. Cotton sheets are the easiest to deal with. Wash them in cool water, then air-dry to minimize shrinkage. As with coolers, going over the dried sheet to brush off any remaining hairs is the usual final touch.

A final word on the subject of blanketing: Contrary to what some people believe, horses don't "hair up" with long, thick coats because of falling temperatures. That response comes as a result of the reduced number of daylight hours as winter approaches. Blanketing may help keep a clipped horse's coat from growing out, but it doesn't in itself cause shedding. That's a result of the longer hours of daylight that come in spring.

Your Horse's Health and Other Veterinary Matters

People who are just starting out as horse owners often complain that caring for horses is like caring for babies: Like very young children, horses are unable to come right out and tell us when and where something is wrong.* But after time these same people discover just how well horses can call our attention to their aches and pains. What's more, they even help pinpoint the problem. All it takes is learning how to listen to what the patient is "saying."

Illness and injury are more than just the opposite of normal good health; they're the absence of it. That's why a basic understanding of veterinary mat-

---

*There's a critical difference, though. Human babies aren't thousand-pound patients that instinctively react to pain by trying to flee from it. An ailment or an injury can cause even the most good-natured equine to react unpredictably, so taking a horse's normal behavior for granted may become the first step toward needing medical attention yourself.

ters begins with learning what is normal, a knowledge of which can come only from observation and hands-on contact. Watching a sound horse walk, jog, and lope establishes the standard from which anything else indicates the animal is "off." Running your hand down his leg to feel its normal warmth teaches you how to recognize the presence of the heat that soreness generates. Similarly, a familiarity with the contours of a horse's "normal" leg, including tendons, other subcutaneous structural elements, and any individual lumps and bumps, provides the basis that will alert you to any changes.

The shelves of bookstores, tack shops, and libraries are full of how-to-be-your-own-veterinarian manuals. Magazine articles are regularly written on equine medical subjects, too. But unless and until you reach the point that you're as knowledgeable as their authors or at least have enough "mileage" to qualify as an experienced horse owner, relying on the expertise of a veterinarian is essential. Not only does a trained professional possess the necessary knowledge, he or she also has access to specialized equipment to diagnose and treat large animals. Not to belabor the point, but you and your horse will be safer and sounder if you use a vet.

That's not to say that you can't be a participant. While the doctor is with your horse, ask questions and take notes. Watch the vet demonstrate procedures and, with permission and under supervision, try such hands-on work as taking the animal's pulse or listening to his heart or stomach. Such training will make you a useful member of your horse's health care team.

First-Aid Supplies

In addition to the following very basic items that your barn's first-aid kit should contain, your veterinarian will recommend medications for specific ailments or conditions.

- thermometer
- hemostat or long-neck pliers
- hair clippers
- restraining twitch
- syringe (without needle, for flushing out wounds)
- antibacterial ointment
- petroleum jelly

- stethoscope
- scissors
- hoof pick and knife
- speculum
- antibacterial powder
- iodine soap
- sterile saline solution

- iodine solution
- isopropyl alcohol
- Epsom salts
- gauze patches
- roll of cotton
- paper toweling

- boric acid powder
- ethylene blue
- gauze bandage roll
- wound pads
- elastic tape

People say about an insurance policy that "you never need it till you need it, and then—boy, do you need it!" The line applies equally well to first-aid equipment. Emergency situations require immediate access to these supplies, so if and when you take out that pair of scissors or roll of bandages to use, return or replace it as soon as you finish with it . . . *before* you need it for an emergency.

In addition to veterinary supplies, another essential item in any barn consists of two twenty-foot lengths of ropes or belting strong enough to pull a horse to his feet. Every so often a horse will lie down and become wedged in his stall in such a way that he can't get to his feet. That's called being "cast." It's not very common, but it does happen, and when it does, you'll need to summon help as urgently as for any medical emergency.

This point cannot be overemphasized: Dealing with a panicked horse unable to get to his feet requires skill and strength. Someone will have to slip one or more of the ropes or belting around the horse's body and/or legs, then other people must help pull the animal to his feet. Unless you know from experience exactly what you're doing, attempting to extricate the animal by yourself is certain to lead to serious injury to the horse and to you, too.

Indicators of Health—or the Lack of It

The most important indicators of medical problems are pulse, temperature, respiration, capillary refill rate, and stomach sound. Become familiar with each one *before* a problem occurs; even before acquiring a horse is not too early to start learning what is normal and what is not.

TEMPERATURE

Normal temperature for an adult horse is anywhere between 99° and 105°F, the higher end coming in the late afternoon and after strenuous exercise.

The range for a foal is approximately one degree higher, and for a mare in heat, two degrees above normal. The thermometer should be shaken down until it reads below normal, lubricated with petroleum jelly, and inserted into the rectum with a rotating motion. Because greased glass is hard to hold and even harder to retrieve, horsemen tie a two-foot piece of strong string to a clip at the end of the instrument, then clip the other end of the string to the horse's tail.

Taking the temperature for three minutes will give an accurate reading.

PULSE

Pulse indicates heartbeat rate. Normal is between 35 and 42 beats per minute when the horse is at rest. Anything faster is an indication that the animal is unwell and quite possibly in pain. You take a horse's pulse by placing your index finger on one of the pulse point arteries. The easiest one to manage is the one under the jawbone on the inside surface. Others, which are more difficult to get to, include one behind the knee and another at the widest point behind the fetlock.

One of the easiest places to take a horse's pulse is behind his jaw. (The Quarter Horse Journal)

Exploring the American West on horseback is always a highlight of a guest ranch vacation.

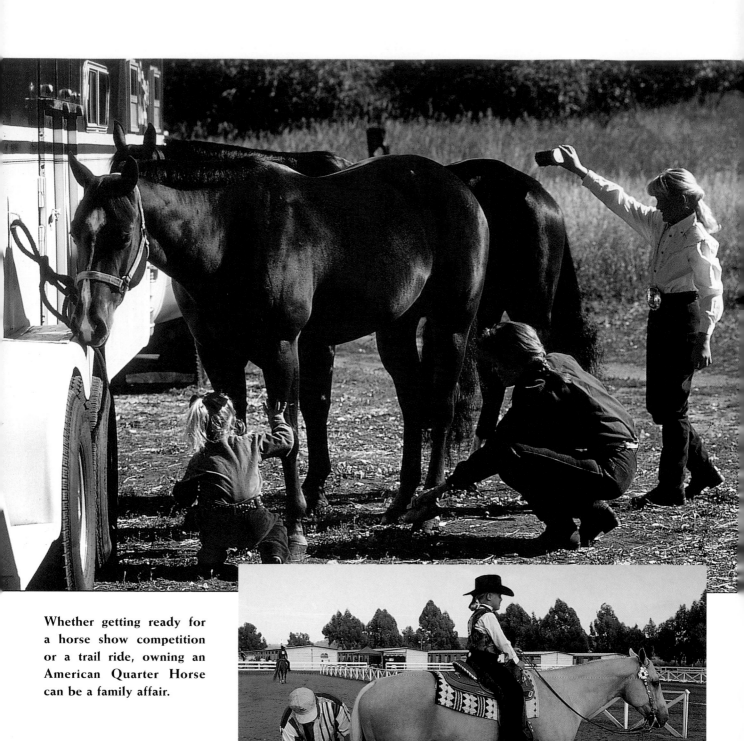

Whether getting ready for a horse show competition or a trail ride, owning an American Quarter Horse can be a family affair.

A hunter class calls for an elegant and athletic effort over a course that simulates obstacles found in the foxhunting field.

No technological innovation offers a better way to work cattle than how it's been done since the opening of the West: in partnership with an American Quarter Horse.

(photo by Wyatt McSpadden)

(photo by Wyatt McSpadden)

Trail rides can range from an informal outing with a friend to an AQHA-organized group event. It's the American Quarter Horse that puts the "pleasure" in pleasure riding.

The American Quarter Horse's powerful hindquarters and overall balance and agility become spectacularly evident in a reining pattern's sliding stop.

(photo by Wyatt McSpadden)

An alternative method is to use a stethoscope. Place it on the horse's chest right behind the left elbow.

If you wish, you can count the number of beats in a full minute. A faster and equally accurate technique is to count for fifteen seconds and then multiply by four.

A horse at rest that has a pulse above 60 beats per minute, especially if he shows signs of distress or pain, needs immediate veterinary attention.

RESPIRATION

A standing adult horse at rest breathes between 8 and 16 times each minute. Young horses breathe faster, with foals registering up to 30 times a minute. Exercise, stress, and illness will increase the rate.

Using a watch or clock with a second hand or a digital readout of seconds, count the number of times the horse's flanks rise and fall in thirty seconds. Doubling that number gives the respiration rate per minute.

CAPILLARY REFILL RATE

Capillaries, the small blood vessels located near the skin, are excellent indicators of blood flow. See for yourself, on yourself. Fold the fingers of one hand as if making a fist and press your thumb against the nail of your index or middle finger. The skin under the nail will turn white. When you release the pressure, blood will flow back into the capillaries under the nail. Or you can try the same experiment in front

Capillary refill time, or how long until gums return to normal after pressure is applied and then removed, is another indication of a horse's health. (*The Quarter Horse Journal*)

of a bathroom mirror: press a finger against your gums. Anything slower than immediate refill indicates impaired circulation.

A healthy horse's gums are pink and moist. To reach the capillaries there without losing a finger in the process, use the same technique as you do to insert a bit: Press the horse's lower lip against the bars of his teeth. Holding your fingers there will make the horse keep his mouth open, or you can insert a speculum. Once his mouth is open, press against the horse's gum and see how rapidly the white area turns pink again after you release the pressure. One to three seconds is normal. This test is used to help indicate colic and sunstroke or heatstroke, among other conditions.

LISTENING TO A NORMAL STOMACH

Using a stethoscope or holding your ear against the abdomen, you can hear the workings of a horse's stomach. The normal sound is a steady gurgling. Anything else, whether a sound like a rushing river or especially no sound at all, indicates a digestive problem.

First Aid

The vast majority of situations that require medical attention are of the first-aid variety. Parallels in our lives would be a scraped knee, a sprained ankle, or a bee sting, and similar to a human mishap, many equine first-aid cases require minimal treatment. Others can be very serious, though, and all require immediate attention.

We'll begin with external emergencies.

WOUNDS

ABRASIONS: A wound is considered an abrasion when only the surface layer of skin is injured, as in a minor scrape or a girth sore. All that's required in the way of treatment is to wash the wound with a saline solution or witch hazel. Then apply a thin layer of petroleum jelly and let nature take its course. Keeping the horse's environment as free as possible from insects will guard against possible infection and almost certain discomfort, since insects are attracted to wounds the way flies are drawn to honey.

LACERATIONS: The word describes wounds with irregularly torn tissue. They can be caused by barbed wire, broken glass, or another sharp object. The bleeding must be immediately stopped or, if you discover the injury some time after it happened, the wound must be cleaned and medicated.

How the blood is flowing is often a clue to what was injured. A cut artery will spurt bright red blood with each heartbeat or pulse beat, while blood from a vein comes out more slowly but steadily, and its color is a darker red.

The first step in treatment is to confine and calm the patient. If at all possible, move the horse to a comfort zone, a familiar area such as his barn. Since human presence tends be more reassuring than being cross-tied, see whether someone is available to hold the horse. A twitch around the patient's nose may be necessary; tighten it only enough to distract and immobilize the horse.

If the wound is bleeding, try to halt the blood flow with a clean cloth or gauze pad by applying steady pressure for several minutes. A roll of bandages or a piece of wood as a splint can help by adding pressure. If the bleeding doesn't stop, try again; you may not have applied enough pressure or have held the cloth in place long enough. In some cases, several layers of bandages may be needed to stop the flow.*

If the bleeding hasn't stopped after a second effort, fasten the bandage firmly in place with elastic, other bandaging, or cord, then call your veterinarian.

In addition to a vet treating wounds that will not stop bleeding, professional help is necessary for wounds over tendons or joints, since both are particularly susceptible to infection. A laceration or a puncture to the foot needs special attention, too, since foot injuries can affect future hoof growth.

Suturing is the fastest way to promote the healing of almost any laceration that reveals pink flesh (except, however, for muscles, which don't hold stitches well). Whether stitches are appropriate is a decision for your horse's doctor. So is the course of treatment, including medication and bandaging.

More times than not, your horse will have cut himself when you weren't around. By the time you see him, the wound may be partially clotted and full of dirt, grass, or other contaminants. In that case, clean the wound with a piece of clean cloth, sponge, or paper toweling dipped in an antiseptic soap or saline solution. Wipe away all foreign objects, including loose hair, until the wound is clean down to pink flesh. Don't worry if your efforts cause blood to flow again; fresh bleeding is a useful and natural way to promote cleaning.

---

*As for tourniquets, some veterinarians recommend them, while others feel that the amount of pressure can cause permanent damage. Follow your own vet's suggestion.

A fully clotted wound will be just as dirty, but even more difficult to clean. It may also be swollen and tender to the touch. Use a hose to flush the wound with cool (not ice cold) water for at least ten to fifteen minutes. Again, don't be concerned about any fresh bleeding. In addition to cleaning, the cool water will help reduce any swelling.

Once the wound is flushed out, proceed with stopping the blood flow and cleaning the wound as outlined above.

PUNCTURES: A puncture wound makes a hole, as when a horse steps on a nail. These wounds tend to be deep, and because nails—rusty or otherwise—open the way for tetanus, puncture wounds require a veterinarian's attention. While the doctor is on the way, clean the wound with cool water from a hose, then stop any bleeding with a clean cloth (watch out for the horse's other hooves while doing so).

As your vet will point out, puncture wounds often heal first on the outside unless the wound is thoroughly cleaned with iodine or methylene blue.

A wound that isn't completely clean will result in an abscess that produces pus. The pressure of pus that cannot escape is painful, and it often leads to more serious complications. That's why your vet will drain the abscess and then begin a treatment of antibiotics and poultices.

BRUISES

Put two or more horses together, and sooner or later one is bound to be kicked. The resulting bruise is known medically as a contusion, which is an injury that doesn't break the skin. As we humans are all too aware from our own bumps and bruises, just because there's no blood doesn't mean there's no pain—or the possibility of serious consequences.

If you're fortunate enough to see the injury happen, you'll be able to pinpoint its location. Otherwise, routinely inspecting your horse's legs, where the majority of bruises occur, will reveal any swelling from broken blood vessels. Hosing the area with cool water should relieve the swelling, but anything that doesn't go down within a day or so calls for a visit from the vet.

Overreaching—where a hind foot strikes the back of a front one—can cause tendon damage when the impact is above the foot. Treat a resulting bruise and any accompanying cut as you would similar wounds, then have a word with your blacksmith about corrective shoeing. Bell or overreach boots worn on the forelegs are another option.

FISTULAS

A fistula is a deep abscess on the poll, withers, or shoulder resulting from a sharp blow or a bruise. When the fistula comes to a head, your vet will lance it and drain the pus, then apply antibiotics to prevent infection.

SNAKEBITES

Horses are inquisitive creatures. They also are grazers. Both characteristics cause them to keep their head near the ground, and if a rattler or another type of venomous snake happens to take issue, you'll have a snakebite victim on your hands.

The prognosis will depend on the amount of venom the horse received and the amount of time between the bite and the beginning of treatment. And there are effective treatments. An antivenom injection may be useful for a recent bite. A bad bite may put a horse into shock, for which intravenous fluids are essential. In any event, the immediate attention of a veterinarian is essential.

Getting to a telephone to call the doctor becomes the most immediate concern. That may be difficult if you're on the trail in an isolated area. Although the impulse to gallop home or in search of the nearest phone is understandable, restrain that impulse. Strenuous exercise will increase the rate at which the venom enters the horse's bloodstream. A slow and steady pace that will not excite the horse is a far better prescription for survival.

Then, while you're waiting for the vet, place ice packs or cold running water on the bite to reduce swelling.

ALLERGIES AND POISONS

Similar to snakebites, some insect stings and the sap or leaves of some plants can cause life-threatening allergic reactions. The danger comes from an anaphylactic shock, during which sensitive horses (like sensitive humans) experience suffocating swelling of the nasal and throat passages.

Panicked by this loss of air, the horse's instinct is to thrash wildly. Since that behavior can produce further injury, it's up to you to try to restrain the animal in his stall or another confined space, but only if you can avoid being injured yourself. Then put in a rush call to your vet.

CHOKING

Another type of choking has nothing to do with suffocation. It happens when food—often a chunk of carrot or apple treat—becomes lodged in the esophagus and the horse cannot swallow. Unlike most instances of choking in humans, the windpipe is not affected; nevertheless, the horse is greatly distressed.

Because the horse cannot swallow, he drools a frothy saliva overflow from his nostrils and mouth. Another telltale sign of choking is when the animal extends his neck in an effort to get rid of the blockage pressure.

If gently massaging the obstruction does not work it down the horse's throat, call your vet immediately. And watch out for thrashing while you work on your horse; large animals often become unintentionally dangerous when upset.

Choking often happens to greedy eaters that wolf down their feed. One solution is to place large rocks or bricks in the feed bin so the horse is forced to pick around them and take smaller bites.

SUNSTROKE AND HEATSTROKE

Horses are susceptible to the effects of extreme heat; the consequences of sunstroke or heatstroke are just as dangerous as they are to humans.

Exercising any horse on a hot, humid day opens the door to the possibility. Be alert for a horse that stops sweating and starts to pant. He also will struggle to move and will appear disoriented. When you check his vital signs, you will find his pulse rate increased, his temperature up to 103°F or higher. His capillary refill rate will fall below normal, and his gums will appear blue instead of their usual pink.

Before you do anything else, get the horse to the nearest shade as quickly as possible. If he won't be led, then push or pull him there. If he still won't or can't move, make a tent over him with whatever is handy—whatever it takes to get him out of direct sunlight.

Because pouring or hosing down with cold water will shock the horse's system, sponge cool water over his head and along his spine. Moisten his mouth, but do not give him any water to drink. Then let him rest.

Immediately call your vet to look for any long-lasting damage. The doctor may recommend electrolytes to replace lost minerals, and you'll probably be reminded that any horse that once suffered from sunstroke is more susceptible to it again. Therefore, you will want to adjust your exercise schedule accordingly.

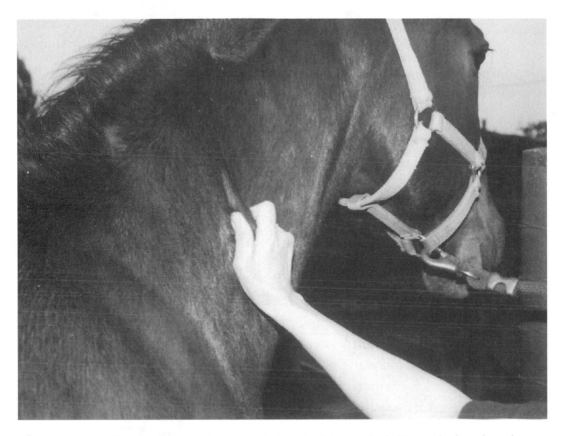

The pinch test indicates whether a horse is dehydrated. If the pinched skin in the horse's neck immediately returns to normal when you release it, he is well-hydrated. (The Quarter Horse Journal)

And since prevention is always the best cure, try to schedule any hot-weather equestrian activity for early morning or late afternoon to early evening. You'll enjoy it more, and so will your horse.

Internal Illnesses

COLIC

Although colic is the general term for any degree of bellyache, it's never a trifling matter.

Colic comes in three forms. One type is caused by blockage. Because a horse cannot vomit, everything he eats must be passed through his system. A blockage such as undigested hay or fecal matter that prevents normal bowel movement produces a impaction that is painful and, if left untreated, eventually fatal.

Symptoms include sweating, above-normal respiration rate, slow capillary refill rate, and the absence of a normal gurgling or roaring sound in the stomach. More obvious signs are the horse's trying to relieve the discomfort by nipping at his flanks, lying down and rolling, and/or continuously moving around.

Since the extent of real or possible blockage is not externally apparent, every case must be treated as serious. After placing an emergency call to the veterinarian, make every effort to keep the horse moving by slowly leading him around. In an effort to relieve or escape the pain, the animal may try to lie down and roll. Don't let him, because a twisted intestine caused by rolling will create an even worse problem.

Even without rolling, a section of intestine may become displaced. This "twisted gut" variety is the second type of colic and may appear to have the same symptoms as the type caused by blockage.

The third type, spasmodic colic, may be the result of the abdominal pain of trapped gas or improperly digested food. It comes from drinking very cold water, or no water at all (especially during winter weather, when horses are reluctant to drink chilled water). Parasites, abrupt changes in feed and hay, lush pasturage, and overeating can also bring on spasmodic colic. Immediately alert your vet, who will determine the cause and extent of the problem. Dosing with mineral oil often facilitates the passage of whatever might be causing the blockage. An injection of a muscle relaxant can help in that regard and also reduce the pain. In severe cases, surgery may be necessary to remove the obstruction or straighten out a section of twisted gut.

EDEMA

An edema is a swelling caused by excess fluid between cells within body tissue. Its symptoms are relatively easy to spot: a swelling of the hind legs (called "stocking up") or in the lower abdomen in mares. The treatment is exercise and, where helpful, support bandages until the swelling disappears.

ENCEPHALITIS

This serious viral condition, transmitted by certain species of mosquitoes, attacks the central nervous system and causes brain damage. There are three types: Eastern equine encephalitis (EEE or its equally well-known nickname "sleeping sickness"); Western equine encephalitis (WEE); and Venezuelan equine encephalitis (VEE).

The Eastern variety is carried by birds that live near water. Mosquitoes draw blood from them and then transmit the virus to animals and humans.

EEE proves fatal in between 70 and 90 percent of horses that contract the disease. Symptoms are a high fever, a drooping lower lip, and often blindness. There is a reluctance to move and a loss of coordination, often expressed by aimless circling. Death occurs within three days.

The Western type shares the same symptoms, but it is fatal in only 10 to 30 percent of cases.

As for VEE, although it seldom occurs north of Mexico, cases have recently been reported in the United States.

Since horses are capable of contracting more than one type, vaccination against all three usually is recommended. Two shots three to four weeks apart produces immunity.

EQUINE INFECTIOUS ANEMIA

EIA, or swamp fever, is a circulatory problem caused by a virus that the horse's natural antibodies are unable to eliminate. Symptoms are a sudden fever that spikes to 105°F or higher, together with rapid weight loss. The anemia, which lasts from one to four weeks, almost invariably proves fatal.

Dealing with the disease is essentially preventive, with horses quarantined before being introduced into a new facility with other horses. In addition, the well-known Coggins test determines the presence or absence of EIA, so all horses should undergo this procedure on a regular basis.

Because EIA is spread by the transfer of infected blood, keeping barns and pastures free from mosquitoes and horseflies and practicing other aspects of conscientious stable management is essential. Similarly, using disposable hypodermic syringes eliminates the problem of contaminated needles infecting healthy horses.

RABIES

This viral and always fatal disease is transmitted in the saliva of infected small animals. Foxes, skunks, raccoons, rodents, and bats have become the most common carriers. Symptoms appear after an incubation period of from two to eight weeks; the lameness, sluggishness, loss of appetite, and choking may mimic the symptoms of colic, influenza, or encephalitis.

An annual vaccination is essential. So is prevention: If you happen to spot a carrier species of animal that shows signs of erratic behavior (the most obvious sign of rabies), alert your vet or your county or state animal control agency immediately.

PARASITES

This category refers to ailments caused by a variety of worms and insects that invade the horse's system and attack organs and other body parts. In addition to showing symptoms that are specific to individual conditions, horses that are affected by any type of parasite will show a loss of coat bloom and an equally noticeable loss of energy.

Routine worming and sound pasture management go a long way toward reducing the chance of these devastating conditions afflicting your horse.

STRONGYLES: Pronounced "STRONG-jyles," this ailment is caused by bloodworms that attach themselves to the large intestine. The eggs they lay are passed in manure and infest pastures. Horses eat the eggs, which when ingested become larvae that cause blood clots, brain damage, and colic. Indications of strongyles include high fever, constipation or diarrhea, loss of appetite, and general lethargy. Because an infected horse's throat will swell, a reluctance to drink is another symptom.

Prevention is the best medicine. Worming medication administered every two months will rid the body of bloodworms. Removing manure from pastures and mowing grass to expose worm eggs to sunlight are good practices. So is rotating pastures to keep horses away from concentrations of manure. Lime in stalls kills eggs, larvae, and adult worms that have made their way indoors.

ASCARIDS: Ascarids are roundworms that hatch in intestines, then move to the lungs, where they are coughed up into the stomach and pass out of the horse. While inside the horse's body, they cause damage to the liver, heart, and lungs; they also can cause circulatory and intestinal blockage that produces ruptures.

The ascarid cycle lasts about ten weeks, so two months of worming medication reduces the amount of damage.

PINWORMS: A horse that rubs his tail against fence posts or other solid objects may be trying to tell you he has pinworms. The itching sensation they cause leads to hair loss from scratching and secondary infections. Again, routine worming and pasture control are the most effective preventive steps.

BOT FLIES: Bots are not worms, but flies that usually deposit their eggs on the hair of a horse's forelegs, although they also can appear on the flanks

Deworming is often done with a paste administered by a plunger tube. (The Quarter Horse Journal)

and hind legs. The horse responds to the itching by licking, which causes the eggs to enter the system and hatch into larvae in the stomach.

Treatment begins with scraping the eggs off the hair with a knife blade or washing them away with hot water. A dose of worming paste will kill any eggs or larvae that already have been ingested.

POTOMAC HORSE FEVER

First isolated in Maryland in 1978, Potomac horse fever is not limited to the Eastern part of the country. It occurs during summer months and primarily in areas near rivers, giving rise to the as-yet-unproved hypothesis that an insect may be the carrier. Symptoms are high fever and profuse and watery diarrhea that lasts for up to ten days. Many horses also develop severe laminitis.

Treatment begins with fluid and electrolyte administration to counter fluid loss from diarrhea. The vet also will prescribe antibiotics for the fever and anti-inflammatory medication for the laminitis. A vaccine has proved effective against this disease.

TETANUS

The bacterium that causes tetanus lives in ground soil. It enters the body through puncture wounds, a compelling reason to be alert to the presence of nails, wires, hooks, or any other sharp objects—especially rusty ones.

Initial symptoms appear within seven to ten days. One is a rigidity of the horse's jaw that gives rise to the nickname "lockjaw." The animal's ears and tail will stand erect, nostrils flare, and the third eyelid roll up. Leg muscles become stiff, so the horse assumes a "sawhorse" stance.

Although the infection has no cure and recovery is unlikely, tetanus toxin inoculations given two to three weeks apart and annual boosters are highly effective in prevention. Since mares can transmit the disease to unborn foals through the umbilical cord, they must be inoculated in the final three to six weeks of pregnancy.

Horses that have not been inoculated will receive ten to twelve days of protection from a tetanus antitoxin after infection.

While we're on the subject, every human who spends time around horses should be inoculated against tetanus. You'll need periodic booster shots, too.

AZOTURIA

Although this condition is now rarely found among horses that have access to pasture or paddock, azoturia needs to be mentioned in case your horse does "tie up."

Also known as "Monday morning sickness," azoturia is the result of working a horse strenuously (as over a weekend), then giving him a day of rest (Monday) without cutting down his grain or giving a laxative bran mash. The resulting buildup of glycogen causes paralysis of the hindquarters' gluteal muscles. The muscles lose definition and become tight to the point that the horse is unable to move. Other symptoms are heavy sweating and coffee-colored urine.

A horse that shows these signs should be kept quiet until the vet arrives. Rest, warmth, and a laxative will be the immediate treatment. Another necessary bit of business will involve you and the doctor reassessing the animal's diet, feeding, and exercise schedules that caused the problem.

LYME DISEASE

Named after a town in Connecticut, this disease has become prevalent along the East and West Coasts. Its cause is a bacterium that is carried by deer ticks.

One trainer described horses that are affected as "not acting themselves": A good athlete will become a poor athlete, while a formerly friendly animal will suddenly shy away from being handled. "Edgy" and "unsettled" are other words that describe a horse that's suffering from Lyme disease.

The usual sequence of events is that once a veterinarian has eliminated other possible causes for the change in performance or behavior, the animal will be given a titre test. Evidence that he's producing the antibodies that counteract the disease is proof positive that he has Lyme.

Treatment consists of antibiotics. Although a preventive vaccine has been developed, veterinarians are divided on its effectiveness. Then, too, Lyme disease becomes systemic, so it can reappear even after a horse appears to be completely cured.

HYPERKALEMIC PERIODIC PARALYSIS

Hyperkalemic periodic paralysis (HYPP) is an inherited disease that leads to uncontrolled muscle twitching or profound muscle weakness. In severe cases, the result may be collapse and/or death. In most cases, however, the condition can be treated through diet and medication.

As of the late 1990s HYPP has been traced to only the descendants of one American Quarter Horse stallion, Impressive (#0767246).

AQHA rules list HYPP as a genetic defect. In an effort to deal with its consequences, AQHA has instituted testing and notification procedures.

Structural Ailments and Impairments

PARROT-MOUTH

Parrot-mouth is an inherited condition in which the upper jaw overlaps the lower jaw, resulting in overgrown front teeth; as horses with parrot-mouth have difficulty eating, a bad case can lead to malnutrition. Little can be done to rectify the problem. AQHA will issue registration certificates for horses that have parrot-mouth; however, the registration certificates and the AQHA records will indicate the condition.

CRYPTORCHID

This inherited condition results in a blockage that prevents one or both testicles from descending into the scrotum. Stallions with the condition may be subfertile. Geldings that are affected may be aggressive because the removal of the scrotum during gelding did not rid the horse of his testes nor the hormones that cause the aggressiveness usually associated with stallions.

Surgical removal of the retained testicle (or testicles) is the proper treatment. Horses with cryptorchid that have undergone treatment should not be adversely affected in their performance. AQHA will register such horses, though their conditions will be designated on the registration certificates and the AQHA records.

LAMENESS

You lead your horse out of the pasture one morning and notice that he's not walking normally. Or within two minutes of riding at the jog or trot you find yourself muttering that "something feels funny." Although American Quarter Horses are blessed with sturdy legs and feet, no horse owner is totally immune from discovering that his or her horse is lame, the catch-all term for a horse that moves unsoundly.

Recognizing that something is wrong is the easy part. You've based your suspicion on your knowledge of how your horse normally moves. However, unless the animal is obviously "off" in a particular leg, locating the lameness can be far more difficult. But there are clues, which the assistance of another person will make easier to figure out.

The trot is the easiest gait at which to identify lameness, because a horse's weight is evenly distributed at each stride. Ask the person assisting you to lead the horse at the jog-trot across a stretch of firm and level ground. Or if the horse can be ridden, have him or her trot the horse in a circle while posting on the wrong diagonal.*

As in so many other assessments, the key is symmetry. Does the horse move in an even fashion? A lame horse does not. Instead, one foreleg step "in front" or hind-leg step "behind" will almost always be shorter than the other, much the way we humans limp when one of our feet bothers us.

Foreleg problems are easier to isolate than hind-leg. That's a good thing, because most lameness happens in front. A horse that is off in front will favor the unsound leg by raising his head when it strikes the ground, as if trying to escape the discomfort.

---

*That means, when circling to the left, the rider rises when the horse's right foreleg/left hind leg strike the ground.

Unfortunately, horses that are off behind offer no such clearcut clues. Although the hip of the affected leg may appear "hitchy," rising awkwardly when that foot hits the ground, the hip may also drop lower in some instances. In either case, look for such hip movement in conjunction with any unevenness of gait, since the horse will tend to move any sore leg in a shorter stride (that's why the ground is a better vantage point than the saddle).

You can also listen for lameness. A sound leg will make a louder sound when it strikes the ground than an unsound leg does, plus the off leg will seem to hit a beat late. The cause of the unsoundness may be no more than a pebble wedged between shoe and hoof or a visible bruise to the sole. If so, you've gotten away lightly. The problem may be less obvious or there may be heat and/or soreness present that indicates more severe problems. Once again, your veterinarian will be the best person to answer any questions about the cause and the severity of a sudden lameness. A professional and thorough diagnosis will use such tools as ultrasound, X ray, and nerve blocking (the last technique isolates portions of the foot and leg to pinpoint the injured area). Only after diagnosis will the vet be able to prescribe the proper treatment of medication and/or rest and venture an opinion about when the animal may be able to return to work.

SPRAINS

A sprain is an injury to a muscle or tendon (a tendon attaches a muscle to a bone). One of the most common sprains is of the flexor tendon that runs along the back of the front leg from knee to pastern. Inflammation from the sprain causes a puffy swelling, heat, and tenderness to the touch, while fluid from the swelling permeates the tissue around the tendon. As the sprain heals, scar tissue replaces normal tissue and restricts the tendon's flexibility. Repeated sprains to that area force it to curve outward and become a "bowed tendon."

Ice or cold water, which reduce swelling, should be applied up to an hour or more at a time during the first twenty-four hours. If the horse doesn't seem more comfortable after that period, your vet will evaluate the sprain for any damage to the underlying bone, perhaps using an X ray or ultrasound.

Support bandages provide a brace for a weakened leg, while heat or liniment encourages blood circulation after the swelling goes down. If the problem is in fact a bowed tendon, several months of rest allow the bow to "set," or permanently harden. Then the horse usually can return to normal activity.

STRAINS

Ligaments connect bones and support joints. When they stretch more than they should, the resulting injury is a strain.

The suspensory ligament runs below the flexor tendon down to the fetlock, then divides into two parts that cross the pastern. This ligament is particularly susceptible to strain, and when either branch stretches too far, the horse will show soreness and swelling.

As with sprains, hosing with cold water or packing with ice will reduce the swelling that accompanies a strain. Subsequent treatment includes wrapping, anti-inflammatory medication, and prolonged rest.

Another site of strains is the plantar ligament along the rear of the hock. Following a severe strain (to which badly conformed horses are particularly prone), the inflamed bone beneath the plantar thickens. This is a condition known as "curb," which takes the form of a bulge about four inches below the point of hock. Rest aided by supportive wrapping is the treatment, from which the horse will usually recover quite well.

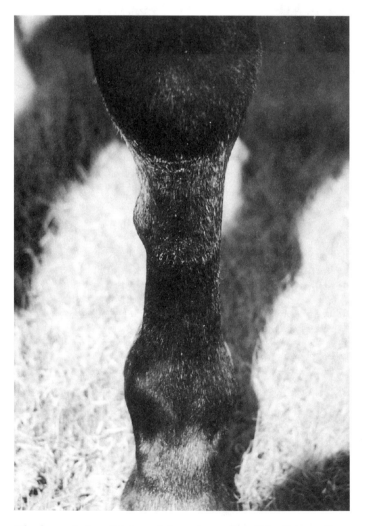

The bump below this horse's knee is a splint. (*The Quarter Horse Journal*)

SPLINT

The splint bone lies on the inside of the cannon bone. When the ligaments that attach the two bones are torn, perhaps by a kick or by pounding on hard ground, the calcium that fills the space produces irritating hard knots.

The good news for owners of older horses is that animals older than six years seldom, if ever, come down with splints. However, if a splint does happen, the vet may apply an irritant blister to harden the ligament, after which the horse will recuperate following a period of rest.

FRACTURED AND BROKEN BONES

What may appear to be a sprain or strain may in fact turn out to be a fracture (yet another reason why your vet should be asked to pass judgment on any questionable injury). Telltale signs are reluctance or inability to place any weight on the injured foot or leg, and, in extreme cases, a broken bone protruding against or through the skin.

All you can do after spotting a fractured or broken bone and calling the vet is to keep the horse calm. The animal's innate protective mechanism may help by sending him into shock.

Some fractured bones can be reset and, with time, will heal. Others, however, will not. In the unfortunate event of the latter, you must face the sad but humane option of having the horse euthanized.

JOINT AND LEG PROBLEMS

SPAVIN: The word describes any of several conditions of the hock joint. A bog spavin is a puffy swelling on the front of the hock about one-third of the way down the leg. More a cosmetic blemish than an ailment, a bog will not cause a horse to become lame.

This is not so with a bone spavin, a calcium enlargement on the inside of the hock joint that produces a buildup of fluid.

Poor conformation of hocks tends to be the cause of both kinds of spavins. Prolonged rest helps make the problem subside, while wrapping or draining a bog spavin reduces the amount of fluid.

THOROUGHPIN: Thoroughpin is an inflammation of the deep flexor tendon that runs from knee or hock to pastern. Fluid that builds up in the tarsal sheath covering the tendon produces a swelling above and behind the hock or knee. Thoroughpin will not cause lameness, and there is no treatment or cure.

WINDPUFFS: A similar swelling of the flexor tendon sheath at the ankle is called windpuff. It comes in two varieties and is most prevalent among horses with straight shoulders and pasterns.

A nonarticulated windpuff is only a cosmetic blemish, but its articulated relative is more serious. Located between the suspensory ligament and the cannon bone, an articulated windpuff is the product of irritation. A veterinarian must determine whether the windpuff has caused any bone damage and, if so, whether surgery will help.

CAPPED HOCK AND CAPPED ELBOW: Bursa are sacs that secrete fluids that lubricate joints. Stress or injury can cause a bursa to become inflamed. Too much fluid will be produced, and that results in swelling.

When that happens, a cap-like, sizable nodule appears. Two classic locations are the point of hock and the elbow. Although the blemish may be no more than cosmetic (lameness may or may not result), a veterinarian may want to check for a more serious underlying problem.

Extended rest is the usual cure for capped hocks and elbows, but surgery is sometimes indicated in extraordinary cases.

RINGBONE: Ringbone is a general term for any bony enlargement below the fetlock. A common variety is a sort of arthritis that affects the pastern or the coffin joint of the foot. Its usual cause is a sudden or chronic strain. Forelegs are most commonly affected; the symptoms of ringbone are lameness and acute swelling, and permanent lameness may result. Although no cure has yet been found, corrective shoeing and prolonged rest often extend the usefulness of a horse with this condition.

SIDEBONE: Sidebone is an inflammation of the cartilage under the side of the coronet band where it joins the hoof. The horse experiences temporary lameness while calcification takes place in the inflamed area; he becomes sound again when the calcium sets in place to form a new bone.

Sidebone is extremely rare among American Quarter Horses that don't race (and uncommon among those that do).

SESAMOIDITIS: This pain and swelling occurs at the rear of the fetlock. Caused by a strain to the ligaments of the sesamoid bones, its treatment is anti-inflammatory medication and rest.

STRINGHALT: This condition is caused by a contraction of the hock's flexor muscles. You'll spot it by the pronounced and unmistakable hop by one or the other hind foot at the walk and trot. There is no known cure for stringhalt, which interferes with a horse's action but does not necessarily render him useless.

HOOF AND FOOT PROBLEMS

CONTRACTED HEELS: This particularly painful—and easily avoidable—condition happens when the heels are allowed to grow toward each other. It can be avoided through proper and timely trimming and shoeing.

BRUISES: A bruise is the result of a blow or another trauma to the sole or, less typically, another part of the foot. A horse so afflicted will limp and favor that foot. Bandaging and corrective shoeing are the cure.

CRACKS: A crack is a split in the hoof wall. Depending on location, it will be distinguished as a toe, quarter, or heel crack, all under the general heading of sand or grass crack. Cracks come from an injury, excessive growth, or dry or thin walls.

A crack that's left alone usually leads to lameness. Infection is likely when the tissue beneath becomes exposed (bleeding is a sign). Corrective shoeing is called for, with footwear that often includes clips to hold the hoof together. Another treatment involves filling the crack with liquid fiberglass or another durable adhesive material.

LAMINITIS: Also known as founder, laminitis is an inflammation of the laminac of the foot. One function of the laminae, which contain blood vessels and nerves, is to secure the coffin bone in place. When inflammation weakens the laminae until the horse's weight forces the bone down into contact with the ground, lameness results.

The primary cause of laminitis is digestive: overeating in general, or, more specifically, too much fresh alfalfa, clover, or another rich legume pasturage. Allowing an overheated horse to drink cold water can also lead to the problem, and so can overworking an unfit animal on hard ground.

Laminitis affects only the forefeet. The most obvious indication is what's known as the "founder stance": hind legs well under the body in an effort to relieve the forefeet of as much weight as possible. Other signs are heat and soreness in the afflicted foot, sweating, labored breathing, and other signs of pain.

Your vet will administer medications to reduce the inflammation and relieve the pain. Feed will be reduced or even withheld for one or two days, followed by small quantities of grass hay (a general change in diet will probably be in order). Corrective shoeing that lowers the heels and protects the sole often helps reestablish the blood supply.

Two layers of laminae interlock between the hoof wall and the coffin bone; when founder causes these two layers to separate, a condition known as "seedy toe" happens. It acquires its name from a white flaky substance that comes out of the space between the hoof wall and sole.

Treatment begins by removing the affected hoof wall and applying antibiotics and disinfectant. Then the exposed laminae are covered and a corrective bar shoe provided to support the foot. Since a foot grows at approximately one-half inch per month, a completely new hoof wall may take up to a year to be produced.

THRUSH: Thrush, an infection of the frog, also often penetrates underlying tissue and structure. Its causes are strictly a function of poor stable management: allowing a horse to stand in a dirty wet stall, neglecting his feet, and shoeing that puts pressure on the frog.

Thrush is among the easiest of conditions to recognize by its inky black discharge and unmistakable foul odor (no one who has been near a thrushy foot will ever forget the smell). Treatment begins with cutting away the damaged portions of the frog, then applying a commercial medication or perhaps a solution that the veterinarian has mixed. Returning the horse to a clean, dry environment helps ensure that the condition will not return.

NAVICULAR: Like laminitis, navicular almost always affects one or both forefeet. The word describes a degeneration of the navicular bone and inflammation of the bursa and their neighboring deep flexor tendon. The rear surface of the bone wears away, and the jagged edge cuts into (and thus progressively weakens) the tendon. A horse with navicular moves in a choppy, stumbling gait when he tries to place his forefeet down toe-first. Standing still, he will extend his front feet as a way to relieve the pressure.

Poor shoeing that puts excessive pressure on the navicular bone often leads to the condition. So does lots of hard work on unyielding surfaces. Another cause is a function of conformation: Horses with straight shoulders and pasterns tend to put more pressure on the navicular bone.

Sad to say, navicular can be only accommodated, not cured. Anti-inflammatory medication such as phenylbutazone relieves the problem, while corrective shoeing, often with a bar shoe, also helps. Removing a nerve in the afflicted foot may provide additional but not permanent relief.

Respiratory Problems

COUGH

As with humans, an occasional horse cough is no cause for alarm. However, persistent and prolonged bouts of coughing, especially if they cause the animal distress, are reason for investigation.

Try to detect whether there's a pattern. Does the horse cough after heavy exercise? Or light exercise, or none at all? When he's in his pasture? His stall? In the arena or out on the trail? During the day, at night, or both?

Hand in hand with coughing is the animal's general respiration. Does he breathe harder or faster at particular times? Does he inhale normally, but require extra effort when he exhales? These are all clues to determining the type and extent of the respiratory problem.

INFLUENZA

Influenza is a viral respiratory problem that is easily spread through coughing and sneezing and even infected tack and grooming equipment. Even humans can spread the disease to horses (sounds like the way we catch colds and the flu, doesn't it?). Although the actual infection lasts up to a week, the horse's weakened condition invites more serious ailments such as pneumonia.

Flu symptoms include a fever that can reach 106°F and last for three days, a cough that may last up to two weeks, labored breathing, and general loss of alertness and energy. Treatment involves fever-reducing medications and a minimum of three weeks of complete rest in a clean space. For secondary bacterial infections, antibiotics may be prescribed.

A vaccine provides immunity, but because the vaccine wears off and because influenza can recur every four to five months, horses that come into contact with others at shows and other events need to be inoculated every three to four months.

RHINOPNEUMONITIS

Equine viral rhinopneumonitis is a highly contagious upper respiratory infection (it also can cause abortion in mares in the later stages of pregnancy and death in newborn foals). Caused by a herpes virus, its symptoms include a high fever, runny nose, loss of appetite, labored breathing, and difficulty in moving. Vaccination is an easy and effective way to prevent rhinopneumonitis. A primary shot is followed by a booster about a month later. Booster shots every three months are recommended for horses that come in contact with other horses on a regular basis. Quarantining new horses before letting them into the general barn population is a wise idea, at least until you're satisfied that they're disease-free.

HEAVES

Also known as broken wind or, more formally, chronic obstructive pulmonary disease, heaves is an allergy to mold, pollen, and/or dust. It can also be set off by bronchitis. Heaves is a subtle condition, in that it can build up slowly and remain unrecognizable until it reaches a full-blown stage.

Chronic coughing is a primary symptom. Others are sluggishness, loss of weight, and shortness of breath marked by normal intake of air but extra effort to exhale.

Allergy tests similar to those given to humans are useful in determining the root cause. The results may call for a change of environment. For example, if dust or mold is the culprit, giving up a barn stall in favor of an outside paddock is an option. Similarly, pellets or cubes will expose the patient to less dust than hay does, while changing the bedding from straw or shavings to shredded paper will also reduce exposure to offending allergens.

In severe cases, your vet may recommend antihistamines, or perhaps cortisone or steroid medication.

VIRUS

A mucus discharge from both nostrils is often the first sign of a virus. It will be accompanied by fever and labored breathing.

Just as a human cold will run its course without any extraordinary treatment, most veterinarians are reluctant to prescribe anything for a light virus. However, a thick mucus discharge and high temperature may indicate a secondary bacterial infection and usually call for an antibiotic. The condition must be closely monitored, since a virus is too often the forerunner of much more serious pneumonia or pleurisy (infections of the lungs or the lining around the lungs, respectively).

A mucus discharge from only one nostril may indicate a sinus infection that requires surgery to drain the sinus cavity.

STRANGLES

Not to be confused with strongyles, this ailment is also known as distemper or, because of its prevalence among horses that have been transported, shipping fever.

It is an inflammation of the nasal mucous membrane that produces abscesses in the lymph glands below the jaw. Symptoms are a profuse nasal discharge, a high fever that can reach 106°F, and a characteristic rattle sound from the horse's throat that sounds as if the animal is being strangled (and gives the condition its name).

The infection, which lasts from two weeks to a month, responds to antibiotics. Inoculation against the strangles bacterium requires two shots two to four weeks apart and annual boosters.

ROARING

You'll know it when you hear it: Strenuous exercise produces a gargling or roaring noise. The cause is a vocal cord that covers the trachea and prevents enough air from getting to the lungs. Surgery to remove or reposition the vocal cord is the treatment.

Skin Problems

DANDRUFF

Horses are just as vulnerable to dry, flaking skin as humans are. The treatment is much the same, too: a wash with antidandruff veterinary shampoo followed by rinsing with clean water. Conscientious grooming that stimulates the skin and removes loose dander helps minimize, if not eliminate, the problem.

RAIN ROT

Hard scabs caused by a fungal organism in dust particles grow after long periods of rain when secretions from a horse's skin promote their formation. Not only do scabs appear, but there is hair loss under and around them.

Your vet or your expert friend will show you how to work in a lather of antidandruff veterinary shampoo, gently but firmly working the scabs loose with your fingers. You'll then apply a medicated salve that the doctor recommends.

RINGWORM

Another type of fungal organism manifests itself by hair loss in round bald spots. It is passed by direct contact, and is extremely contagious to all animals, including humans. Accordingly, keep the horse isolated, and wear gloves as you apply an antifungal cream. Disinfect or dispose of all equipment that comes in contact with any afflicted animal.

CRACKED HEELS

Despite the name, it is the hollows of the pasterns that are affected by this scaling and scabby condition. The cause is prolonged exposure to water, usually from mud or flooded pasture or paddock land. Infection is likely if it is not caught and treated early.

After you wash the pastern with soap and water and thoroughly dry the area, apply a coating of petroleum jelly or an antiseptic ointment.

TUMORS

Although not strictly a dermatological problem, tumors begin as lumps and bumps on the skin. Most are harmless, but in the event your horse develops a lump that continues to grow or becomes tender to the touch, call the matter to your veterinarian's attention. A biopsy may be needed for diagnosis.

Older gray horses are prone to a type of tumor called melanoma. Although the lumps tend to be unsightly but benign, many are not, and only a veterinarian can determine whether a melanoma needs to be surgically removed or treated in another way.

Eye Care

The horse has the largest eye of any land mammal. To protect this vulnerable organ, nature gave the species several specialized features. In addition to lids and tear ducts is a muscle that allows the eyeball to retract part of the way back into the socket. A pad of fat behind the eyeball acts as a kind of shock absorber. In addition, the third eyelid, a thin, retractable membrane, acts as a "windshield wiper" whenever a foreign object like a speck of dirt or an insect touches the eye's surface.

Although you won't be able to protect your horse from dust, bugs, and all the other objects that can fly into his eyes, you can keep stalls and pastures as free from them as possible. You certainly can make periodic inspections to make sure that nails, hooks, and other projections aren't accidents waiting to happen. That sort of awareness is the best preventive medicine in the world when it comes to eliminating eye problems.

However, despite both the animal's well-adapted features and conscientious human care, injuries and ailments do occur.

INJURY

This catchall term encompasses any trauma to the eye area. For example, a cut on the eyelid will be accompanied by bleeding, swelling, and obvious pain. The veterinarian will stitch the wound, making sure that the cornea isn't scratched and the lid is working as it should. An antibiotic ointment or powder helps ensure that no infection results while the wound heals.

INFECTION

Usually the result of a cut or scratch, an infection will cause the affected eye to discharge a watery fluid or pus. Sometimes the discharge is seen as only dried crust on the eyelid or eyelash. Another way to spot the problem is to see whether the pupil is contracted; it will appear smaller than the pupil of the other eye.

The vet will treat such infection with an antibiotic ointment and, in the case of a contracted pupil, a muscle relaxant. The eye's extrasensitivity to light may require the horse to be confined to a stall with subdued lighting.

EQUINE RECURRENT UVEITIS

A horse's eye is composed of three layers, of which the uvea is the middle one. An infection of this layer, equine recurrent uveitis, is more familiarly known as "moonblindness." The leading cause of equine blindness, it appears as a teary eye, a constricted pupil, and a cloudy cornea often accompanied by pus discharge. The symptoms last for a week or so and then vanish (the ailment was once thought to be related to the moon's changing phases, hence the nickname). Nevertheless, symptoms will return.

Because ERU is likely to cause blindness if not caught in time, calling the vet as soon as you spot the symptoms is essential. Another compelling reason for promptness is that the ERU may be a secondary reaction to another problem that will need to be identified and treated.

Medication includes steroid and anti-inflammatory ointment and pills. Keeping the horse away from bright light is usually prescribed, too. Although your vet may continue treatment after the horse seems to have recovered, the idea is to prevent recurrence of this dreadful condition.

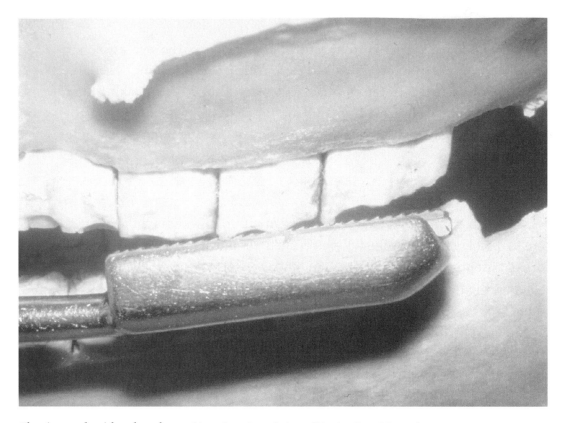

Floating teeth with a dental rasp. (American Association of Equine Practitioners)

CONJUNCTIVITIS

The conjunctiva is the membrane that covers the insides of the eyelids and the eye's surface. Just like the condition in humans, the membrane turns red when it's irritated (the result of increased blood flow).

If this redness is the only symptom, with no puffiness or fluid discharge, the condition is likely to disappear on its own in a day or two. If it doesn't, call your vet, because something more serious may be present.

BLOCKED TEAR DUCT

Excessive tearing without any further symptoms is the sign of a blocked tear duct. Opening the duct with a catheter, your vet will irrigate with a saline solution, then apply an antibiotic ointment.

CATARACTS

Cataracts tend to be a function of the aging process (although some hereditary conditions will affect horses when they're just foals). As in humans,

the lens clouds or "milks over." Even before the condition becomes visible to the human eye, the horse will not react to visual stimuli as he once did.

In many cases, the lens can be removed without causing blindness, but the horse will lose some ability to perceive details.

Ear Care

Problems affecting a horse's ears aren't nearly so easy to isolate as those that affect eyes, because the parts of a horse's body that deal with hearing are hidden from sight. That's why a horse owner must be particularly alert to those changes in attitude that may be clues. These include sensitivity to being touched around the ears while being bridled; shaking, tossing, or tilting the head; and the same sort of loss of balance and coordination that humans experience from middle-ear disorders. More obvious symptoms are growths or infection in the visible portions of the ear. In any case, any sort of irregularity is a reason to call the veterinarian.

The advice that doctors give to their human patients also applies to horses. When you're grooming and bathing the animal, avoid flooding the inside of the ears with water. Instead, wipe the outside and inside of the external ear with a damp sponge or cloth. And as for trying to clean the middle or inner ear, remember the line about never inserting anything smaller than your elbow. Translation: Don't even try—cleaning that part of the ear is a job best left to a veterinarian.

Teeth Care

Horses have from thirty-six to forty-four teeth: twenty-four molars, twelve incisors, and anywhere from no canines to four, and no wolf teeth to four of them, too.

As grazing herbivores, horses developed teeth that are well suited to the tasks of nipping and then grinding forage. Domestication, especially in the form of grain added to their grassy diet, has had an important impact: The hard husks of oats and corn, for example, offer enough resistance to grind against a horse's teeth just as the teeth grind the grain.

A horse's teeth continue to grow throughout the animal's useful working years, and so need periodic attention. That's especially true in those cases when horses are fed sweet feed or pelleted rations that are softer than oats or corn. Moreover, experienced horsemen are aware of a link between a horse's teeth and his well-being. Even minor dental problems, which are more common than many people would think, will affect performance as well as health.

POINTS

Sharp enamel points are perhaps the most common dental problem. They result from the fact that upper molars are set slightly wider than the lower ones. Because horses chew in a circular grinding motion, the inside edges of the uppers and the outer edges of the lowers wear away faster than other parts of the surfaces. The points that are created can become sharp enough to irritate and even cut the tongue.

Floating (the word for filing down the points) is the treatment. If your vet's practice doesn't include doing such work, he or she can usually recommend a horse dentist. The specialist will first prop the horse's mouth open with a speculum, then file away the offending points until the surfaces are smooth.

HOOKS

A formation called a hook develops on a cheek tooth when there is no opposing tooth to match (and grind down) the tooth. Due to misalignment, the first or last tooth is most often affected. It's a serious matter, because hooks on bottom teeth can grow tall enough to penetrate the roof of the mouth and even the nasal passage.

A vet will cut tall hooks with a molar cutter or remove smaller ones with a float rasp.

TALL TEETH

Similar to hooks are tall incisors and cheek teeth. A "tall" tooth happens when the opposing tooth is lost through decay or extraction. With nothing to stop them, incisors and cheek teeth continue to grow. A tall tooth can injure the opposite gum, which will in turn throw the rest of the cheek teeth out of alignment. The vet will cut a tall tooth until it is level with the rest of the grinding surface, then float it smooth.

Tall or sharp canine teeth (known as tushes) are most prevalent in older geldings and stallions. They can interfere with the bit (and do some real damage when the horse decides to bite). When these canines grow to a certain length, a vet or horse dentist will cut or float them down to size.

MALOCCLUSIONS

A purely structural form of misalignment happens when the top and bottom teeth fail to meet. Heredity is the most common cause of a "parrot-mouth,"* or an overshot or undershot upper jaw.

Misalignment also can be a result of age; an estimated 30 percent of middle-aged and older horses have some structural problem that affects their eating and/or performance. The dental equivalent of corrective shoeing sometimes helps: The teeth are floated until the bite is as level and even as possible.

WOLF TEETH

Not all horses develop wolf teeth, which are one or two small and incompletely developed teeth that are usually in place when the animal is seven months old. Much more prevalent in the upper jaw, a wolf tooth can cause discomfort when it interferes with the bit or irritates the gum. A vet will easily and routinely extract wolf teeth.

TOOTHACHES

Horses get toothaches, and for the same reasons that humans do. Food becomes lodged in cavities and decomposes into bacteria that cause pulp and gum infection. Symptoms include bad breath, swollen jaw or face, and/or eating slowly or not at all. (The accompanying unwillingness to work is completely understandable, because any creature with a toothache has other things on his mind.)

The veterinarian will extract the infected tooth, then treat any infection with antibiotics.

Examining and treating a horse's teeth is a job for a professional, and not just because he or she knows what to look for: Inexperienced examiners have been known to lose fingers. There are, however, certain things that any owner can and should do.

That begins with becoming familiar with your horse's eating habits. Spilling or dropping feed while chewing, or showing discomfort while chewing, is often a symptom of dental problems. Broken teeth, bad breath, a lacerated tongue, and white or yellowish gums also are danger signs.

---

*AQHA considers the parrot-mouth condition an undesirable trait that reduces the animal's value for breeding. The condition is indicated on his registration certificate.

Similarly, a horse that suddenly becomes unwilling to accept a bit, or one that fusses excessively or tosses his head when he's bridled, may be trying to tell you that the mouthpiece has become uncomfortable. So is a horse that becomes difficult to ride, especially when it's time to slow down or halt (he's trying to run away from the painful bit). Before you switch to a stronger bit, consider having your vet check to see whether a sharp, broken, loose, or infected tooth might be the culprit.

Alternative Therapies

Paralleling a growing interest in nontraditional treatment of human illnesses, the veterinary world has developed alternatives to conventional medical treatment. According to supporters, the approaches go beyond treating symptoms of ailments to focus on underlying causes of restricted motion (including lameness), discomfort and pain, and loss of energy. Treatment techniques make use of the body's own healing powers by releasing painkilling endorphins, relaxing muscles, correcting skeletal misalignments, and restoring chemical and physical balances.

Some alternative therapies are more widely accepted than others, but all are worth hearing about in the context of veterinary options (you probably know about most of them and may yourself have benefited from one or more).

CHIROPRACTIC

When the vertebrae that make up the spine are out of alignment, the resulting condition (called subluxation) restricts movement, blocks transmission of nerve impulses, and produces pain.

Chiropractic corrects the problem by realigning the vertebrae. The chiropractor first examines the horse's spine, then makes a series of short, rapid adjustments to return the vertebrae to their natural positions and release tension. Several sessions may be necessary before the horse shows any improvement. In addition to treatments for specific problems, regularly scheduled periodic adjustments are widely used as a form of preventive medicine.

ACUPUNCTURE

Acupuncture is based on the theory that specific points on the body can be stimulated to trigger certain biochemical and physiological reactions. All of these points (a horse has some one hundred) are located in the depressions between bones and muscles. They are tied to the central nervous system and are said to affect musculoskeletal, hormonal, and cardiovascular systems. Stimulation comes from the insertion of sterilized thin needles at certain places where the acupuncturist finds muscle spasms or sensitivity to touch. The insertion increases circulation, stimulates the nervous and defense systems, and releases endorphins. In some cases, small amounts of electricity will be used to increase stimulation. Horses don't seem to object to the needles, which remain in place for an average of fifteen minutes; in fact, the released endorphins often cause them to doze off. A variation known as acupressure massage involves stimulating acupuncture points manually.

Repeat sessions from one to three times a week over a four- to six-week span may be required, although improvements are often apparent after four to six treatments.

MASSAGE

Massage is the use of the hands to knead and rub muscle tissue to relax contracted muscle fibers. Massage increases blood flow to muscles and skin, removes toxins, releases endorphins, and promotes tissue healing.

The massage-giver (the masseur or masseuse if you insist) starts at the horse's upper neck and works along the body and then the legs.

Massage is often combined with chiropractic and acupuncture to increase effectiveness. It is also used along with such other modes of treatment as laser, ultrasound, magnets, and hydrotherapy.

MAGNETS

Since the body is in part composed of substances that respond to magnetism, magnets can be used to encourage healing by increasing blood flow deep within a horse's tissue and bone. As blood flows through magnetic fields created from special blankets, pads, and leg wraps, ions in the blood increase circulation. This therapy is used both to accelerate healing after the swelling has gone down and as preventive medicine.

OTHERS

Homeopathy is the administration of microdoses of herbs, minerals, or animal products to combat diseases and promote health. Botanical therapy uses plants and their derivatives as healing and therapeutic agents. Neutraceutical therapy involves nutrients and nutritional supplements to promote healing.

Because they include doses of some substances than can be toxic if misused, these three approaches are the most controversial of alternative therapies.

The role of a qualified practitioner is as important in alternative therapies as it is in conventional medicine. Here, too, the primary source is your horse's veterinarian, with whom you should discuss whether your animal might benefit from such attention. If your vet agrees, he or she should be able to refer you to a qualified therapist. Look for a specialist whose credentials and experience indicate competence and who will be willing to work in conjunction with your horse's vet. In the best of situations, the therapist also will be a licensed veterinarian who can quickly and accurately identify any problems the therapy might create.

FOR FURTHER INFORMATION

Your Horse's Health. Dr. Tom Lenz is well known for his popular *America's Horse* equine health care presentations on ESPN. Now, four of these presentations have been consolidated into a single, comprehensive video source. Learn the important facets of keeping your horse healthy as Dr. Lenz discusses, in plain language, equine diseases, parasites, vaccinations, and deworming. 19 minutes.

In addition, the American Association of Equine Practitioners offers *A Veterinarian . . . for the Life of Your Horse,* a fifteen-minute video with helpful suggestions on preparing for your horse's exam and communicating with your veterinarian. Available on loan only from AQHA, the video may be purchased by calling the American Association of Equine Practitioners at (800) GET-ADVM.

IV

Enjoying Your American Quarter Horse

Equine Behavior

Although this book isn't a how-to-ride manual, understanding the fundamentals of how horses behave and why, and especially how they perceive and process information, will improve your riding as much as your stable-management skills—and your overall enjoyment of your American Quarter Horse.

Horses gather information through their senses. Let's start with the eye.

Vision

A horse's eye does not focus the way a human's does. The lens can't change its shape, so the animal must move his head until his eye receives the clearest picture.

The position of the eyes, set back on either side of the head instead of close together (as human eyes are), creates a blind spot in front of the horse's face and under his nose. Raising or lowering or turning the head compensates for, or eliminates, the spot. On the plus side, this eye position enables the animal to see well behind him, with only his rump blocking an almost 360-degree panoramic view.

Horses also lack the acute three-dimensional vision and accompanying depth perception that we have. Almost as if to compensate, each eye receives and registers a picture that the horse's brain is able to process separately.

Biologists tell us that horses perceive objects way out of proportion. We humans appear as giants, perhaps nine or ten feet tall, and our huge size may help explain why horses are willing to submit to our demands.

Equine eyesight does not distinguish colors; horses see only in shades of gray. Their eyes also adapt to changes in light conditions somewhat more slowly than ours. Moving from a dark stall into a bright light or from a stretch of bright sunny trail into the shadows of a stand of trees, a horse will instinctively want to pause until his eyes adjust.

Hearing

Like other species that have long, funnel-shaped ears, horses have a far more acute sense of hearing than humans. Using the thirteen pairs of muscles in each ear, a horse is easily able to turn one or both of his two "satellite dishes" in any direction to pick up sounds. Those include sounds so faint that a horse senses them far earlier than his rider.

Apart from the function of hearing, horses use their ears to indicate objects or stimuli that have caught their attention or to "telegraph" upcoming behavior. For example, excessive leg or spur pressure from a rider usually causes the horse to lay back his ears in the direction of the irritation. As for "telegraphing," a horse will often pin back an ear a few strides before a jump that he plans to run out on, signaling with the ear on the side where he plans to misbehave. Similarly, a horse that plans to refuse a fence will lay both ears back.

Smell

A horse's sense of smell is just as sharp as his sense of hearing. The moment he picks up an unfamiliar scent, he'll try to identify whether the odor is coming from a friend or foe. The possibility of danger is almost impossible for a horse to disregard: Carnivores possess an unmistakable musky smell to which horses almost always react to some extent, even if it's coming from the family dog. Using two senses in combination, horses that see or hear something unfamiliar will inhale, looking for an odor to help determine whether danger is at hand.

Any natural or man-made occurrence that reduces or deprives a horse of his sense of smell—or, for that matter, vision or hearing—is cause for concern: What if a predator is nearby and the horse can't sense its presence? That's why heavy rain (especially when accompanied by thunder), bright lights, darkness, and crowd noises make a horse wary.

Touch

Information that a horse receives through the sense of feel comes primarily by nuzzling. Two horses establish bonding connections by blowing into each other's nostrils and by grooming each other. People who want to take part in that blowing-bonding technique should be aware that some horses may respond by nipping, and at a time when the human's nose is in a very vulnerable position.

Another aspect of the sense of touch or feel is most apparent on hot summer days. Even the most thick-skinned animals will nip or kick at insects buzzing around or touching them, especially around their flanks and bellies. That calls to mind a well-known anecdote about a beginning rider who complained that her horse wouldn't listen to her cues. "Are you telling me," her instructor boomed back, "that your horse will twitch at that little ol' horsefly on his rump, but your stick and your heels can't get his attention?"

The rest of the lesson went much better.

Flight or Fight

No species, especially those that figure prominently on the menu of carnivorous predators, survives for millions of years without developing a healthy respect for personal safety. When the choice is (a) stand their ground to investigate or fight back or (b) run away from even a hint of danger, horses choose (b).

That deeply ingrained instinct explains why horses don't stop to consider whether an object is a real peril, like a rattlesnake along a trail, or a piece of garden hose or drainpipe. Only after they've put a distance between them and the danger (real or otherwise) do they settle down.

Only rarely will a horse stand and fight. Except for stallions establishing herd dominance or mares protecting their young, horses will turn on their attackers only when there is absolutely no alternative, especially when there is no opportunity to flee, as in the case of a horse that is threatened while he is cornered in a stall.

That's not to say that horses always behave passively toward each other. Many become belligerent when another horse enters their domain. A newcomer to a pastured herd will need to sort out his place in the pecking order, and probably take a few lumps in the process.

Antagonistic behavior also arises when one horse "invades" another's immediate space without the latter's consent. A horse that moves too close, whether loose in a field or under saddle during a trail ride, may be greeted by laid-back ears or bared teeth, if not a nip or kick.

Herd and Homing Instincts

A sense of safety in numbers against predators is the likely basis of the herd instinct, an inherent preference for the company of other horses. You'll see how strong this instinct can be when you ride away from the others when you're out in a group. Even if your horse doesn't protest very hard, he's likely to look back with the equine equivalent of separation anxiety. By the same token, when the rider at the head of the group picks up the pace from a walk

In this example of herd instinct, the horse that is leaning his head on his neighbor's back is displaying another sort of bonding behavior. (The Quarter Horse Journal)

to a trot or a lope, you'll see how quickly the other horses make every effort to keep up.*

Home is where the herd is, and so are food and shelter. Given a choice, horses prefer to stick close to their barns and paddocks (except when they get it into their heads to become escape artists). And when horses are away from home, they're eager to return. The classic example is a horse that's sluggish on the way out on a trail ride but invariably picks up his pace heading back to the barn.

This behavioral trait can manifest itself during arena work. Horses that have to be urged when tracking away from the ring's gate, especially when the barn is just beyond, often need to be steadied when turned and heading toward "home." However, this homing instinct can also work to tragic disadvantage in the case of barn fires. Horses with an otherwise strong sense of survival have been led to safety, but then break away and race back to perish in their stalls. In their panic, they've reverted to the "home = comfort zone" equation.

---

*This herd instinct can be a useful training tool. A horse that is reluctant to cross a stream or jump a fence will often do so when another horse (and rider) leads the way.

The herd instinct applies even when horses are separated by stall walls. (AQHA photo by Wyatt McSpadden)

Temperament

The most general statement that can be made about equine temperament is that horses are individuals. Some are more aggressive than others, while other prefer to be passive. Some enjoy human presence, while others barely tolerate or even acknowledge people. Some horses are inquisitive and even what we'd call in humans "fun-loving"; they delight in breaking out of pastures or shredding blankets just for entertainment. On the other hand, there are horses that couldn't seem to care less about amusement.

Horses are not very good at hiding their emotions. They communicate their feelings by expressive, unmistakable body language: Eyes that roll, ears that are laid back, a curled lip and bared teeth, and a cocked hind foot are all signs of annoyance or outright anger. An anxious or frightened horse will snort, roll his eyes wide enough to show the whites, and tense his body. Eyes that are open and ears pricked forward indicate curiosity, alertness, or both. Half-closed eyes and drooping ears and lower lip announce that a horse is becoming tired or that he's asleep.

There are vocal cues, too. Their volume and context are clues to what the neigh-sayer is trying to communicate. The horse may be lonely and is trying to attract the attention of another horse or a human. A more gentle nicker is often a sign of anticipation, as is the "chatter" of high expectation when the feed cart starts its rounds.

Whether equine nature includes a competitive streak has been frequently debated. Trainers and jockeys can point to some horses they say "just don't like to lose." Those are the runners that, seemingly defeated, summon up a second effort to finish in front. And who's to say that some instinct to prevail is not part of their makeup?

Although certain show horses seem to thrive on competition, saying that they understand and appreciate winning is more of a stretch. No horse is able to reason along the lines of "I'd better do a stronger reining pattern today than I did last week because this is the Nationals," or "Anything less than a clean round means I'll lose the jumper championship." It's more realistic to suppose that a horse that "thrives on competition" has an ability not to be distracted by arena sights and sounds—as well, of course, as the talent and the training to win.

Nor do horses understand they've won a horse show class, at least not the way humans do. Although the animal that takes home the blue ribbon may enjoy all the petting, carrots, and the rest of the fussing that accompanies an outstanding performance, the equine mind is simply unable to grasp that the attention comes as a direct result of being the best at dally roping or Western pleasure that day.

Interaction with Humans

Are horses able to sense human emotions? Most experts would say yes, especially with regard to fear. All frightened mammals emit a distinctive odor, a "smell of fear" that equines are quick to pick up. Another clue that horses perceive is a person's body language. A horse accepts human control because the person is in a real sense the alpha-leader of that horse's herd, even if the "herd" consists of no more than one horse and one human. A frightened person lacks the essential commanding presence without which the horse has neither the instinctual nor the learned basis to obey.

How often have you heard riders, especially beginners, complain, "I just can't get that horse to perform. I don't think he likes me." The reason is usually less a dislike on the animal's part than his reaction to the rider's indecisiveness. Horses, particularly the veteran riding school variety, often "test" riders. They

A reassuring rub goes a long way toward establishing trust. (*The Quarter Horse Journal*)

make every effort to get away with as little work as possible, such as gravitating to the center of the ring and standing still or taking every opportunity to head back to the barn.

Unless the rider responds immediately and firmly to such "tests," the horse cheerfully concludes there's no reason not to be the one that takes control. That's likely to escalate the conflict: Out of frustration or anger, the rider ends up giving conflicting or contradictory cues that only make the problem worse. Now you have both sides having temper tantrums. Because of his greater strength and stubbornness, the horse ends up the winner. And what's worse, at least from the standpoint of the rider and owner-trainer, the horse has learned one more lesson in the art of evading work.

The Learning Process

The system by which horses learn is known as conditioning, and it's no more than repetition and reward. You squeeze your legs at the girth or tap with

Horses communicate by touch and smell as well as by sight and sound. (*The Quarter Horse Journal*)

your spurs, and the horse moves forward. Why? Because he has been conditioned to do so.

This type of conditioning is very different from the way other species of animals are taught. Dogs, for example, are trained by a system known as positive reinforcement. You press on Rover's hind end and say "sit." When he gets around to sitting, you give him a biscuit and lots of pats. You repeat the process until at some point his doggy brain associates the act of sitting with receiving affection and food. And because responding to the word "sit" has now become a conditioned reflex, Rover will sit at the command "sit" even after you stop handing out pats and biscuits.

Positive reinforcement doesn't work on horses. They learn by negative reinforcement, using unpleasant experiences to create an option to perform the desired effect. For example, you as the trainer apply leg pressure, which (especially when reinforced by a stick or spur) evokes a response. A horse has the same response to all unpleasant or unfamiliar stimuli: He instinctively tries to escape them. If the horse moves forward, you reward him simply by removing

157

A horse points his ears in the direction in which he is interested. Here he shows he's listening to the rider's cues. (The Quarter Horse Journal)

the unpleasantness; you stop squeezing and tapping. But if he moves sideways or backward or doesn't move at all, you continue squeezing and tapping until he gives you the desired response of moving forward. And so the horse becomes conditioned. (Such positives as patting the horse's neck and saying "good boy," while no doubt appreciated, are secondary reinforcements; affection and words will not in themselves train a horse.)

Horses also learn on their own through negative conditioning. The disconcerting shock that comes from brushing against an electric fence "teaches" them to avoid that type of barrier, and often any other kind of fencing they come across.

Another mental feature is an excellent, if selective, memory. A horse that doesn't otherwise object to strangers entering his stall will lay his ears back and cock a hind foot at the approach of a veterinarian who performed an unpleasant procedure six months earlier. Similarly, a spot along a trail where a horse was once startled by a deer may evoke a skittish reaction even years later.

As good as a horse's memory may be, however, he cannot connect a misbehavior with a correction made more than several seconds later. The "wait till your father gets home" time-lag approach just doesn't work. If corrections aren't given *immediately* after a disobedience, the connection is lost forever. The horse will feel unfairly abused, and the consistency at the heart of any successful training system will be eroded.

Consistency is very much the essential element in any training situation—and horses are trained whenever they are ridden or handled. For example, they cannot be counted on to distinguish between a cue given during a trail ride and the same one given in a showring. Although you may be able to distinguish between an unimportant pleasure riding situation and an all-important (to you) competition, your horse can't. As a result, asking for or allowing a sloppy canter depart under one circumstance and not under another, then expecting your horse to understand the different contexts, does neither you nor the animal any good. Partnerships work because both participants agree on the ground rules and "speak the same language," and that's never truer than in the partnership between you and your horse.

Tack

Saddles

THE WESTERN SADDLE

The Western, or stock, saddle is the functional and spiritual descendant of the saddle that the Spanish conquistadors introduced into North America four centuries ago. These explorers needed a secure perch from which they would not be easily dislodged by the impact of a lance or the thrust of a sword, and the seats with high pommels and cantles that they inherited from their mounted warrior forebears provided such an advantage.

Form followed function in the development of the stock saddle. In the flat grassland areas of Mexico, cattle-herding vaqueros were able to work their herds by means of the long lance-like poles that were used in Spain. But north of the Rio Grande, especially in the parts of Texas where brush and ravines made keeping a herd together more difficult, poles gave way to the *reata* or rope lariat.

That in turn led to the development of the saddle horn, around which the rope could be wrapped. But even with the new technique of roping, regional necessities led to specialized innovations. For example, in California's open country, where long lariat throws were possible, vaqueros-turned-cowboys had the luxury of plenty of time to wrap their ropes around the horn and play the rope to absorb some of the impact. That procedure became known as making a dally, from the Spanish phrase *dar la vuelta,* "to give a turn." However, working cattle in the brush and ravines of Texas's hilly terrain required shorter ropes, shorter tosses tied "hard and fast," and quicker turns and stops. That led to the more secure double-cinch rigging on saddles, as opposed to single cinching on California saddles.

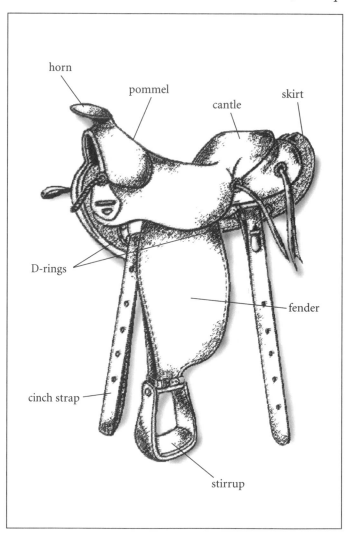

The heart of the Western saddle is the tree, or frame, made of laminated wood, fiberglass, or aluminum and covered with rawhide or bullhide. Trees come in several styles: the full–Quarter Horse, designed to fit a horse with a broad back and relatively flat withers; the semi–Quarter Horse, for average backs and withers; and the regular, for a sloping back and normal withers.

The tree's four components are its fork, horn, bars, and cantle.

The fork consists of the gullet, the space formed by the fork's shape, and the swells, or the area on the sides of the horn.

The horn itself, made of leather-covered wood or metal and usually bolted onto the fork, ranges in height from two to four inches, the higher ones found on roping and cutting saddles.

Bars, the two panels that rest on the horse's back, measure about six inches wide and are often are reinforced with steel.

The cantle of a stock saddle is dish-shaped and relatively high (two to four inches), wide (twelve to fourteen inches), and deep. Padded with rubber, the cantle usually is covered with rawhide or suede for additional comfort and security.

Underneath all four main parts is the skirt, the lowest panel that rests against the horse.

Billet straps, to which cinches and girth are attached, come in three types, all of which are used on a Western saddle. The front girth is attached to the off billet, a folded double layer of leather on the right side of the saddle. A "half-breed" strap wraps twice through the cinch ring, then buckles to the billet for additional security. The third type is the latigo, or tie-strap, fastened to the saddle's left side. One end is tied to the rigging ring; the other looped through the cinch's ring and then secured by a tie knot or cinch tongue.

Two rear billets are identical, each tied to the saddle's rear rigging D-rings and buckled to the flank cinch.

Stirrup leathers are fastened by double-pronged buckles with sliding metal loops that keep the prongs in place. Foot-long thongs called stirrup leathers, or hobble straps, wrap around the leather above the stirrup and prevent the stirrup from slipping out of position. Western saddles usually include fenders, the wide leather panels that keep the rider's legs from being chafed by the leathers.

STIRRUPS: Rawhide-covered wooden stirrups come in several shapes. The Visalia type is bell-shaped with a one-inch-wide tread. Ropers use a wide and flat-bottomed type that permit quick and smooth dismounts. Bronc riders and others who want secure support, however, prefer a narrower "oxbow" shape with a rounded bottom that surrounds the arch of the foot.

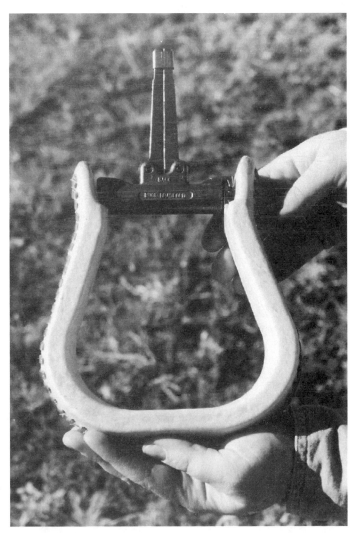

A rawhide-wrapped oxbow stirrup. (*The Quarter Horse Journal*)

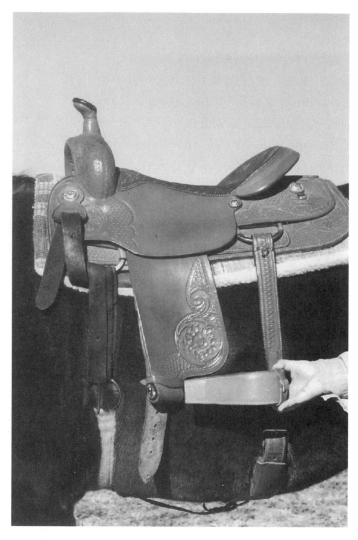

Center-fired rigging. (The Quarter Horse Journal)

Western stirrups can be covered by tapadaros, or taps, hoods that were originally used for protection against thorns, cactus needles, and other sharp objects. They're now especially visible as a parade saddle accessory.

RIGGINGS: The term "rigging" (sometimes called "girthing") describes how one or more cinches are attached to the saddle. Western saddles originally were rigged with two straps, one that passed around the center of the fork and another that ran over the rear of the tree, the cantle. The ends of both were joined to large rings on either side of the tree.

As rigging became more specialized, the types were named in terms of their location. A center-rigged or center-fired cinch is suspended under the center of the saddle seat. Forward-rigged describes a cinch that is suspended from any point ahead of the center, while full-forward or front-fired has the cinch below the pommel.

Ropers needed a more substantial system, so they shortened their two cinch straps and attached each one to its own ring. That system has become known as full-rigging, double-rigging, or rim-fire.

CINCHES AND GIRTHS: Western cinches (a term for girths) are made of approximately seventeen braided mohair or cotton cords with additional cords in the center to keep the shape and add support. Rings at both ends attach to the saddle's latigo and off billet strap. A generous width distributes the tension across the horse's belly; roping cinches are even wider and have a sturdy leather reinforced center.

A saddle with a two-cinch rigging gives even greater security. The front cinch is made of cording and the rear, or flank, strap of leather. The flank strap is not cinched tight; a two-inch leeway puts it into use only when the saddle is pulled forward, such as when a cow is roped. A strap that connects the two cinches keeps the rear one from swinging against the horse's belly, an irritation that might cause the animal to buck.

TYPES OF STOCK SADDLES: The most popular stock saddle is the general-purpose, or all-purpose, model. Built for comfort and versatility, it has a deep seat, high swells, a relatively small horn, and ample padding in the seat. It weighs approximately thirty to thirty-five pounds.

An equitation saddle has a high cantle and deep seat that's built up in front to place the rider in the correct position for Western horsemanship. The leather on these saddles usually is embossed with intricate designs.

The parade saddle, the kind seen on horses in such festivities as New Year's Day bowl parades, is even more ornate. It sports hand-tooled engraved leather and inlaid silver filigree work; equally splendid matching bridles and breast-plates set off the ensemble.

The band of rubber around the horn of this roping saddle keeps the rope from slipping after the rider makes a wrap. (Greg Thon/Cowboy Tack)

The roping saddle, a true workhorse of a rig, is relatively heavy (at least forty pounds). It has a high, sturdy horn that can accommodate making dally turns of a rope, and its relatively low swells and cantle allow easy and quick dismounts. As was pointed out earlier, sturdy extra-wide cinches and flat, wide stirrups are the customary accessories.

Cutting saddles have flat seats that help riders stay in balance and keep up with their horse's athletic moves. Oxbow stirrups are customary on this tack.

Since weight is a factor in barrel racing, saddles used in that event can be as light as twenty pounds. Undercut swells provide maximum security during tight turns made at top speeds. The skirts are usually rounded and as small as possible to cut down on poundage.

BLANKETS AND PADS: The traditional Western saddle blanket is a thirty-inch by sixty-inch wool cloth decorated in Native American motifs. Folded in half, it is placed fold-forward across the horse's back. In addition to or instead of a blanket, a foam pad helps protect the horse's back from the rider's weight.

SADDLEBAG: Although not strictly a piece of tack, a saddlebag is a handy way to carry items you don't feel like stuffing in jacket or pants pockets. Basically two leather pouches joined at the middle, the bag is tied behind the cantle.

FITTING AND BUYING A WESTERN SADDLE: The first step in selecting any saddle is to know that trying it out on your horse is essential. That's because an individual's conformation will determine the correct fit. Broad withers require a saddle with ample width between its bars; one that's too narrow will sit too high and have a tendency to pinch. On the other hand, the bottom edges of the bars resting on the horse show that the saddle is too narrow. As for excessive width, if only the top sides of the bars rest on the horse, there will be an uneven distribution of the weight of both saddle and rider.

The gullet should be high enough so you can insert two fingers between it and the horse's withers. If not, the saddle will pinch.

A rider's own conformation is relevant with regard to seat size. An all-purpose saddle should place you comfortably in the center of the saddle with your legs easily in their correct position. A seat that's too small forces your body forward and your legs far back; one that's too large pushes your body backward, which in turn forces your feet forward "on the dashboard."

Perhaps you're currently using a saddle that suits your purposes and will fit your new horse. Before you consider buying it, make sure it's in safe

This horse is in his ranch "work clothes," including a bosal bridle and a tie-down. (Cowboy Tack)

condition. That means asking your adviser or another expert to show you how to feel that the tree isn't cracked or broken. You'll also need to make sure the leather and stitching are in good shape.

Buying such a "tried and true" used saddle eliminates any breaking-in period. Or you might consider purchasing a new saddle of the same brand and model. Most tack shops will let you take a new saddle home on trial. Take advantage of the opportunity, but be careful not to damage any piece of tack that you might need to return.

THE ENGLISH SADDLE

The so-called English saddle (even though it was developed throughout Europe, we still refer to it as "English") was created in response to a radically new style of jumping. Until the late nineteenth century, riders leaned back over fences and other obstacles they encountered during a cross-country gallop, often while foxhunting; old sporting prints illustrate that uncomfortable spine-wrenching position.

Shortly before the turn of this century, an Italian cavalryman named Caprilli had a radical idea. He shortened his stirrups, which closed his hip angle, a position that helped him to maintain his balance over a jumping horse's center of gravity all the way from the takeoff to the landing. Calling the new technique the forward seat, Caprilli saw it catch on throughout the military and civilian worlds.

In response, saddlemakers angled the tree of the flat saddle in vogue then until it was at a forty-five-degree angle to the horse's back. They also lowered the pommel, raised the cantle, and added knee and thigh rolls under the saddle's flaps. The result was a saddle that supported a jumping rider's legs, seat, and upper body.

Over the years, this saddle's older, rigid, solid-wood tree gave way to fiberglass or laminated wood. Another innovation was spring trees, two steel strips that return the frame to its original position whenever it bends (as it does during a jump). The springs also more easily transmit the rider's seat aids to the horse's back.

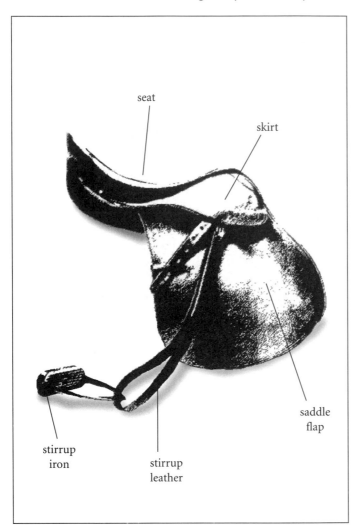

seat

skirt

saddle
flap

stirrup
iron

stirrup
leather

Seat panels are now padded with leather, wool, or foam rubber for the comfort of both horse and rider. Divided panels under the seat are stuffed with felt, wool, hair, or foam rubber that cushions the horse's back.

Jumping saddles have undergone even further modifications in response to more recent riding styles. Riders no longer brace themselves on their knees over the tops of fences; they now sit deeper and use their seats to drive their horses between fences. This gave rise to the so-called close-contact saddle, with its smaller knee rolls, no thigh rolls, and lower cantles.

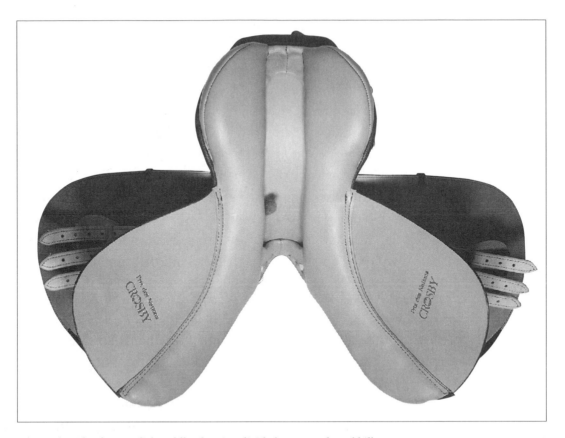

The underside of an English saddle, showing divided seat panels and billet straps. (Miller Harness Company)

The all-purpose saddle is a good choice for general riding. As versatile and comfortable as its Western counterpart, it can be found at riding academies, on bridle paths and the foxhunting field, and in horse show arenas. It has a forward-cut flap, knee rolls, a generous twist (the section of the tree between the rider's thighs), and a short, deep seat.

Eventing saddles are similar in design to the all-purpose variety, but, since they're used in three-day eventing and other forms of combined training, they are somewhat sturdier so they can cope with the rigors of cross-country galloping and jumping.

Dressage riders need to sit centered, erect, and deep, essential for using their driving aids for impulsion and to brace their back to collect their horse. Deep spring trees of dressage saddles facilitate this position. These saddles also have noninterfering straight panels and flaps and stirrup bars located directly under the rider's thighs, all of which maximize the length of the rider's legs.

Racing saddles are little more than leather pads, or support systems for stirrups. Since weight is a constant factor in a jockey's career, these saddles are designed and constructed to be as light as possible, weighing from one to two pounds.

Comfort is especially important for endurance riders, who are in the saddle over all sorts of terrain in competitions that can range up to a hundred miles. That's why the endurance saddle has a high, rounded pommel and cantle between which the rider is practically wedged; the design provides thigh support and also minimizes chafing and blisters.

Although the vast majority of endurance saddles are made with heavy-duty leather, modern technology has opened the door to ones made from nylon or other synthetics. They're lightweight, easy to clean, and inexpensive, but they're not nearly as durable as their cowhide cousins (since the natural oils of real leather weaken nylon, the stirrup "leathers" and girth also must be made of less durable synthetic fabric). But these saddles have their enthusiasts, so much so that they're also available in all-purpose and Western models.

GIRTHS: Girths come in a variety of materials. Leather girths may be one piece, or they can be the "shaped" variety made of three or four strips of braided leather that lie flat to reduce chafing.

Elastic pieces between buckles and girth make tightening the girth easier.

String cotton cord girths are lightweight and allow air to pass through. That helps healing when a horse has a saddle sore or another type of wound. Another lightweight girth is made of wide fabric, usually canvas.

Sleeve-like sheepskin or synthetic fleece girth covers reduce chafing. They're especially useful on horses that tend to get girth sores.

Girths are buckled to billets, the straps on each side of the saddle that are securely attached to the tree. Although there are three straps, only the outside two are used (the center serves as a spare). Billet flaps, or small leather panels threaded through the straps, keep buckles from rubbing against the rider's thighs.

STIRRUPS: The most common English stirrups are the stainless or nickel-plated steel straight-sided Fillis models. Alternatives include heavier hunt stirrups with arched sides.

Offset stirrups tilt inward to facilitate the cocked ankle position that is correct for hunt seat equitation. A recent innovation is a tread that swivels to help riders drop their heels.

Instead of a metal outside arm, the peacock (or the release, or "safety") stirrup has a sturdy rubber band that fastens to the tread. In the event of an accidental fall, the rubber band releases and the foot slips out. The idea, of course, is to prevent the rider from being dragged.

Most English-style stirrups are fitted with rubber tread inserts that prevent boot soles from slipping out far better than the stirrup's bare metal does.

Whichever style of stirrup you choose, its width must accommodate your foot at its widest part. Anything narrower is likely to wedge the foot in case of a fall, with being dragged as a frighteningly dangerous consequence.

STIRRUP LEATHERS: Stirrups are held in place by belt-like straps called leathers. They range in size from ⅞ of an inch to 1½ inches wide, with the wider end of the range used for foxhunting and eventing. Leathers slide under the saddle's stirrup bars and through the openings at the top of the stirrups, then buckle to themselves. Many leathers have numbered holes to help riders keep their stirrups even.

People who ride at the same "hole," never adjusting the length of their leathers, run the risk of having the buckle cut into the leather. Eventually the

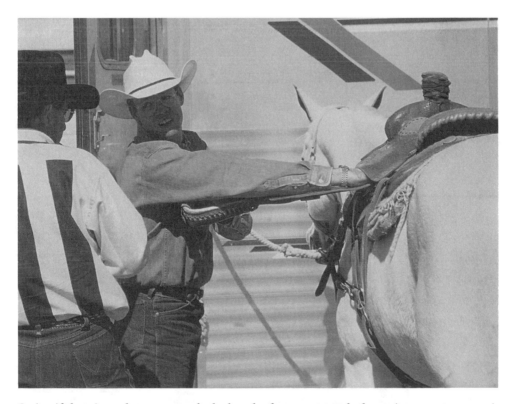

Seeing if the stirrup bottom extends the length of your outstretched arm is a way to approximate the correct length. (AQHA photo by Wyatt McSpadden)

strap will wear through, but that can be avoided by checking the condition of the leathers and replacing worn ones *before* an accident happens.

SADDLE PAD: Sheepskin, cotton, wool, or synthetic fleece saddle pads absorb sweat, keep dirt and sweat off the saddle's underside, and cushion the impact of the saddle and rider. Either square or contoured to follow the saddle's outline, a pad also may have pockets for foam rubber inserts under the cantle.

Pads are held in place with straps with an opening through which a billet strap passes.

Additional cushioning for English saddles comes in the form of thick keyhole-shaped foam rubber "bounce pads." They rest between the saddle pad and the saddle and stay in place when the girth is tightened.

FITTING AND BUYING AN ENGLISH SADDLE: English saddles come in seat sizes that range from fourteen to eighteen inches, based on the distance between the nail below the pommel and the center of the cantle. But just because a saddle is your correct seat size doesn't mean it will necessarily fit any horse, or even you. Too many variables among manufacturers and even among models from the same saddler make the process of fitting an English saddle to horse and rider a complex process.

Just as with Western saddles, fitting the tack to the conformation of the horse is of paramount importance. A horse with prominent withers needs a saddle with a high pommel or a cut-back pommel, with the latter having the advantage of a closer fit.

Both panels should sit squarely on the horse's back for even weight distribution.

A saddle with a narrow twist allows a rider to sit deep, but a wide twist forces the rider back toward the cantle. Forward-seat hunter-jumper riders whose weight belongs on the front of their seatbones and who hold their lower legs slightly behind the girth need to find a saddle with a twist and a seat that let them keep their bodies in the correct position.

Anyone thinking about buying a used English saddle needs to make certain the tree is in good condition. One that's cracked or broken is worse than worthless, it's a hazard to the comfort and safety of both horse and rider. Leather and stitching shouldn't be in such poor shape that they can't be easily and inexpensively restored if need be.

Pay particular attention to the stirrup bars that hold the leathers. The hinge at the end must be workable so a falling rider's weight will snap it open and let the leather slide out. As with a Western saddle, trying a prospective purchase on your horse is essential. Ask your adviser to inspect the fit before and after you tighten the girth and again after you mount and then ride in the saddle.

Bits and Bridles

There's no such clearcut distinction between Western- and English-style bits as there is between Western and English saddles. Types of curb bits and hackamores once closely associated with cow ponies have become common in the jumper ring, just as Western-trained horses are introduced to bits and bitting through traditional English snaffles.

Look through a tack-shop catalog or stroll through the store itself, and you'll encounter displays of bits in bewilderingly large numbers, sizes, and shapes. How, you may ask yourself, can you determine which one (or several) is appropriate for your horse?

The first step is to become familiar with how bits work. Bits exert pressure on certain sensitive pressure points on the horse's head. These consist of the bars of the mouth (the space between molars and incisors), the roof of the mouth, the lips, the tongue, the nose, the poll, and the "curb groove" behind the chin.

Horses react by moving away from the source of the pressure. To give a common example, as a reaction to the direct pressure of a snaffle against the bars and corners of his mouth, a well-trained horse will shift his weight from his forequarters to his hindquarters until he comes to a halt (a horse that reacts that way quickly has learned from experience to anticipate greater discomfort if he doesn't halt at the first feeling of bit pressure).*

TYPES OF BITS

Bits are divided into three broad categories: the snaffle, the curb, and the hackamore.

SNAFFLES: The snaffle is marked by a level horizontal mouthpiece that applies pressure to the bars and lips. Some snaffles have a solid, unbroken mouthpiece, while many others have two short arms joined in the middle. The jointed variety produces an additional pincers-like effect against the horse's

---

*It should also be pointed out that not all a bit's action is designed to signal a horse to stop; another effect influences how he carries his head.

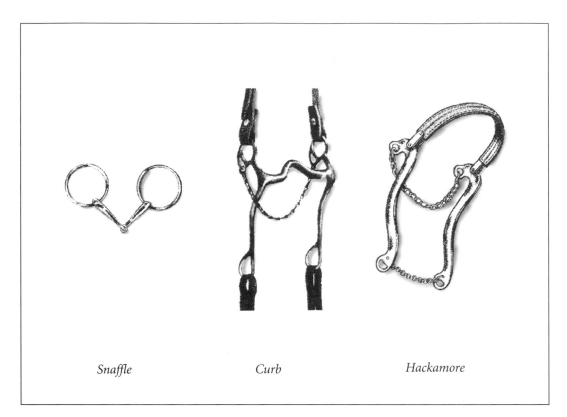

Snaffle   *Curb*   *Hackamore*

tongue. Although snaffles are considered the mildest of bits, their severity is affected by the following:

- the shape of the mouthpiece. A plain snaffle is milder than one with corkscrew-like twisted arms.
- the thickness and composition of the mouthpiece. A "fat" mouthpiece is milder than a thin one. A rubber-covered mouthpiece is milder than a plain metal one.
- the tension of the joint. Tighter joints between the mouthpiece's arms are milder than looser ones.

The size of the rings to which the reins are attached also influences a bit's action. Small rings are more likely to be pulled into the horse's mouth, thus producing more pressure. When this reaction isn't wanted, you would choose a snaffle with larger rings. Or you might select one with full or half cheekpieces; these are arms that rest against the horse's cheeks and keep the rings outside the horse's mouth.

Among the more specialized bits best left to experienced hands, the gag snaffle works on the poll as well as the mouth. Pressure from the reins makes the bit slide upward in the horse's mouth while a pulley effect from the bridle's crownpiece works against the poll.

CURBS: The curb bit is distinguished by its port, the elevated portion of the mouthpiece, and by the extended shanks to which the reins are attached. The long shanks act as levers that move the port against the roof of the horse's mouth. The horse reacts by arching or flexing his neck, which shifts his body weight back onto his hocks for impulsion and instant responsiveness.

The bit's effectiveness is increased by a strap or chain fitted in the so-called curb groove behind the horse's chin. In addition to pressing on that sensitive area, the strap or chain keeps the port from moving too far forward against the roof of the mouth.

The action of any curb is affected by the following factors:

A plain bridle with a snaffle bit is the tack most commonly found in a hunter class. (AQHA photo by Wyatt McSpadden)

- the size and shape of the port. A small, wide port is milder than a tall, narrow one.

- the length and angle of the shanks. Short, rear-curving shanks are milder than long, straight ones (the curved shanks of the "grazing bit" are specifically intended to let a horse get his head down to eat grass).

- the tension of the curb strap or chain. Looser straps or chains are milder than tight ones.

This horse is wearing a bridle with a one-ear headstall and a grazing bit. A breastcollar keeps the saddle in place. (Cowboy Tack)

HACKAMORES: When is a bit not a bit? When it's a hackamore, a device that goes not in the horse's mouth but over his muzzle.

Hackamores originally consisted of three parts: the bosal, a leather-covered nosepiece with a rawhide core; the fiador (sometimes pronounced "Theodore"), a rope that goes over the horse's poll and knots behind the jaw to keep the bosal in place; and the mecate, another rope that ties to the back of the bosal and acts as reins.

The mechanical hackamore is a variation made of a bosal with long metal shanks. Its curb strap or chain creates a curb-like lever effect to tighten the bosal.

Hackamores are most often seen on horses that have been schooled to neck-rein and thus need no bit pressure to change direction. They're also worn by horses with especially sensitive mouths (including animals that are recovering from an ailment or injury to their mouths).

"HYBRID" BITS: As if the many varieties of "pure" snaffles and curbs aren't perplexing enough, a range of hybrid bits combine the two. For example, the Kimberwicke is basically a snaffle with a port mouthpiece. A more common example is the Pelham, a one-piece snaffle and curb, the curb having shorter shanks than usual. It uses two sets of reins, with the snaffle reins carried outside the curb's reins. The Pelham is often considered a tasteful way to compensate for a horse's small head or short neck.

Similar to the Pelham is the Weymouth, also known as the double bridle or full bridle. Mandatory at dressage's upper levels, it is composed of two separate bits: a thin snaffle (called a bradoon) and a curb. Each is attached to its own headstall and its own set of reins. As with the Pelham, the Weymouth gives the rider literally a handful of tools with which to set the horse's head carriage with precision.

*This hackamore is properly fitted, with the mecate coming out of the top of the wraps. (*The Quarter Horse Journal*)*

Almost all bits are made of nickel-plated steel or stainless steel. A horse is more responsive to a bit when he is salivating, and copper mouthpieces encourage this reaction more than those made entirely of steel.

Some horses, especially young ones, will accept a bit more willingly when they have something they can mouth or chew. Copper "cricket" rollers or dangling "keys" on a mouthpiece encourage such acceptance (some older horses seem to get along better when they, too, have "toys" to play with).

CHOOSING A BIT

The large number of variations and hybrids among snaffles, curbs, and hackamores is the result of centuries of experimentation. There are bits that attempt to provide the cure for horses that bolt, or lean on their rider's hands, or carry their heads up like "star-gazers" or down toward the ground . . . A problem doesn't exist that someone hasn't tried to fix by coming up with a new kind of bit.

Another determining factor is the stage of a horse's schooling. Sophisticated equipment like a Weymouth or a spade curb bit would be appropriate only for more advanced training and for competition. The rider's ability is another important consideration, a point made clear by the expression that a severe bit can be "a razor in a monkey's hand."

Despite the dazzling array of bits in saddle shop catalogs and well-equipped tack rooms, your choice of bit will be easy. Nine times out of ten, one in which your new horse had been going for his former owner will work just as well for you. But if your adviser or instructor thinks a problem cannot be corrected through horse and/or rider training and a bitting change is advisable, knowledgeable horsemen always choose the mildest bit that works. You can always switch to a more severe one should the need arise.

Whichever bit you choose, it must fit. Ask your instructor to help you determine if a bit is the correct width.

BRIDLES

Something must hold a bit in place. That's the job of the bridle. The basic parts of every bridle are the headstall (or headpiece) and cheekpiece. The headstall fits over the bridle path behind the horse's ears and runs down the sides of the head. One end of the cheekpiece buckles to the headstall, the other to the ring of the bit. Another buckle on the strap lets you raise or lower the bit for a correct fit.

Since a headstall and cheekpiece alone aren't always the most secure arrangement, horsemen have developed a number of ways to keep them from slipping. Common to both Western and English bridles is the throatlatch, a strap at the back of a headstall that buckles loosely behind the horse's jowl and keeps the bridle from being slipped off by its wearer.

Traditional Western bridles have an earpiece worn over the horse's off (right) ear. Some are sewn onto the headstall, while others, known as sliding earpieces, are adjustable. The English bridle has a browband worn across the horse's forehead. Many modern Western bridles borrow from their English equivalents, with many trading the earpiece for a browband. However, unlike the plain letters used for English browbands, the Western styles often sport horse-hair tassels, horsehair braiding (called "hitching"), or other decorations.

The caveson, or noseband, is a strap around the horse's muzzle worn approximately midway between cheekbone and mouth. Its primary function is to hold a martingale or tie-down, but even when there is none, tradition dictates that a caveson be worn (although it's prohibited in some horse show classes). Another use is to keep horses from gaping their mouths open, which diminishes the bit's effectiveness.

Most complex is the double bridle apparatus for a Weymouth bit. The headstall and cheek-pieces that hold the bradoon snaffle and the ones that hold the curb bit share just a browband; otherwise they are two separate bridles.

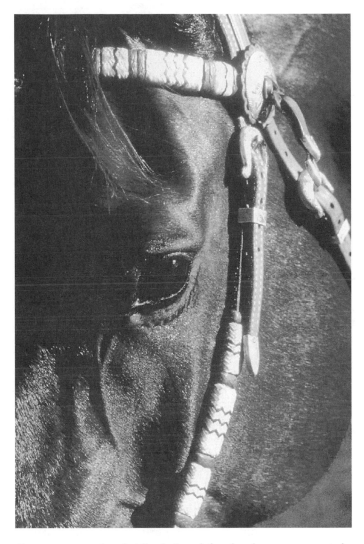

Ornaments mark a bridle designed for the show arena, not for everyday use. (AQHA photo by Wyatt McSpadden)

REINS: Reins for a Western bridle come in two distinctive styles. Texas-style split reins are a pair of straps, each six to seven feet long. Carried in one of the rider's hands, they are never tied together. The California fashion is a single closed eight-foot rein of braided rawhide. Attached to a loop or ring at midpoint is a four-foot strap called the romal. One hand grasps the reins just behind the romal, with the trailing piece held in the other hand. That long end can be used as a crop or quirt if need be, which is why many have a noise-making popper.

This photo shows correct hand position when using a romal.

Reins for an English bridle are, like Texas-style reins, two plain straps, but they are buckled at their ends to form a single loop. They can be braided, laced, covered with dimpled rubber, or (if made of canvas) have leather cross-pieces, all to make gripping them easier when they're wet with rain or sweat. Widths range from ⅜ to ⅞ of an inch, with the larger sizes used for foxhunting, the cross-country phase of combined training, and other strenuous activities.

Bradoon snaffle reins of a Weymouth bridle are slightly wider than those of the curb so riders can tell them apart by feel, without having to glance down.

A novel and useful rider training aid are color-banded reins. A different color every twelve inches makes it easy to tell whether your rein length has changed (such as by slipping through your fingers).

Supplemental Tack

BREASTCOLLARS AND BREASTPLATES

Sometimes more than a cinch or girth is needed to keep a saddle in place. For example, a saddle is likely to slip when it's on a horse with high or low withers, when horse and rider are climbing a steep hill, or when the full weight of a roped steer pulls against the saddle horn.

That's why many horses routinely wear a breastcollar, composed of a broad leather strap across the horse's chest and another strap across the withers. A Western style that's frequently used in conjunction with a tie-down or martingale is the ring type. Two leather, nylon, or cotton cord pieces are joined in the center by a metal ring to which the tie-down is snapped (see illustration on page 174). Two straps buckle or snap to both sides of the saddle, and a third to the girth through the horse's forelegs. The two sections move independently, and the minimal restriction makes this type of breastcollar a favorite for roping, cutting, and barrel racing.

In the English-style breastplate, straps that attach to D-rings on either side of the saddle meet at a ring in the center of the horse's chest. A single strap attached to that ring passes between the horse's forelegs to the girth. As with the Western breastcollar, the center ring accommodates a martingale.

Saddles, bits, and bridles are the basic items that help with the fundamental chores of starting, steering, and stopping a horse while staying on his back in the process. But there are situations—and horses   for which basic gear is inadequate: A horse may evade the bit when asked to perform parts of a reining pattern, or toss his head during trail rides. Most items that have been designed to correct these problems do so simply by increasing the effectiveness of basic tack.

MARTINGALES AND TIE-DOWNS

A horse that raises or tosses his head can be more than a nuisance, especially when he decides to stick his nose in the air just as you lean forward—there's no doubt whose nose will get the worse of the encounter. Some horses also move their heads to escape listening to their rider's hands, an attitude that usually leads to a tug-of-war that the horse with his superior strength will invariably win.

The most basic solution is the standing martingale, which Westerners call a tie-down. That latter term describes it very clearly: a leather strap that runs between the horse's forelegs from the girth or breastplate ring to the caveson or, in the case of a Western bridle, to a thin strap around the horse's muzzle. Adjusted so there's no tension during normal head carriage, the standing martingale/tie-down comes into play only when the horse raises his head.

There may be times, such as during a high and wide jump, when you want more latitude in head carriage than a standing martingale allows. That's the advantage of a running martingale. That strap extends from the girth through the forelegs, but then divides into two sections, each ending in a metal ring through which a rein passes (the rings are kept from sliding forward against the bit by small rubber stops on the reins). The effect is a kind of pulley arrangement that operates only when the rider, by changing rein length, wants it to.

Sometimes the problem is a horse's attraction to clumps of grass. That's a job for a strap that runs from the pommel of the saddle to the top of the bridle's cheekpiece. Although this antigraze sidecheck can restrict steering, the device has saved many a novice trail rider (adult as well as youngster) from being pulled over a horse's head.

NOSEBANDS

Nosebands have other uses besides holding standing martingales. That's why they come in more styles than the plain caveson.

Bits are at their most effective when the horse's mouth is closed. Many horses learn to evade the pressure by opening their mouth, for which a dropped noseband is the antidote. When fitted approximately three inches above the nostrils and snuggly buckled, it keeps the mouth firmly shut. A bosal acts as a Western alternative.

Because a dropped noseband does not accommodate a standing martingale, a flash caveson (with straps that buckle behind the horse's jaw) or a detachable hinged noseband that fastens to a plain caveson is necessary if a martingale is also required.

A figure-eight noseband runs from behind the muzzle, crosses the center of the horse's face, and buckles behind the jaw. Stronger than the other types, the figure eight works as a sort of hackamore by pressing against the sensitive part of the horse's nose.

HALTER

How many Western movies have we seen where cowboys ride into town, dismount, and then loop the reins around a hitching rail? In truth, that works only in the movies. Tying a horse that way in real life leads at best to broken reins and at worst to an injured mouth when the animal pulls back.

The one piece of tack worn more than any other is the halter. It's the way to tether a horse, lead a bridle-less horse, or keep a horse from wandering off even when he's wearing a bridle. Basically a combination of a caveson and a throatlatch, the halter buckles or snaps around the muzzle and the poll, with another strap in the back that goes from throatlatch to noseband.

Halters are made of nylon or cotton rope, nylon webbing, or leather. The last is traditional for more formal occasions such as horse show breeding classes (which is why they're known as halter classes).

Halters come in various sizes and can be adjusted to correct size by tightening or loosening the muzzle/poll strap. When two of your fingers can easily slip under the noseband at the horse's cheeks and at his jawbones, you'll know the halter fits correctly. The strap behind the face also should

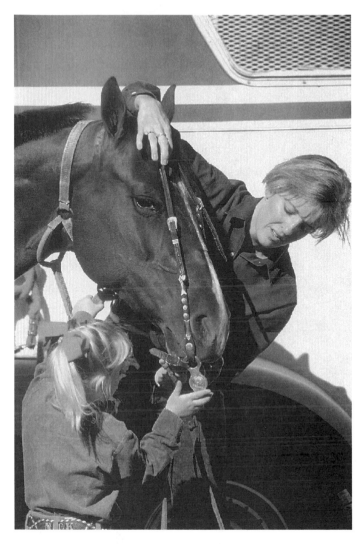

Keeping a halter around a horse's neck until the bridle is in place prevents the animal from wandering off. (AQHA photo by Wyatt McSpadden)

be loose enough to allow plenty of room for breathing.

General Thoughts on Buying Tack

Good-quality tack that's in good condition is important for more than just reasons of appearance. It can be a matter of survival: A cinch that breaks, a saddle bar that snaps off, or bridle stitching that gives way often results in serious injury.

Buying the highest-quality items you can afford makes good sense, because settling for second-rate tack is false economy. A well-made saddle, bridle, or accessory will last for many years when you take good care of it. You can rely on products from nationally recognized manufacturers, especially those that have earned endorsement from AQHA. Until your own expertise has developed, you also can rely on advice from your expert adviser and from reputable tack dealers, who will do their utmost to earn your ongoing patronage.

Look around a professional horseman's tack room and you'll see a dazzling array of items. Don't feel that *you* need all of them, too. Stick to the basics unless and until your adviser or trainer tells you otherwise: He who has the most tack does not necessarily win.

Cleaning and Storing Tack

Because sweat and dirt shorten the working life of leather, tack should be cleaned after each use. A thorough application of glycerin saddle soap cleans and also coats leather with a protective waxy layer. Work in the lather (without too frothy a head) with a damp sponge in a circular motion. Rinse the sponge frequently to remove accumulated dirt.

Completely cleaning your tack is a more complicated, but no less essential, chore. It should be done at least once a month. Start by taking the saddle or bridle apart. Bits, stirrup irons, and any other metal pieces should be placed in a bowl or bucket of clean water, while cotton or synthetic girths and saddle pads and blankets go into a washing machine and dryer.

Thoroughly clean each piece of leather with saddle soap. A piece that appears especially dry or dirty (which is often a sign that you've been neglecting the chore) requires a coat of a commercial leather dressing or conditioner to restore the leather's natural oils. Too much soap or dressing clogs the leather's pores, so follow the directions on the container.

Remove the metal pieces from their bath and apply metal polish. Take particular care to remove all traces of polish from the bit.

Before you reassemble the tack, polish the cleaned leather with a soft, clean cotton cloth or chamois for a nice finish. Another professional touch is using a toothpick to remove any leftover soap or conditioner from stirrup leather holes and other tiny out-of-the-way crevices.

Rain, snow, and fording deep streams will soak tack. Excessive water robs leather of its natural oils, weakens stitching, and promotes mildew. Before cleaning wet leather, let it dry first at its own rate (this advice also applies to riding boots and chaps). Sunlight, a radiator, space heater, or any other source of direct heat causes leather to dry out too fast; the loss of natural oils leads to cracking. Once the leather has been allowed to dry slowly, treat it with conditioner.

Just as grooming a horse is an opportunity to look for cuts, scrapes, and loose shoes, so cleaning tack lets you check for wear and tear. Keeping stirrups buckled at the same hole stresses the leathers, so pay particular attention for any potential weakness there. If you're not handy with awl and thread, most tack shops have repair departments. And for safety's sake, any equipment that is questionably salvageable should be replaced.

Storage

Tack-room saddle racks and bridle hooks are there for a reason: to prolong the good condition of equipment.

Laying a saddle flat on the ground will damage its tree, so it belongs on a rack whenever it's

Because sweat and dirt shorten the working life of leather, tack should be cleaned after each use. A thorough application of glycerin saddle soap cleans the leather and coats it with a protective waxy layer. (AQHA photo by Wyatt McSpadden)

not on a horse. Run up the stirrup leathers of English saddles, or let the fenders of Western tack hang down. If no rack is available, lean the saddle upright on its gullet against a wall or tree.

That's also a good technique for transporting saddles in a car or truck. One way to avoid scratches and scrapes during shipping is to keep the saddle in a canvas carrying case. And whether you use a case or not, make sure your saddle is securely anchored in the back of your truck or trailer. That way, if your vehicle hits a bump, the saddle won't go flying and land flat on its tree.

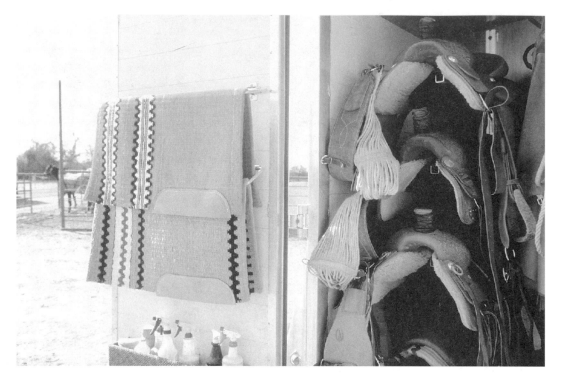

A well-organized tack room saves time and energy, whether at home or on the road in the back of a trailer. (Greg Thon/Cowboy Tack)

Standing a saddle on its end keeps the tree from being damaged. (Cowboy Tack)

FOR FURTHER INFORMATION

Everyone who competes in AQHA horse shows must know and comply with what is considered legal or prohibited tack for particular divisions and classes. Details can be found in the AQHA *Official Handbook of Rules & Regulations.*

Apparel

As you've discovered from your own riding and by watching others, appropriate clothing and footwear for your kind of riding involves more than just looking the part. No matter what the activity, its clothing evolved or was designed for comfort and safety.

Western

BOOTS

Like so much of the cowboy's outfit, Western boots descended from the gear of Mexican vaqueros and their Spanish forebears. Because ranch work involved riding through cactus and brush, ranchers chose knee-high boots made of sturdy leather. Hand-tooled tops were for more than individualized decoration: The tooling strengthened the leather. Curved tops allowed for ventilation and ease of pulling on and off.

To make mounting and dismounting as easy as possible, Western boots developed narrow pointed toes that could slip easily in and out of stirrups. Heels became higher and underslung so a rider's feet were less likely to slip through narrow stirrups while the wearer was trying to stay aboard a bucking horse. This design was also useful on the ground: A cowboy could dig in his heels and brace against a cow at the end of a rope.

Because high-heeled boots can be uncomfortable, if not precarious, to run in, "roper" boots with wider and flatter heels became popular with calf ropers. The style has gained in popularity with horse show judges and others who spend lots of time standing on their feet.

SPURS

Spurs come in countless styles, from mass-produced, inexpensive models to custom works of art. While spurs can be useful aids in guiding horses into gaits and through maneuvers, they usually are not recommended for beginning riders.

PANTS

It's a long sea voyage from France and Italy to the gold fields of northern California, but that was the route of the garment that's mostly closely associated not only with the American cowboy but with America itself.

"Stacked" jeans legs straighten out to cover the entire leg when the wearer is on horseback. (Wrangler)

Whether you call them jeans (from the French word for the Italian city of Genoa) or denims (*de Nîmes,* or "of Nîmes," a French city also noted for its fabric manufacture), the pants were originally made of durable canvas sailcloth. The first pairs were not intended for riders, but for the forty-niner prospectors who worked gold mines.

It didn't take Westerners long to discover that the fabric was equally well suited for ranch wear. The wide legs and baggy seat of the original cut were narrowed to eliminate chafing in the saddle and to fit snugly over boot tops.

Not very much has changed over the century and a half since jeans first saw the light of day. The indigo shade of blue remains the color of choice, and although the addition of stretch fabric allows for a bit of give, most Western riders choose all cotton. They also prefer tapered legs worn longer than the rider's actual inseam so that the jeans bunch up around the boot from the hem to the upper ankle. The bunched fabric is commonly called "stacks," and when the wearer is in the saddle, the extra length extends to cover the entire leg.

Alternatives include the boot-cut style with a slightly flared bottom for tucking your pants legs into your boots (especially useful in keeping the bottoms clean when working around cattle or mucking out stalls).

Women enjoy a wide range of colors in their jeans, especially for dressy occasions and for certain horse show and rodeo events.

BELTS

Why do Western riders wear wide tooled-leather belts with big buckles? To keep their jeans up. And when the buckle is a prize the wearer won at a horse show or rodeo, the belt becomes a walking trophy case.

CHAPS

The word "chaps" (pronounced "shaps") comes from a Spanish word that means leggings. The first chaps were leather aprons worn by vaqueros against cactus thorns, mesquite brambles, and other sharp objects they encountered in the course of herding cattle. At some point the apron was refined into twin leggings fastened around the leg by leather thongs.

Variations of the basic straight-legged "shotgun" style include flared "batwings" held in place by snaps and conchas; their open backs are well suited for warm climates. Colder weather called for warm sheepskin linings.

Apparel for Western pleasure classes includes a Western hat, long-sleeve shirt, chaps, and Western boots.
(AQHA photo by Wyatt McSpadden)

Chaps for daily wear remain relatively plain, but those worn for competition are often custom-made and embellished with silver conchas, fringe, and hand-tooled leather. The decorations frequently feature the owner's initials, ranch brand, or other distinctive pattern.

Fringed chaps in a variety of colors remain popular in Western horsemanship (equitation) and other horse show performance classes.

The style known as chinks, or armidas, short chaps that stop at the knee or slightly below, seems to be coming back into favor. They're especially popular among working ranchers who don't want to drag longer chaps along the ground while doing such chores as branding or castrating cattle.

Women and girls who take part in halter and showmanship classes favor brightly colored formal outfits. (AQHA photo by Wyatt McSpadden)

SHIRTS

The earliest Western shirts were wool or flannel collarless pullovers. There was a very practical reason for their popularity: Button-front shirts meant the possibility of losing buttons, and sewing was never a favorite activity either in the bunkhouse or (especially) out on the range.

When button-front shirts did come into vogue, a popular style had a lapel-like flap of cloth that buttoned across the chest. The style helped keep trail dust from blowing inside, while the extra layer of fabric was especially welcome in cold weather.

Fancy fabrics and styles like fringed sleeves, yokes, and snap fasteners came less from ranch life than from country-and-Western entertainment and Hollywood's idea of what singing cowboys should wear. Much more prevalent are long-sleeve dress shirts, often sporting a designer logo, found from informal riding settings to horse show competitions.

NECKWEAR

Few pieces of clothing had so many uses as the cowboy's bandanna or neckerchief. It protected his neck from summer sun, winter cold, and year-round wind and dust. Worn across the face (think stagecoach bandit), it protected the nose and mouth against dust and swarms of insects. Soaked in cool water, the bandanna kept the cowboy's neck cool in summer. Wrapped and tied around a hat crown and under the chin, it kept the hat from blowing away. And in a pinch, it served as an ever-ready bandage or tourniquet.

Bandannas are still worn, even under collared shirts, for their decorative effect. Traditional alternatives for more dressy occasions are string ties and, more recently, bolo ties with ornate sliding keepers.

In horse show competition, neckties remain popular accessories for men in halter classes, as do short at-the-collar styles in Western performance classes.

VESTS, JACKETS, AND COATS

The layered look long has been an integral part of ranchwear, thanks to sleeveless leather vests that provided insulation against wind without restricting the rider's—and especially the roper's—arms. Their pockets could hold many items and offered easier accessibility than pockets on jeans. Winter cold brought out sheepskin-lined versions.

It didn't take cowboys too long to match long-sleeve waist-length multi-pocketed denim jackets with their jeans. More recent additions for nippy and downright cold weather are goose down or synthetic-filled vests, quilted parkas, and duct jackets in many styles.

Wet weather required as large a waterproof or water-resistant covering as a cowboy could wear. A raincoat made of rubberized canvas and called a mackintosh (after the man who invented the process) covered a rider and his saddle. Later made of vulcanized rubber, they were the forerunner of the slicker, a coat or poncho that's now made of durable vinyl or plastic. When not in use, a slicker or poncho is carried rolled up and tied behind the cantle of the saddle.

Another enduring item is the duster, a canvas coat that reaches the wearer's ankles. As the name suggests, it protects the wearer against blowing soil and other dust. Not too many people wear dusters these days, but those who do are part of a great Western tradition.

Tying a rain slicker to the back of a saddle keeps it close at hand. (AQHA photo by Wyatt McSpadden)

HATS

The only piece of apparel that might rival cowboy boots in both popularity and in identification with the American West is the cowboy hat.

Like boots, the so-called cowboy hat evolved from a distinctive piece of vaquero apparel, the sombrero. But the sombrero's very high crown and wide brim tended to make it fly off during a good lope (the chin cord with which vaqueros kept their hats in place could strangle a careless cowboy). To the rescue came an Eastern hatmaker who designed a beaver felt model with a lower crown and narrower brim.

The rest, as they say, is history. Cowboys found almost as many uses for their headgear as they did for bandannas. Depending on the season, a hat gave shade or warmth. It was used to fan campfire embers or stir a reluctant cow, and as a water cup or bucket.

The most popular colors are still white (known as silverbelly) and black. The most expensive felt hats contain an amount of beaver (the designation of a number followed by an "X" indicates the proportion of beaver) in addition to rabbit fur. Felt hats often give way to lightweight natural straw when warm weather comes.

Wearers express their individuality in how they crease the crown and brim; many styles are associated with a geographic area or an activity, such as the Canadian or roper crease.

Hats are required for most horse show classes and rodeo events, so first-time contestants need to check the requirements before entering.

English

BOOTS

The knee-high riding boot associated with English-style riding is the descendant of footwear worn by eighteenth-century gentlemen and by cavalrymen throughout the ages. Typical showring attire includes the plain-front calfskin "dress" boot, with black as the basic hunter-jumper showring color.

Since a snug fit around the ankle is as desirable as one around the calf, some riders prefer field boots that are laced in front to the top of the ankle.

Hunt boots, black with mahogany brown top cuffs, are proper for the foxhunting field, but only for the Master of Foxhounds, his staff, and gentlemen members of the hunt (all others wear plain black boots).

Newmarket boots are named after the racing center in England. They're made of heavy canvas and rubber and can be cleaned with a water hose or bucket, making them extremely practical for riding in wet weather or walking across soggy ground.

Dress (left) and field boots are appropriate for hunt seat and jumper classes. (Miller Harness Company)

Any top boot will drop at the ankle when it's broken in, so allow for that change in height when being fitted.

Although ankle-high paddock and jodhpur boots may not support and protect the calf as top boots do, they are far more comfortable when you're walking or standing. They're also easier to get on and off, especially if you wear the kind with zippers or elastic side gussets.*

PANTS

Old-style breeches, the kind seen in paintings and photographs before the 1960s, had flared (or "pegged") tops that fit comfortably around the hips. That look ended with the advent of two- and four-way stretch fabrics that give breeches a sleek look from waist to calf. Khaki and tan are the most popular showring colors, with white worn for hunter and jumper stakes classes.

As a practical matter, almost all English-style riders wear snug jeans for informal and practice situations. Worn with paddock boots and snug-fitting chaps, they virtually eliminate the chafing that can come from keeping your lower legs against the girth. An alternative that's particularly popular among endurance and dressage riders is stretch tights especially designed for riding, with padding where it helps.

SHIRTS AND NECKWEAR

For showing, women wear shirts with detachable choker collars, while men wear dress shirts and ties. Stock ties, either ready-tied or tied snugly to prevent chafing, are correct for foxhunting and upper-level dressage trials. Otherwise, turtlenecks and polo shirts seem to lead the list for pleasure riding and informal schooling sessions.

COATS AND VESTS

Riding coats were once virtually indistinguishable from sports jackets and suit coats: three buttons, narrow lapels, and slashed pockets. Although streetwear fashion may have gone to two-button or double-breasted styles with wide lapels, the formal riding coat and hacking jacket have remained the same.** AQHA

---

*Once upon a time, young English-style riders wore jodhpurs with low boots ("jodhpur," named for a state in India, evokes that nation's traditional leggings). Although the low boots with which they were worn are less expensive to replace than high boots, all but the youngest show riders now appear in tall boots and breeches.

**A word of caution about wearing "street" jackets for riding: The shoulders of riding coats are cut more amply so riders can extend both arms in the jumping rein-release movement. When you try that movement while wearing a buttoned "street" jacket, you'll notice that your upper body is restricted. You may even hear the sound of tearing cloth.

Traditional hunt seat apparel: hunt cap, choker-collared shirt, breeches, and high boots. Rust-colored breeches were originally designed for wet weather; the color hides the effect of rain and mud. (AQHA photo by Wyatt McSpadden)

English show competition calls for traditional, conservative colors such as navy, dark green, gray, black, or brown.

English-style pleasure riders wear all sorts of jackets and vests, from athletic warm-up or jeans jackets to down vests and quilted parkas. The common thread is that the cuts and fabrics are nonconfining and durable.

The wax jacket is a foul-weather item from Britain that has caught on in this country. The glycerin wax with which the cotton fabric is impregnated makes the garment water-resistant (although not waterproof). Some styles with double vents and storm tab collars have been designed with riding in mind.

HATS

Helmets have become standard equipment for all potentially hazardous sports, and horse sports have been in the forefront in that regard. Jockeys and polo players have worn helmets for many years, while reinforced hunt caps and

Helmets with chin straps are recommended for all levels of riding and especially for novices. (AQHA photo by Wyatt McSpadden)

derbies are no newcomers to the foxhunting field. In the showring, hard velvet-covered hunt caps have been mandatory in hunter, jumper, and hunt seat equitation classes. Although the basic style has changed little, the strength of the helmet material has been improved. Brims are now flexible (rigid brims can snap on impact); chin straps are now required and are strong and secure harnesses.

The brimless, shell-like jockey helmet, sometimes known as "Caliente" after the Mexican racetrack, also is standard combined training gear. Worn with a black cover, it doubles as a hunt cap for the dressage and stadium jumping phases, while with a distinctive colored or patterned cover, it can be coordinated with the rest of a rider's cross-country outfit.*

Endurance riders have popularized lightweight ventilated helmets that many pleasure riders wear during hot weather. Whichever style you choose, all the technology and safety features in the world won't be of any value unless the hat fits properly and you fasten the chin harness.

---

*In eventing's cross-country phase, riders must also wear reinforced "flak jacket" vests that offer protection to the chest and back in case of a fall.

More fundamentally, the point is to wear a hard hat. They are required for all AQHA English-style show riders. With sensible urging from insurance companies, almost all public and private stables have made them mandatory for lesson programs and, more often than not, for all riders. There's a lesson to be learned here: Whether jumping or not, whether riding English or Western, falls do happen—and hard hats reduce the likelihood of serious injuries.

Known as helmets, hunt caps, and hard hats, this protective gear is worn by young and old alike.
(Miller Harness Company)

Taking Care of Footwear and Apparel

Like saddle leather, boot leather needs to be kept clean and supple. Start by brushing off dust, caked manure, and any other dirt, then wipe with a clean, damp sponge or cloth. Contrary to popular opinion, a little bit of plain clean water will never harm cowhide, calfskin, or any other boot leather, with the exception of suede.

Too much water, however, causes leather and stitching to weaken, if not rot. Boots that are soaked need to be allowed to dry away from direct heat. Stuffing them with newspaper will speed the process and help retain their shape. Then apply a conditioner to retain the leather's natural oils.

After every few wearings, or more frequently if the boot has been out in hot or wet weather, a light coating of saddle soap or commercial leather cleaner will supplement these natural oils. "Light" is the operative word: Too much soap or cleaner clogs the leather's pores and shortens its life span. Mink oil or another waterproof dressing is good protection, and it keeps the leather pliable.

Polish gives boots a nice finish. Use it sparingly, again to keep pores from becoming clogged. Because polish stains not only fabric but a horse's coat, savvy English show riders avoid using it on the side of the boot that comes in contact with their horse.

Boot trees help footwear retain its shape. In addition, cedar trees absorb perspiration and other dampness, while plastic trees just allow air to circulate. In either case, the result is a dry boot that's a pleasure to put on again.

Boot bags keep away dust and prevent scratches, just as garment bags keep jackets and breeches clean, especially en route to horse shows and other competitions.

Any perspiration on the inside of hats or caps should be allowed to dry. Velvet hunt caps can be cleaned easily by a good brushing with a garment brush. That same brush is equally useful in getting dried dirt off coats and breeches. Felt hats can be steamed and reblocked when they lose their shape.

A Final Word on Innovation

Horse sports are a growth industry in many respects, and the variety and diversity of rider apparel is growing right along with them. The past decade has seen the introduction and growth in popularity of such items as riding sneakers with pronounced heels and lightweight space-age insulated gloves and vests.

Even between the time these words are written and you read them, manufacturers are certain to develop new items and improve existing ones. That's yet another reason to pay close attention to magazine articles and advertisements and tack-shop catalogs.

The ABCs of Trail Riding

Ring work may be fine, especially when you're learning to ride, but one of the great delights of the sport is the opportunity to take to the trail. Whether the route starts in your backyard or you have to haul to get there, whether it's a bridle path around an urban park or someplace where you won't see another soul for hours, a riding trail is your highway to enjoyment.

Experienced trail riders know that using commonsense rules of the road puts the "pleasure" in pleasure riding, so take time to become familiar with the following tips:

- Ride only where you're welcome. Signs that indicate posted land and threatening "trespassers will be prosecuted" put you on notice that you have no right to be there.

- Stay on the trail. Leaving a designated riding path is likely to harm the habitat of animals and destroy plants and other foliage. What's more, holes and other hidden hazards may await horses and riders who stray off the path.

- Some trails include stretches that run along paved roads. Keep off the pavement whenever possible, but avoid ditches or tall grass. Hazards like broken glass or holes may be hidden there, too.

- Don't assume that drivers of cars and trucks will automatically reduce their speed when they see people on horseback. Signal speeders to slow down by flagging them with an up-and-down palms-down hand signal. Then thank them for their courtesy with a smile and a wave or a tip of your hat.

- With encroaching development cutting down the amount of recreational land, riders must increasingly share available trails with other sportsmen. Riding on the right side of the trail (just as you drive on the right side of the road) avoids collisions with oncoming traffic, especially with hikers and bicyclists. By the same token, the riding arena tradition of passing oncoming horses on the right applies out on the trail, too. Not everyone understands this custom, so don't take it for granted.

- Take advantage of your horse's acute sense of hearing. Ears that suddenly prick forward and/or a nicker or whinny are the usual signs of someone or something that's approaching. Horses hear things far sooner than humans do, so be alert to their signals.

Ride in the middle of the road only when you're certain there will be no traffic coming from either direction. (AQHA photo by Wyatt McSpadden)

- Horseback riders have the right-of-way over bicyclists and hikers, but don't assume everyone knows that. Anticipate situations where you may be cut off, and then act accordingly—defensive driving is as good a strategy when you're in the saddle as it is when you're behind the wheel. For example, be the first to establish voice contact. Let people know you're there; hikers or bikers may be chatting, daydreaming, or listening to a portable radio and not realize they have company. Waving your hand to establish visual contact is another good idea.

- Backpacks, baby carriages, loud radios, and dogs straining against leashes pose possible spooky threats to horses. You can defuse a potentially dangerous situation by asking people to move to the far side of the trail or, if available, a nearby wider part of the path. Don't let them get behind a tree or bush, which your horse may perceive as an ambush about to happen.

- Nevertheless, no matter how hard you try to head off a dangerous situation, someone may do something that will cause your horse to spook. The first rule is to keep your cool. Then, after you calm your animal, educate the person about proper trail etiquette. An angry attitude is far less effective than a calm and friendly conversation.

- Some people you'll encounter on the trail will want to pat your horse. Whether that's such a good idea depends on the situation. For instance, you may be heading home, and standing still may be the last thing on your horse's mind. Or the weather may be brisk and your horse is feeling good: His tossing head and dancing feet pose a danger to someone trying to get close. In such cases, explain that although you—and your horse— appreciate the thought, keeping a distance will be safer for all concerned.

- If contact is appropriate, explain that a pat on the neck is just as friendly, and far safer, than a pat on the nose. Parents of a small child should be reminded not to thrust their youngster up toward a horse's face; nor should the child's hand get too close to the animal's mouth.

- Don't travel faster than a walk or slow jog-trot around blind corners. You never know when riders or pedestrians are coming the other way, and they can't see you either.

- Riders who come upon each other at different gaits should pass at the slower gait. If you're loping and the other rider is jogging, it's your responsibility to slow down to the trot.

- When riding in groups, ride side by side only when the trail is wide enough. Otherwise, riding in single file does less damage to the environment.

- Some horses that become trail buddies are upset when they're separated. Some horses are leaders that insist on forging to the front; others are followers, happiest when they're not in the lead. If any such behaviors apply to the animals in your group, arrange the order accordingly.

- Maintain a distance of one horse length. Riding any closer leads to crowding and an opportunity—if not an outright invitation—for horses to kick. Any habitual kicker belongs at the back of the group; a red ribbon in the tail is the universal warning sign.

- If you must pass, do so only when there's enough space on the trail to move by without crowding.

- When you get to a steep slope, keep two lengths apart going uphill and three lengths when descending. Those distances will keep horses from crowding in case one slips or slides.

- Unused or unfamiliar uphill trails pose a problem when you can't see very far ahead. In that case, one rider should go first to make sure the trail is usable.

- If your horse misbehaves, use appropriate punishment, but don't administer it in such a way that other horses will react. That's particularly important if your group includes a novice or timid rider.

The position of horses on a trail ride should be based in part on how well particular animals get along with each other. (AQHA photo by Wyatt McSpadden)

- Although the walk is the standard gait for trail riding, a jog-trot now and then is a welcome break. So is a lope, but only if all the riders in your party can handle their horses in a group situation. Remember equine attitudes toward competition and the herd instinct: What starts as a sedate canter often ends up as an All American Futurity stretch drive.

The pace of a trail ride depends on the ability of all the members of your group. (AQHA photo by Wyatt McSpadden)

- Move up to a faster gait only after everyone has been alerted. Being caught unawares, off balance and with long reins, isn't much fun when everyone else takes off.

- Holding a tree branch for the rider behind you is misplaced courtesy. By the time the person gets close enough to reach the branch, it will have snapped back in his or her face. Besides, your horses will have moved too close to each other.

- Gates, however, should be held open. The person who opens the gate holds it until everyone else has passed through. Make sure gates are securely closed and latched; allowing livestock to escape is a very quick way to have the owner stop letting people ride across his or her land.

- Another way to alienate landowners is by dropping trash along the trail (it's also just plain bad manners). On the plus side, informing the owner about something he or she would want to know, such as a broken fence, is a way to earn points. It's also the neighborly thing to do.

- Whether you're out in a group or by yourself, give your horse a chance to warm up and cool off by walking the first mile out and the last mile home.

FOR FURTHER INFORMATION

The AQHA affiliate in your state, province, or country is an excellent source for learning about trail riding opportunities in your area. And if you're contemplating a horseback riding vacation elsewhere, contact the AQHA affiliate at your destination for similar information.

Trailers: Hauling Your Horse

One of the most appealing aspects of riding is the mobility it offers. And there's even more mobility when you're not limited by how far you can travel from home on horseback, perhaps to a horse show or another competition or perhaps to trails that are some distance away. Getting there requires a trailer or van, and having one of your own means you won't have to rely on the kindness or schedule (or hauling fees) of others.

Choosing a Trailer

Even if you're a one-horse owner, consider getting a two-horse trailer. That's called foresight: It's likely that someday soon you'll want go somewhere with someone who has his or her own horse.*

Preliminary considerations in selecting a trailer include the comfort and safety of the equine passenger.

The interior dimensions will depend on your horse's size. Experts recommend the ceiling be a minimum of ten inches taller than the height of his head while he's in his normal resting position. The stalls should be wide enough to allow three inches of lateral movement on each side of the horse. The depth should allow him a little bit of movement between the front wall ahead of him

---

*And in the "could happen" department, owners of one horse have been known to buy a second one.

Several owners might consider going in together on a larger, goose-neck trailer. (Sooner Trailer)

and the butt bar behind. Taking these considerations together, the horse should stand snugly, but comfortably.

The front and sides of the stalls need to be well padded. The butt bar should be padded, too, to prevent injury in case of sudden stops. A chain behind the butt bar is a safety measure in case the rear door accidentally opens.

The floor should be solid, with nonslip rubber mats. You'll remove the mats periodically so the floor can dry thoroughly; otherwise, the acid in urine will accelerate rusting and rotting.

Even just one horse gives off lots of heat, especially during the summer. That's why enclosed trailers need front, side, and overhead ventilation.

You'll also want to be sure that the brake and lighting systems are fully operational.

A fully loaded trailer weighs somewhere in the area of two tons. That's a hefty burden for most cars. If you don't already own a truck or another type of vehicle that can pull a trailer, you'll need to buy one. Trailer dealers, mechanics, and experienced friends can offer recommendations about makes and models. They also will suggest that the hitch (the gadget on the towing vehicle to which the trailer is attached) be welded as well as bolted in place.

Hauling a Trailer

Driving a vehicle with a trailer behind it isn't difficult, but you'll need some amount of practice before you feel confident (leave your horse at home while you learn). The trick is to start and stop gradually, since sudden changes in speed will throw your passenger off balance.

Pay particular attention to the distance and speed required to overtake and pass cars in front of you. However, excess speed, especially when high winds are blowing broadside against you, can make the trailer fishtail along the road.

Backing a trailer should become as natural as driving it forward. Steering is just the opposite: Turn the steering wheel left to back right, and vice versa. Confusing? Not after you've practiced.

Loading Your Horse

Even before your horse sets foot in the trailer, you need to prepare both the vehicle and the animal.

A horse being hauled alone rides in the left-hand stall, which compensates for how roads slope. Lots of straw or wood shavings on the floor makes the trip easier on his legs and feet (a minimum of four inches seems to encourage normal urination). A full haynet is an alternative to boredom. Hang the net high enough so the horse can't step over or into it.

At least two weeks before beginning a long trip, check with your veterinarian about the need for vaccinations against respiratory diseases like rhinopneumonitis and influenza. A negative Coggins test and a health certificate are required for foreign and some interstate travel, and they usually must be presented at competitive events.

Also as a matter of health routine, every trailer needs a first-aid kit to cope with minor scrapes that can happen en route: bandages, antiseptics, wound ointments, scissors, and insect repellent.

Very few "backyard" horses haven't at some point in their lives taken a trailer ride. Because American Quarter Horses have such good attitudes, your horse probably won't think twice about being loaded. However, if some enticement is necessary, a little grain in a feed bucket works well, or, in a two-horse trailer, another more willing horse getting in first should do the trick.

Some horses, however, just don't like trailers. Perhaps they associate the enclosed space with a trip to the veterinarian or some other unpleasant experience.

According to Craig Cameron, the Texas trainer who shared his expertise in *The Quarter Horse Journal* (May 1997), if force created the horse's reluctance to enter the trailer, using additional force won't solve the problem. "When a horse puts one foot in the trailer, that's when most people . . . lay on the whip.

They think, 'well, she's almost there,' so they try to get her in quick. That only justifies all the horse's natural fears of the trailer."

Instead, Cameron suggests the animal be taught to respond to a gentle touch of a crop and a verbal "cluck" as the cue to move forward. Then the horse can be led toward the trailer. At each small step, the handler should wait a few moments for the horse to relax, then ask again for the forward movement. In time and with patience, Cameron contends, the horse will make his way into the trailer.

Once your horse is in his trailer stall, tie him in place. The rope should be long enough so he can maintain his balance, but not so long that he can turn around. One end of the rope snaps to the halter ring, the other is tied to the side of the trailer with either a quick-release knot or an easy-release "panic snap."

When you've reached your destination and unloaded your horse, check his legs and feet for any scrapes or injuries.

Providing drinking water for your horse en route is virtually impossible, for the simple reason that water tends to spill out of any bucket hung in a moving trailer. That's not to say that your passenger shouldn't be offered the chance for a drink whenever you stop for gas or your own creature comforts. Fill the bucket that you've brought along at the service station or rest stop. However, don't be surprised if he turns down the offer: Horses that have any qualms about being trailered will refuse to drink and, moreover, may not want any water for the first ten or fifteen minutes after they reach their destination.

Another method is to soak the hay in the trailer's haynet in water before you leave home, or at a rest stop. Not only will your horse have something to nibble on, but the snack provides the added benefit of slaking the thirst of a horse that won't drink from a bucket on the road.

Vans are all-in-one units for four or more horses. Although they're impractical for an owner of only one or two horses, you and several other nearby horse owners who routinely travel to the same destinations might consider buying one as a group. The same thought applies to larger trailers, which can accommodate up to eight horses.

FOR FURTHER INFORMATION

Sooner Trailers, an AQHA sponsor, offers a five-minute *Safety Video.* Contact them at 1515 McCurdy, Duncan, OK 73533. Phone: (405) 255-6979, fax: (405) 255-9783. Web site: www.soonertrailers.com; e-mail: sooner@simplynet.net.

This AQHA video has information of relevance:

Horse Sense. Judge, trainer, and college equine professor Dr. Jim Heird provides sensible safety, grooming, and halter-breaking tips for the novice horse enthusiast. Basic clipping, bedding, and trailer-loading techniques also are covered. Excellent for 4-H and FFA clubs. 26 minutes.

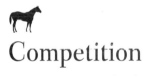

Competition

A two-horse trailer is the ideal vehicle for a first-time owner. (Sooner Trailer)

At some point in your equestrian career, you're likely to take part in some sort of competitive activity. You won't be alone, because millions of other owners and riders have chosen the American Quarter Horse as their partner in a variety of horse sports. Among the many arenas where you can demonstrate your horse's athletic skills—as well as your own— let's begin with horse shows.

Horse Shows

HALTER

Halter classes sometimes go by the name of conformation classes or breeding classes. When taken together, all three terms describe the procedure and purpose of this important competition.

Classes in this division are based on age and gender—for example, two-year-old stallions or three-year-old mares. The horses, which wear no tack other than halters, are led into the arena, then lined up, their handlers making sure the animals stand balanced and squared, relaxed yet alert.

An exhibitor presents her horse in a halter class. (AQHA photo by Wyatt McSpadden)

The judge—or judges, since the larger shows often use more than one—scrutinize each horse in terms of conformation standards of the American Quarter Horse (see this book's appendix for more detailed information about conformation).

In addition to structural correctness and degree of musculature, judges assess balance and soundness. In that regard, handlers are asked to jog their horses a short distance so judges can see whether they are structurally correct while in motion.

Placing halter horses in the order in which they deserve prize ribbons is no easy task. Few owners will enter horses that lack fundamental American Quarter Horse conformation qualities, so evaluating a good animal both in terms of the breed standards and relative to the others in the class takes an experienced horseman.

Then, too, although the winner may be obvious, the judge must determine the complete order of finish. Is the hock on that sorrel worse than the shoulder on that bay? And how do those two horses compare to the less-than-classic head on the dun at the end of the line? Only the final placings

Showmanship classes spotlight the handlers, starting at a very early age. (AQHA photo by Wyatt McSpadden)

will reveal how the person holding the card answered these and other questions.

The halter division is, as it should be, more than just a beauty contest. That's where the word "breeding" comes into play. In principle, only physically correct horses should be used as breeding stock (in the case of geldings, their sires and dams deserve the merit); otherwise, conformation faults are likely to be passed along. Therefore, by rewarding individuals that come closest to the ideal, halter classes are crucial in maintaining the excellence of the American Quarter Horse as a breed.

Western Performance Classes

SHOWMANSHIP

Showmanship, in which youth and amateurs take part, is very much a performance class, but here the spotlight shifts from the horse to the handler.

This class is conducted in the format of a halter class, but with certain adaptations. Each exhibitor leads his or her horse through one of several patterns chosen by the judge. For example, it may begin by entering at the judge's signal, walking the horse to a pylon at one end of the arena, turning the horse to face the judge, and backing to a second cone several strides away. The pattern may conclude with jogging up to the judge, halting and setting up the horse for the judge's inspection, and finally returning to the rail to line up.

Handling a horse in a show situation is very different from doing so at home. Despite the distractions of unfamiliar surroundings and spectator sights and sounds, you as a showmanship exhibitor must make your horse walk and jog alertly and mannerly and, when required, in a straight line. Instead of pulling your horse into a jog, you need to encourage a prompt and willing transition and a smooth and balanced pace. As with any other horse show class, preparation begins at home with plenty of practice.

Standing a horse up for inspection is an art in itself. The horse needs to be balanced on all four legs, standing straight from head, neck, and shoulders back to his hips, and showing a straight top line. An alert yet calm expression with ears pricked forward is always a bonus. A well-groomed horse in excellent condition and wearing a clean and properly fitting halter and lead shank is essential (for that matter, so is the exhibitor's own appearance).

Judges also will take into account how horse and handler fit together, since, for example, a very small person leading a very large horse makes less than an ideal picture.

The most successful showmanship competitors are those who understand how to accentuate their horse's good points and minimize any weaknesses. In that sense, showmanship is salesmanship, convincing the judge that your "product" is the best one to select.

WESTERN PLEASURE

The name of this class tells the story: Judges are looking for American Quarter Horses that give the impression of being a real pleasure to ride. Their gaits are true and comfortable, balanced, and in rhythm and cadence. Their attitude is alert and mannerly, and all their riders need to do (or so it would appear) is maintain the lightest of rein contact—if any at all—and just sit back and enjoy the ride.

Sounds easy, doesn't it? Well, ask any experienced horse show judge, and you'll find that winning a Western pleasure class takes skill. It also takes a pretty nice horse.

The foundation of a successful Western pleasure horse is good gaits. As you've discovered from your own riding education, the walk should be four distinctive beats at an easygoing, flat-footed, and square pace and cadence. The jog is a true two-beat diagonal movement, with the front legs flat (that is, not snapping at the knees). There should be no sign of forging, winging, interfering, or lameness. A smooth top line at the trot, one that's level from poll to croup, lets the rider sit easily and comfortably. (In fact, a horse that carries his head lower than his withers at any gait for more than five strides will be eliminated.)

Western pleasure classes spotlight the horses' "way of going." (AQHA photo by Wyatt McSpadden)

A three-beat lope reveals a horse's natural balance better than the walk or the trot because any lack or loss of equilibrium is most evident there. Judges reward a horse that takes and holds the lope on the correct lead and moves forward at that easy three-beat cadence. Straightness is valued, not only in the horse's way of going, but in his top line, too.

Horses in this division may be asked to show at the extended gaits, most often the extended jog. Judges want to see the horse reach out with his legs, lengthening the stride while maintaining a steady pace.

Western pleasure horses are required to back easily and stand quietly. Anyone that stiffens his jaw, opens his mouth or otherwise resists, moves in a crooked line, or simply refuses to back up will be severely penalized.

Perhaps just as important as the gaits themselves is how a Western pleasure horse makes transitions from one gait to another.

Transitions show how well broke a horse is to the rider's cues. The less visible the cues, the better. Transitions also demonstrate how balanced the animal carries himself. Judges are interested in seeing a horse change gaits without changing body position. A horse that, for example, "collapses" onto his forehand while going from the lope down to the jog obviously lacks the hind-end engagement to carry himself in a balanced fashion.

"Engagement" is an important concept. The term refers to how a horse's hind legs should work under him, propelling him forward and letting his forelegs become free and light. Engagement produces the desirable soft, graceful, and fluid movement of a Western pleasure horse.

Another crucial aspect of a Western pleasure horse's way of going deals with how the animal flexes, or carries his head and neck. Carrying his face at the vertical is the ideal. Overflexion, where the neck is bent so far that the horse seems to be staring at his front feet, will create a "downhill" action. (It may also be the sign of an intimidated animal.) The opposite extreme is "star-gazing," or carrying the head too high; the horse is forced to hollow his back. Neither position allows a comfortable or athletic movement at any gait.

Horses compete as a group in the Western pleasure horse class. After they have worked in both directions in the arena and at all three gaits, the judge will ask the riders to line up side by side. Then comes the command to back up. Here the judges are looking for those that back in a straight and balanced way, with no evidence of resistance or a sour attitude.

When asked what he looks for in a top Western pleasure horse, one judge said simply, "The horse that I'd like to ride myself." Watch a class closely, and chances are you'll say the same thing about the winner.

REINING

Reining classes have sometimes been accused of being "showboat" classes. That's true to the extent that their spins and sliding stops are real crowd pleasers. But there's also no better way for a horse to show he has the athletic ability and responsiveness to be a superior working stock horse than to

A reining horse's hindquarters "melt" into the ground at the end of a sliding stop. (AQHA photo by Wyatt McSpadden)

perform the moves that reining patterns call for. Perhaps the best summary comes from the National Reining Horse Association's definition:

"To rein a horse is not only to guide him, but also to control his every movement. The best reined horse should be willfully guided or controlled with little or no apparent resistance and dictated to completely. Any movement on his own must be considered a lack of control. All deviations from the exact written pattern must be considered a lack of control and therefore a fault that must be marked down according to the severity of deviation . . . credit should be given for smoothness, finesse, attitude, quickness and authority of performing various maneuvers, while using controlled speed which raises the difficulty level and makes [the horse] more exciting and pleasing to watch to an audience."

The order of movements varies from pattern to pattern. Whichever one is called for, riders and trainers break it down into its individual movements. That's because it's the way judges assess performances, so let's examine the movements that way, too.

Circles and figure eights are at the heart of all reining patterns. Ask a judge what he or she expects to see in a good circle, and the answer will be "roundness." A circle isn't an oval or a wiggly, drifting ring. It's round, and the only way a horse can properly make a circle (or a figure eight, which is no more than two linked circles) is by arcing his body from nose to tail into a smooth bend. The pace of the circle also must be smooth and steady; a horse that varies his speed isn't under maximum control.

Figure eights are done at the lope, with flying changes of lead required at changes of direction. Although judges are looking for the forelegs and hind legs to swap leads simultaneously, the rules permit a leeway of one stride. Crossfiring, or cross-cantering (the forelegs on one lead and hind legs on the other), is penalized. So is any anticipation or reluctance to change, varying the pace, or excessive cues from the rider.

In the rundown, the horse lopes or gallops down the center line or along the rail from one end of the arena to the other. Although this movement leads to stops, rollbacks, and other movements, judges consider rundowns as more than just preparation. They look for a smooth, even pace that demonstrates the horse's balance. The speed, which should be appropriate for that particular horse, needs to be consistent throughout the run.

The most spectacular part of any reining pattern is the sliding stop. At a signal from the rider, the horse drops and "melts" his hindquarters into the ground, without changing the relative position of the hind legs. Simultaneously, the forelegs keep moving, maintaining the horse's balance until he comes to a complete stop. With regard to the rider, only the slightest cue should be needed to initiate the stop, since an upper body that leans up the horse's neck or too far back will interfere with the horse's own balance. A smooth and straight halt with no anticipation or resistance will receive high marks.

Many reining patterns incorporate rollbacks. The sequence calls for a combination of a stop, a 180-degree turn on the haunches, and a departure, all done in one fluid motion; hence the term "rollback."

Another movement is the spin, in which the inside hind foot acts as a pivot. It remains firmly planted while the horse moves his forequarters around in one or more 360-degree circles, one or the other forefoot remaining in contact with the ground. The turn should not appear rushed or forced; judges want to see a consistent speed, a straight body, and an overall fluidity of motion.

The back-up is just as important as any forward movement. As the horse works off his hocks, his neck should not be overflexed (causing the impression that the rider is forcing him, even if that's not the case). The impression the judge should have is of willingness and, above all, straightness.

Scoring a reining class is done on the basis of each movement. Each horse begins with a score of 70, to which 1 full or ½ point is added for well-executed movements. Those that have been poorly done have full or half points subtracted. The total score determines the placings.

TRAIL

Unlike reining classes, there are no flashy edge-of-your-seat sliding stops or multiple spins to be found in trail classes. Instead, what's highlighted are horses with the handiness and calm attitude that you'd be happy to be mounted on during a ride out in the country. Worth their weight in gold, they have the intelligence and good sense to cope promptly, confidently, and above all safely with whatever they might encounter along the way.

Trail class course designers have a range of items to choose from, and the most imaginative designers come up with fair and inviting yet demanding combinations and sequences of obstacles. Although which ones they use depends on the abilities of the riders, all courses must include a gate, a series of logs to be walked or jogged through, and a backing obstacle.

A turn within the box obstacle in a trail horse class. (AQHA photo by Wyatt McSpadden)

For example, a course may begin with the gate, which the rider must open, guide the horse through, and then close. After walking across a grid of logs, the horse is asked to back through and around at least three markers, then stand while the rider puts on and removes a rain slicker that was tied to the back of the saddle. Next come a circle at the jog and another at the lope, followed by crossing a wooden bridge. After a side pass of several steps, the course ends with the horse again standing quietly while the rider removes a letter from a mailbox.

Other obstacles include carrying a bucket or another object; riding a serpentine series of S-curves between poles; and pivoting 360 degrees inside a five- to seven-foot-square box made of ground rails.

Each obstacle is scored. Additional impression marks are given for the horse's gaits, manners, attitude, and style.

When you ask judges what they look for in a top trail horse, you'll hear such terms as "alert," "energetic," "interested," and "personality." That last one refers to a horse that performs the test neither mechanically nor with obvious boredom, but studies each obstacle and then answers its question in a straightforward manner. You can tell by the animal's alert eyes, ears pricked forward, and relaxed but responsive movements. That's exactly the sort of horse anyone would be happy to take out on a trail ride.

Western riding classes call for prompt and confident responses. (AQHA photo by Wyatt McSpadden)

WESTERN RIDING

A Western riding class is another event that tests an American Quarter Horse's athleticism and accuracy. Calling for movements that also are found in reining and trail classes, tests here emphasize prompt and confident responses.

The class uses one of two set patterns, with the one to be used designated in advance of the class. Pattern number one begins with the horse entering the arena at a walk, then jogging over a single log and moving into the lope. Once around the end of the arena, the horse continues down the long side, slaloming around five pylons set thirty to fifty feet apart and making flying changes onto the correct lead at each change of direction.

The rider then brings the horse back up the arena in a series of four serpentine loops, again executing flying changes at the midpoint of each loop (and loping over the log when they come to it). At the end of the ring, the horse turns left down the center line to halt and back at the center of the arena.

The other pattern calls for the same maneuvers but in a different sequence.

Of particular importance in Western riding classes are promptness and consistency. The former means the horse must make his transitions between gaits and his lead changes at the lope at the precise moment they're called for. Consistency calls for a steady and suitable pace throughout the pattern, with no sudden accelerations or loss of impulsion. In addition to these criteria, horses are judged on their manners, alertness, and the quality of their gaits.

Although Western riding patterns are relatively easy for any well-broke horse to perform, doing them well is a different story. Judges take each maneuver into account, basing their scores on a starting mark of 70 points, and adding or subtracting up to 1½ points for each well or poorly done move. In addition, major errors like blatant disobedience or hitting the log result in up to 5 penalty points for each mistake.

WORKING COW HORSE

A working cow horse class is a kind of "ranch biathalon": two events that demonstrate first the potential for handling cattle and then actually managing one.

The first segment is known as the "dry work" and involves executing a pattern similar to those in reining classes: circles and figure eights at the lope with flying changes of lead, rundowns ending with rollbacks, and spins by themselves.

The second segment, "cow work," traces its origins to handling cattle out on the range and bringing them into a pen. It begins with the horse and rider "boxing" the cow, or holding the animal along the rail at the end of the arena long enough to demonstrate total control. Then the horse and rider let the cow down the fence, galloping after it along the side of the arena. Horse and rider next head off the cow and turn it first in one direction and then the other. The work ends with moving the cow to the center of the arena (where there's no railing to help) and again turning the cow in both directions.

Turning a cow in the center of the arena in a working cow horse class. (AQHA photo by Wyatt McSpadden)

Judges want to see tight work during the boxing part, the horse "hinging," or moving from side to side in anticipation of the cow's moves as in the cutting class. When the horse lets the cow down the arena, he should "rate," or speed up or slow down as necessary in order to stay with the cow. Staying in tight at the cow's shoulder is essential in turning the animal. The danger here, as well as in the work at the center of the arena, is losing the cow, or allowing it to escape from the horse's control. That's also known as the cow "taking" the horse, and it's nothing any rider or trainer—or any spectator, for that matter—wants to see happen.

Each horse has two minutes to work a cow, subject to the judges' calling time sooner when they're satisfied with the horse's performance. Scores range from 60 to 80, with 70 as average and 80 as the almost-impossible dream. Penalty deductions come from losing the cow, abusing the cow, and obvious and excessive cuing from the rider.

In addition to showing consummate "cow ability" at work, working cow horse classes demonstrate that the movements in reining and Western performance classes have their roots in actual ranch work. And the class is an exciting way for us to be reminded.

CALF ROPING

Many horsemen consider calf roping to be the truest test of an American Quarter Horse's ranch-work education. That's because of all the activities a cow horse does, roping requires the highest degree of partnership between a cowboy and his mount.

A quick dismount as the calf roping horse slides to a stop. (AQHA photo by Wyatt McSpadden)

Unlike rodeo calf roping, the fastest time does not determine the winner. Instead, horse show judges rate a horse's effectiveness and responsiveness in all four phases of a go-round.*

Judging begins as soon as the horse enters the roping box. The judges consider whether the animal walks in, turns, and stands quietly but alertly, ready

---

*One of the first things spectators notice in a calf roping class is the neck rope or foul rope around the horse's neck. The contestant's rope passes through it and goes back to the roper's hands (the other end of the contestant's rope is tied to the saddle horn). The purpose of the neck rope is to prevent an undisciplined horse from running off after the roper dismounts.

to gallop out at his rider's signal. Also rated highly is an eager and prepared attitude, but any show of jumpy nerves or outright reluctance loses points.

Once the calf is released, the horse should respond to his rider's cue by breaking smoothly out of the box without being distracted when the rider swings the rope loop over his head. The horse belongs directly behind the calf, just a few lengths off the animal's tail. Speeding up or slowing down to maintain this position is called "rating," an essential roping-horse skill, because the rider is focused on the calf and can't be bothered having to guide the horse.

Once the rider throws the loop over the calf's head and feeds out the slack, the horse should begin his sliding stop. Unlike reining classes, judges aren't looking for a spectacularly hard and fast halt, which would throw the rider off balance and make dismounting harder. Here, the stop should be quick but smooth, with the horse first dropping his hind end and then bracing his forelegs. A straight stop is also what judges want to see; ducking to either side will mean deductions from the score.

Once the rider is on the ground and running toward the calf, the horse should back up to keep tension on the rope until the roper throws the calf. How hard and how far to back depend on how hard the calf resists. As soon as the calf is thrown, the horse stops backing (continued backing would interfere with the roper's tying the calf's legs). Instead, the horse stands his ground until the roper remounts. At all times the horse should remain positioned facing straight toward the calf.

The horse's work during all parts of the run determines the score (the difficulty of the calf is also factored in). Marks range between 60 and 80, with 70 an average score. Although fast times are impressive, spectators must remember that it's the sum of the horse's skills that judges take into account.

DALLY TEAM ROPING

A roper and his or her horse may be able to rope and tie a calf by themselves, but when the animal grows up to be a steer, more than one horse and rider are needed. That's where dally* team roping comes in. It's another horse show class based on the demands of actual ranch work: two cowboys catching a steer and holding it to be branded, inoculated, or given some other form of attention.

---

*The word "dally" comes from the Spanish phrase *dar la vuelta,* meaning "to take a turn." As soon as header and heeler make their catch, each rider makes one turn of the rope in his hand around the saddle horn.

Unlike rodeo's team roping, where winners are determined by the fastest times, the horse show version takes only the athletic ability and "cow savvy" of the horses into account. Actually, team roping is two classes. In one, "heading," or roping the steer's head, is judged; in the other, only "heeling," or roping one or both hind legs, is scored. Even though two ropers take part, only the header or the heeler horse is scored. In either case, both the header and the heeler have one minute to rope and hold the steer, with time beginning when the steer leaves the starting box.

A dally team roping heeler makes his throw. (AQHA photo by Wyatt McSpadden)

From their positions on either side of the box, the two ropers pursue, swinging their loops above their heads. The header forges forward and throws his loop. The steer can be caught in three legal catches: by both horns, by one horn and the head (the "half head"), or around the neck. Once the steer has been caught, the header tightens the loop and turns the steer off to the left.

The heeler, who has been galloping behind the steer, then throws his loop in front of the steer's hind feet (one or both may be caught). When the steer steps in the loop, the heeler tightens the rope.

Meanwhile, with the heel horse acting like something of an anchor, the head horse is turned to face the steer, leaving it stretched out and immobilized.

The preceding description is a spectator's overview of a go-round. Judges, however, focus on the work of whichever horse is being scored, using technical criteria based on what a cowboy would want in an ideal roping horse.

When headers are being scored, the judges watch how a horse stands in the roping box. High marks go to a horse that breaks quickly and fluidly when the steer is released, preferably taking the left lead so he can turn the steer more easily to the left. The horse should hold a position just behind the steer's left hip, but never directly behind the animal. He should maintain that spot as the rider ropes the steer; any moves like ducking away lose points.

After the header has caught the steer and made a dally, the horse then "sets," or drops his rear end slightly to slow the steer and direct its path to the left. The horse then "quarters," or pivots on his left hind leg, raises out of the set, and leads the steer to the left. The purpose is to set up the steer's hind end so the heeler can do his job quickly and smoothly. It's important for the horse to maintain a fluid movement; lunges or sudden bursts of speed that upset rhythm and timing mean a lower score.

A good heel horse needs the same speed and agility. He begins by coming out of the roping box smoothly, holding a position just off the steer's right flank. Once the header ropes the steer and turns it left, the heel horse's position shifts to off the animal's left hip until the rider ropes the steer's hind legs.

Then the horse makes a quick, solid stop and holds his ground without backing. Holding still and level is crucial, especially while the rider is making his dally; any shift of the saddle horn may cause the roper to miss the turn (and injure a hand in the process). Maintaining that halt, even if the head horse and the steer pull hard, is a way to score big.

As in calf roping, horses are scored between 60 and 80, with 70 counting as average work.

As a display of partnership between horses as well as riders, dally team roping is always a very popular horse show event.

TEAM PENNING

Watch a team penning class, and you'll quickly see why this sport has become Western horse showing's fastest-growing event. It combines ranch-work skills with teamwork, all done in nonstop overdrive.

A signal to the judges ends a successful team penning run-round. (AQHA photo by Wyatt McSpadden)

Each team consists of three riders. Their object is to separate three cows (or calves or steers) from a herd that's held at one end of the arena, then move the trio up the arena and put them in a pen. But life becomes more complicated when one, two, or even all three decide to run back to the herd or a few other cows decide to join them.

Between twenty-one and forty-two cows normally constitute a team penning herd. Numbers painted on their backs are in sets of threes (three cows will wear number 1, another three will wear number 2, and so forth). Prior to the event, all the teams draw numbers that correspond to the numbers on the cows. When a team's turn is called, the three riders enter the arena's far end. The announcer calls out their number as they make their way down to where the herd holders have settled the cattle into a tight bunch. Then, as the herd holders leave the arena, the fun begins.

Each team member has an assigned job. One will cut the designated cows, moving them up to the "turnback" man or woman who works them up the arena. A "hole" rider will keep them from escaping down the narrow gap between the pen and the arena side. But these assignments are not hard and fast: A cutter may see that one of the cows has ducked back and needs to be headed off, while a hole rider may have to leave his or her position to help out.

Since everyone needs to know where the rest of the team is, riders constantly call out orders and requests.

Each team has a maximum of two minutes to pen its cows, with the fastest times determining the winners. A team that pens all three will place higher than one that pens only two, and two will beat one. However, if at any time five or more cattle are across the starting line, the team will be judged "no time."

How well teams do depends on their horses' and their own abilities to make lightning-fast decisions. And there's also the luck of the draw when it comes to the cattle they've pulled.

WESTERN HORSEMANSHIP

Except for showmanship classes, in all the classes with which we've been concerned to this point only the horse is judged. But because riders need just as solid a basic education as horses do, AQHA amateur and youth divisions feature horsemanship classes that spotlight a stock-seat rider's form and control.

Every aspect of correct position* is designed to maintain balance and to exercise control over the horse, and with the least amount of effort.

The lower body provides a base of support for the entire body. The ball of the foot rests in the stirrup at the foot's widest part, with weight in the heel and with the toes turned out at the same angle at which the rider stands or walks. The lower legs hang straight down from the knees, only slightly away from the horse when viewed from the front and in a position to apply calf pressure.

The rider's thighs rest against the saddle with a firm, but not forced, contact, pointed more in a downward than a forward manner. The seat is in the center of the saddle, the hips tilted slightly forward so that the rider's weight is on the front of seatbones (sitting in a chair-like position with weight on the tailbone is incorrect).

The rider's back should be straight, neither slouched nor ramrod-stiff. Similarly, the shoulders are not braced rigidly; they are held square, with neither one ahead of the other.

The head is erect and straight, eyes looking in the direction where the rider wishes the horse to go.

---

*Even though this book isn't a how-to-ride manual, the following brief discussion of what Western horsemanship (and further in this chapter, what hunt seat equitation) judges look for can help readers analyze their own position in the saddle.

The rider's upper arms, from shoulder to elbow, fall naturally against the sides of the body, hanging straight down as if pointing to the hips. The forearm of the hand that holds the reins is carried parallel to the ground, creating a straight line from the elbow to the horse's mouth. The other arm takes the same angle as the upper body and thigh.

Western horsemanship allows a choice of ways to carry the reins and in which hand they may be held, although as a practical matter the vast majority of exhibitors use the split rein style and their left hand. In the split rein technique, both reins are held flat across the palm of the left hand from the index to the little finger, with one finger separating the reins if the rider wishes. The ends of both reins hang down the horse's left side. (The alternative, the romal rein style, requires the reins to be clenched in the left hand, the knuckles facing the horse's head and the reins running up the fist from the little finger out over the thumb. The rest of the reins below the romal is gripped in the right hand, which rests on the rider's thigh.)

Whichever style the rider chooses, the hand that holds the reins is carried above or just in front of the saddle horn in a light, relaxed fashion.

A Western horsemanship class starts with each rider performing a thirty-second pattern that the judge posts before the

Good form for Western riding, with the rider's free arm in the same vertical line as her back and her leg. (The Quarter Horse Journal)

event. Geared to the level of ability of the riders in that particular class, the test may call for straight lines and circles at the jog and lope, backing, side passes, turns on the forehand and haunches, simple or flying changes of lead, spins and rollbacks, and other combinations of movements. Some tests even have the riders dismount and remount.

Judges look for a natural and functional ride. Such faults as looking down, wrapping legs around the horse's sides, flapping elbows, or sliding around in the saddle will be marked down. So will letting the horse lope on the incorrect lead or breaking to the walk when a jog-trot is called for.

The total picture, a catchall expression that includes how well horse and rider fit each other, is taken into account. So is the appropriateness of the rider's apparel (Western boots, chaps, shirt and tie, and hat) and the horse's tack.

High scores in this portion qualify a certain number of riders to take part in the rail work phase. As a group they work both ways of the arena at the walk, jog, and lope. Judges look for correct equitation position, as well as whether the horses are being ridden at rhythmic, cadenced gaits. Especially important are smooth and accurate transitions between gaits.

Following the rail work, the riders line up in the center of the arena. At the judges' discretion, some or all of them may be asked to back their horses. In the event there's still not a clearcut winner, two or more riders may be called back to the rail for further work.

The purpose of horsemanship classes is not to present a beauty contest to acknowledge the prettiest rider on a "push-button" horse. Instead, top ribbons go to riders who demonstrate a clear understanding of correct fundamentals and can put them into practice.

CUTTING

Horses are herd animals, but cattle may be even more so, since they spend their lives in groups even more than horses now do. Cows suffer from acute separation anxiety and will do just about anything to get back to the herd.

The job of the cutting horse is to frustrate this bovine instinct by preventing a cow that he's separated from the herd from returning to the group. What's more, the horse does it with no assistance from his rider.

At the very beginning of a cutting class, a group of cattle is herded to one end of the arena and allowed to settle, or become accustomed to their surroundings. Then the first of the contestants (the riders are known as cutters) enters the ring. With the cutter are four assistants: two herd holders who keep the cattle under control while the cutter is working; and two turnback riders who keep the cow that's being worked from escaping to the far end of the arena.

A face-to-face confrontation in a cutting horse class. (AQHA photo by Wyatt McSpadden)

Each work lasts two and a half minutes. At the sound of the buzzer, the cutter walks his horse into the herd. With the help of the herd holders, he moves a number of cows out from the end of the arena. Focusing on the specific cow he wants to work, the cutter lets the others slip past him until only the one he chose remains apart. Then the cutter drops his reins and lets the horse take over.

Dropping his head and front end until he's eye-to-eye with the cow, the horse stays active and balanced on his hocks. The cow pauses momentarily until its herd instinct takes over, and it tries to swerve around the horse. Ideally, the horse moves in that direction and blocks the way, so the cow tries the other side, only to find the horse there, too.

This battle of instinct and wiles continues, with the horse anticipating the cow's every move, then blocking the cow with maneuvers worthy of an all-star basketball defender or football linebacker. All the while the cutter sits with one hand on the dangling reins and the other braced against the saddle horn, a spectator enjoying the performance from what's been called "the best seat in the house" (although a subtle and judicious use of the rider's seat and legs can help guide the horse).

If and when the cow reaches the frustration point and stops trying to get back to the herd, the cutter has the option of "quitting" the animal and, time permitting, going back to cut and work a second and even a third cow.

Scoring is based on how well the horse works the cow. Each contestant begins with 70 points, and the judges add or deduct points as the work progresses. They look for good herd work with a smooth cut made on a loose rein, then a balanced and athletic horse with nimble moves, quick stops, and the overall ability to control a tough cow. They also reward horses that look interested in outthinking and outmaneuvering a cow, and they reward cutters who select tough cows that make a real contest out of the face-off.

What makes a good cutting horse? Physically, it's speed and agility. Perhaps even more valuable than physical attributes are the eagerness and mental ability to take on and defeat bovines. This "cow sense"—or just plain "cow"— really can't be taught. It's bred in the bone and has been cultivated through selective breeding for generations. In other words, it's the reason why the American Quarter Horse makes the world's best cutting horse.

BARREL RACING

Few events show off the American Quarter Horse's brilliant speed and agility better than barrel racing. Once a sport associated with young girls, it is now widely popular with female and male riders of all ages.

The course consists of three barrels set in a triangular pattern. The two that form the base are twenty yards from the start/finish line. In a full-size course, the barrel farthest from the line is placed thirty-five yards from the other two.

Riders can choose how they run the cloverleaf pattern. The more popular option is to begin with a right-hand circle around the barrel on their right, then cut across the arena to make a left-hand loop around the next barrel. They continue up to make a left-hand circle around the barrel at the far end, then finish with a flat-out dash down across the finish line.

The alternative, often depending on the horse's preference for leads, lets the rider start with a left-hand circle around the left-hand barrel, then completes a mirror image of the route described above.

Not every fast American Quarter Horse makes a successful barrel horse. Although blazing from one barrel to the next or up and down the arena is certainly crucial, agility and balance may be even more important. Horses that cannot make tight turns or change directions and leads not only lose valuable time, they are likely to knock down the barrel they are trying to circle. And with a five-second penalty for each downed barrel added to the actual time, even one knockdown makes a big difference in the score—and the final standings.

An American Quarter Horse carving tight turns around barrels, leaning over so far that the rider's boot practically scrapes the arena dirt, gives new and eye-opening meaning to the words "handy" and "balanced."

POLE BENDING

Pole bending might be considered "in-line barrel racing." In another sense, however, the event requires a different kind of maneuverability. Instead of three 360-degree turns and unobstructed galloping, pole bending calls for running to the end of six poles set twenty-one feet apart, rounding the last

The tighter the turn, the faster the time in barrel racing. (AQHA photo by Wyatt McSpadden)

pole and slaloming back between the others, then circling the pole closest to the start/finish line, slaloming back down the line again, rounding the last pole, and galloping across to the finish line. The fastest times determine the order of finish, with any pole that's knocked over counting as five penalty seconds.

Although the best horses at this event can run down and lean into the first turn like barrel racers, the similarity ends there. A good pole bending horse must make a tight turn, pivot around the pole, and then start the slalom move. Riders help less with rein cues than by using their legs to keep their horses close to the poles without knocking any over; in other words, keeping their mounts

Making the first turn in a pole bending class. (AQHA photo by Wyatt McSpadden)

on as straight a line as they can. For their part, horses swap leads with each change of direction so they're literally certain to have a leg to stand on.

English Classes

HUNTERS

The English-style riding featured at AQHA shows is known as hunt seat, a name derived from the sport of foxhunting. It's based on riding to hounds, which often involves galloping across country for miles at a stretch and negotiating whatever rugged terrain and unyielding obstacles riders encounter while following a pack of foxhounds.

Hunter classes at horse shows originally incorporated such conditions much more closely than they now do. Now, instead of outside courses composed of drop fences, water jumps, and stone walls, arena courses consist of an assortment of post-and-rails,* brush-topped boxes, coops, rolltops, gates, panels, and blocks of wood that simulate stone walls.

---

*The rails (which is what the cross-bar poles are called) rest in cups so they can come down easily in the event a horse's hoof hits them.

Judges look for a long fluid trot in a hunter under saddle class. (AQHA photo by Wyatt McSpadden)

Some fences are verticals, or narrow obstacles, while others are called oxers, which are spread fences that test the horse's form over width. Heights at AQHA shows range from 2 feet 9 inches to 3 feet 9 inches, depending on the class specifications, the rider's level, and/or the horse's age.

Distances between fences are set at multiples of a show hunter's twelve-foot galloping stride. A forty-eight-foot distance, for example, translates into three strides: the three galloping strides, plus the six feet it took to land off the preceding fence and another six for the takeoff at the next jump.

Where the fences are placed is equally accommodating. Horses must make a minimum of eight jumps taken in a combination of outside lines along the arena rail and diagonal lines across the ring. There may be an in-and-out, the term for two fences set one stride apart (based historically on a hunter's ability to jump a fence or hedge out of one field, take one stride across a country road, and jump back again into a second field).

In working hunter classes, only the horses are judged. They are scored according to how well they duplicate the style and grace that a hunter going across country should have. Judges look for a long, low, ground-covering, and comfortable pace between fences. Most important is that the horse jump in an athletic, balanced, and safe form, with a rounded back, forelegs that are evenly folded, and hind legs well tucked under him.

Taking off too far back from a fence can be dangerous. So can leaving the ground too close to it. That's why two heavily penalized errors are "leaving long" and "chipping in," the latter referring to adding an extra half stride in front of an obstacle. Experienced hunter riders develop what is known as an "eye for distances," the ability to regulate a horse's stride to arrive at an optimum takeoff spot at each fence, neither too far away nor too close to the jump.*

Other major faults include refusals, run-outs, hitting or dislodging a fence, being on the wrong lead (as well as failing to do flying changes of lead when changing directions), and breaking to the trot.

A hunter under saddle class (familiarly known as a "hack") focuses on a hunter's way of going at the three basic gaits. Judges look for long, low, ground-covering, comfortable, and athletic strides, exactly what you'd want in a horse that would carry you in the hunting field. The walk should be a rhythmic four-beat gait. The trot should be low and straight from the shoulder in a flicking "daisy-cutting" style. The ideal canter has a relatively slow pace and long, low, and fluid strides at a regular three-beat cadence. Some judges want to see hand galloping: an extended and faster canter, but always at a controlled pace.

Good manners also are taken into account. The horse's head is minimally restricted: The rules call for light rein contact and no martingales.

The hunter hack class combines "over fences" and "under saddle." Horses are judged on how well they jump two low fences set from 2 feet to 2 feet 9 inches and then how well they move at the walk, trot, and canter while working on the rail.

Because the foxhunting tradition from which these classes evolved is based on centuries-old traditions, hunters wear conservative tack: unadorned bridles with snaffle or Pelham bits and close-contact or forward-seat saddles over plain white saddle pads. Manes and tails are traditionally braided. The riders' apparel is equally conservative: black, navy, or dark green coats over tan or light gray breeches and high black or brown boots. Men wear ties, women wear choker-collar shirts, and everyone wears a velvet-covered hunt cap with a safety harness.

---

*Human high jumpers develop the same skill at regulating their own stride to hit their takeoff point.

JUMPERS

Unlike the hunter division, jumper classes call for no subjective opinions on the part of the judges. They are scored objectively, by the number of faults, or penalties, incurred around the course. Nor is the horse's style or rider's form taken into account. All that matters is whether the fences stay up and whether horse and rider finish the course within the time limit.

Successfully negotiating a jumper course calls for an athletic, well-trained horse. Fences, which are set from 3 feet 6 inches to 4 feet high in the first go-round, are varieties of verticals and oxers, as well as walls. Unlike the subdued and plain colors of hunter fences, they are often made of brightly colored rails and panels, the latter often bearing the names and logos of AQHA and horse show sponsors.

A jumping class's oxer fence tests a horse's ability to jump width. (AQHA photo by Wyatt McSpadden)

Designers of jumper courses place the obstacles around the arena individually or as combinations of two or three fences set with up to three strides between the elements. An innovative designer can place fences in such a way that their relative location creates as many problems as their height or width.

Anything that measures other than multiples of the normal twelve-foot gal-loping stride means that a rider has to decide whether to lengthen or shorten the horse's stride to get to the optimum takeoff spot.

Although horses do not see the course until they enter the ring for their rounds, riders may walk the course in advance of the class. They stride from fence to fence, memorizing the route and converting their own steps into horse strides (four human three-foot steps equals one equine twelve-foot stride).

The way a jumper class is scored makes it easy for spectators to follow along. Each knockdown (the term for hitting an obstacle and knocking part of it down) counts as four faults. A refusal, in which the horse evades the fence by ducking out to one side or by flatly refusing to attempt to jump, counts as three faults for the first disobedience, an additional six faults for a second stop at the same or a subsequent obstacle, and elimination in the event of a third.

In addition, time faults are given for exceeding the time allowed, within which the horse and rider must complete the course. Going off course or the fall of horse or rider is grounds for elimination.

A round in which horse and rider incur no faults is called a clear, or a clean, round. In the event that two or more horses finish with the lowest score, a second round takes place. Called the "jump-off," it adds the element of speed. Competitors go in their original order over a shortened, usually twistier course. The fastest times determine the final placings in the event of another equality of faults.

Because controlling speed and direction is crucial, jumpers are shown in a variety of bits (including no bit at all—hackamores are not unknown in this division), and they often wear standing or running martingales. As for rider apparel, the same tall boots, breeches, conservative coats, ties, and hunt caps found in hunter classes are customary here, too.

American Quarter Horses have proved themselves to be successful show jumpers at the highest levels of competition. For example, one named Threes and Sevens won several major Grand Prixes and took part in the prestigious international Volvo World Cup series in the early 1990s.

HUNT SEAT EQUITATION ON THE FLAT

Like Western horsemanship, hunt seat equitation classes call for a demon-stration of rider form and control, but here it's the skills necessary to train and show a hunter (and, by implication, jumper) on the flat and over fences.

Proper hunt seat form begins with the rider's base of support. The ball of the foot rests in the stirrup with the heel down and toe out at a forty-five-degree angle. The lower leg rests against the horse's side just behind the girth. The rider sits toward the front of the saddle, with most of the weight resting on the front of the seatbones.

The upper body belongs at or slightly ahead of the vertical, depending at which gait the horse is moving. The rider's back should be flat, but not rigid. Elbows belong close to the sides, with the forearms angled to form a straight line between elbows and the horse's mouth. Hands are carried with the knuckles at a thirty-degree angle inside the vertical. The head is held erect, eyes looking in the direction the rider wishes the horse to go.

In addition to form, judges look for the effectiveness that equitation tests and courses ask for.

The class begins with each rider performing the same predetermined pattern. All patterns include the trot and canter; depending on the level of the rider's abilities, the pattern may

English riding form and control are judged in a hunt seat equitation class. (AQHA photo by Wyatt McSpaddcn)

also include circles, figure eights, halts, backing, and a hand gallop, along with more advanced maneuvers. In the event the judges wish to see more after this first phase, further testing is used to rank the riders. Any equitation errors, such as lower legs that slip back, elbows that flap, or seats that "dig" to make the horse move ahead, are marked down. Incorrect diagonals at the trot or wrong leads at the canter are more obvious and highly penalized errors.

Inclining the upper body keeps a hunt seat rider in balance with her horse's center of gravity at the extended canter. (AQHA photo by Wyatt McSpadden)

EQUITATION OVER FENCES

In "over fences," or jumping, classes, each rider negotiates a course of a minimum of six hunter-style fences set a height of either 2 feet 9 inches or 3 feet. Courses are built in the same patterns as in hunter classes.

Judges consider the horse's performance only with regard to how the animal responds to the rider's influence. Instead, they focus on the rider's position, especially during the approach to each fence, the jump itself, and after landing. Form during the approach is based on the half seat (or "two-point") position at the canter: The lower legs support the body (the buttocks are out of the saddle), while the upper body is inclined slightly ahead of the vertical. The horse's hind-end thrust during the takeoff closes the rider's hip angle, and the rider's hands slide forward to release the horse's head and neck. In the air, the rider remains in balance over the horse's center of gravity. The impact of landing is absorbed by the rider's ankles and knees, with the upper body coming back toward vertical and the hands continuing to maintain contact with the horse's mouth as horse and rider move on to the next fence.

High scores in over fences classes go to fluid, well-executed rounds in which the rider remains in balance with the horse throughout the course. Being left behind (thrown back in the air) or letting the horse "chip" by adding an extra half stride in front of a fence is unlikely to win a top prize. Nor will allowing the horse to be on the incorrect lead or break to the trot. Other major faults include letting a horse refuse or run out at a fence (three refusals are cause for elimination), losing a stirrup, and dropping the reins. Less obvious equitation errors are lower legs that slip back in the air, and hands that catch the horse's mouth.

As with Western horsemanship classes, hunt seat equitation and equitation over fences are the proving ground where riders in the youth and amateur divisions demonstrate mastery of the basics. It's no wonder than the most successful adult and professional hunter and jumper riders from local shows all the way to the Olympics started out winning top ribbons in these classes.

PLEASURE DRIVING

Pleasure driving classes hark back to an earlier era in which Americans measured their transportation in the original sense of horsepower: The family horse was hitched to a buggy or buckboard and then driven to church, on a neighborly visit, or on a shopping trip to town.

Buggies and buckboards have given way to the showring's two-wheeled cart. The horses that pull them perform at three gaits: a flat-footed but smooth and lively walk; a stylishly elegant medium trot known as the park gait; and an extended and more animated trot called the road gait. After working at these gaits in both directions, the horses are lined up in the center of the arena and individually asked to back several steps. Then they line up again and stand until the class is pinned.

Similar to the way pleasure classes under saddle are scored, judges reward those horses that give the overall impression of doing their job with effortless enjoyment. Pleasure driving horses should be good movers, balanced and symmetrical at all three gaits. They need to carry themselves in an appropriate manner to the American Quarter Horse breed, not with the arched necks or high-stepping trot of Saddlebreds, Hackney Ponies, or other breeds associated with fine harness driving.

Speed should not be a factor. In fact, extreme speed is penalized. So are bad manners and, on the part of the driver, dangerous driving. The important criterion is elegance in motion, which also is reflected in properly fitted harness and the formal attire of the drivers.

A pleasure driving class winner displays a World Championship garland. (AQHA photo by Wyatt McSpadden)

In addition to classes held at AQHA-sanctioned horse shows, American Quarter Horses can be found competing at other English-style events.

DRESSAGE

Dressage is a French word that is often translated as "training." It means much more than that, however. Dressage is a system of progressively improving a horse's responsiveness and athletic ability.

Dressage is similar to Western reining classes in that all the horse-and-rider teams execute the same test composed of series of movements. The arena in which the tests are performed is marked by letters around its perimeter, in addition to which is an imaginary "X" that indicates the center of the arena. Tests are written in terms of these letters: For example, "FXH—working trot, rising" calls for the rider posting at a working trot that moves off the track at the "F" marker, passes through the arena's midpoint, and rejoins the track at "H".

Dressage tests at the lower levels require no more than what any well-trained horse should be able to do: halt, walk, trot, and canter. Unlike more informal riding, however, dressage riders work at achieving correctness, or regularity, of their horses' gaits: a square halt, a four-beat walk, a two-beat trot, and a three-beat canter. Other goals are straightness, smooth bends around corners, round circles, and impulsion at all three gaits.

The letters around a dressage arena indicate where transitions between gaits and changes of direction should be made. (The Quarter Horse Journal)

Tests at higher levels add collection and extensions, half passes and other leg-yielding movements, flying changes of lead, and pirouettes. The most advanced tests contain two examples of highly collected trot: the passage (pronounced "puh-SAHZ"), where the horse appears to float across the arena; and the piaffe ("pee-AFF"), which is a trot in place.

Each movement and transition of the test is scored from 0 (not performed) to a rarely awarded 10 for excellent. Judges give high marks for accurate and prompt transitions at the designated markers. They also consider the horse's degree of impulsion and the rider's position and application of the aids.

Until several decades ago, most American horsemen viewed dressage as something alien and artificial. That attitude changed when we saw how such systematic education is not very different from the way good horsemen of all disciplines school their horses. A particularly impressive example happened at an exhibition at the prestigious Dressage At Devon (Pennsylvania) show: Horses ridden by a dressage rider and a Western American Quarter Horse trainer performed a *pas de deux* that incorporated many classical dressage movements. At the conclusion, the riders swapped horses and, to the spectators' applause and delight, they repeated the test on each other's mounts.

COMBINED TRAINING

Combined training, popularly known as eventing, developed from a cavalry officer's need for a well-schooled and versatile horse. One day the soldier might take part in a parade or other ceremonial occasion, where he needed a calm and obedient animal underneath him. On the following day, when he might be ordered to deliver a dispatch across rugged terrain where there were huge solid obstacles to be jumped, his horse needed to be fit and bold in order to gallop at speed for many miles. A battle might take place on the next day, where the cavalryman's very life depended on the energy and responsiveness his horse held in reserve after the demands of the previous day.

These military requirements translate into the three phases of combined training. The competition* begins with a dressage test appropriate to the level of the horse's amount of training. Then comes the speed and endurance phase, the very heart of combined training. At the higher levels, the day begins with a few miles of warm-up called roads-and-tracks, which is followed by a gallop over steeplechase brush fences. After another roads-and-tracks comes the cross-country: up to four miles over unyielding obstacles—piles of logs, fences made of timber or stone, embankments, ditches, and knee-deep ponds (to be jumped into and galloped through.) Penalty points are given for refusals, falls, and exceeding the time allowed.

Eventers are quick to point out that every effort is made to safeguard the horses' welfare. Cross-country obstacles usually have alternatives to the most direct (and most demanding) lines. Then, too, compulsory veterinary checks before and during the speed and endurance phase and the following morning ensure that any horse deemed unfit to continue is eliminated from the rest of the event.

The final phase, stadium jumping, presents a course of show jumping fences that makes the horses show whether they still have "enough gas left in

---

*The competition is called a "horse trial" if it takes place over one or two days; if longer, it's a three-day event.

A variety of unyielding obstacles awaits horses and riders in combined training's cross-country phase. (*The Quarter Horse Journal*)

the tank" after the cross-country. Knockdowns, refusals, and time faults are taken into account. Stadium jumping scores are added to dressage scores and any cross-country penalties to determine the overall winners.

Combined training's popularity is due in large part to appreciation for the variety the sport offers. And although other breeds are more closely associated with eventing, an American Quarter Horse gelding nicknamed Giltedge carried David O'Connor to an Olympic team silver medal at the 1996 Atlanta Games.

FOR FURTHER INFORMATION

Winning with the American Quarter Horse, written by Don Burt, a leading judge and commentator (and former AQHA President), published by Doubleday, 1996, analyzes all the AQHA-recognized divisions and classes from a judge's perspective.

The booklet *Your First American Quarter Horse Show,* available free of charge from AQHA, contains basic information about preparing for and taking part in competitions.

Another booklet, *Competitive Horse Judging,* was designed as a guide to develop a successful horse judging team. In addition to an explanation of the criteria for each horse show division, the booklet suggests language with which a judge can explain his or her placings.

A set of casebooks published by AQHA is intended to complement the *AQHA Official Handbook* with regard to scoring individual runs and rounds, the criteria for awarding points for superior work and subtracting points for faults, and detailing legal (and prohibited) equipment. As of this writing, casebooks are available for roping (heading, heeling and calf roping); working hunters; hunt seat equitation; equitation over fences; showmanship at halter; and Western horsemanship.

AQHA offers the following videos on the subject of competition:

Best Seat in the House (Cutting). Matlock Rose and Tom Lyons, two respected cutting horse trainers, explain basic training techniques for cutting horses. Lyons focuses on training two- and three-year-olds, while Rose discusses attributes of a cutting horse and the philosophy of the event. Scenes of outstanding cutting horses are included. Suitable for beginners and experienced horse enthusiasts. 28 minutes.

The Reining Horse. Experienced judges and trainers Bob Loomis and Bobby Ingersoll discuss reining, the foundation for any performance competition. Each discusses his philosophy of a good reining horse. Loomis focuses on basic training while Ingersoll notes differences between East and West Coast styles of reining and explains snaffle bit, hackamore, and bit reining. Also available in Spanish. 25 minutes.

Team Roping. Ropers at all levels appreciate these pointers on the selection of ropes, techniques, and timing in team roping competition. Training and selection of team roping horses and AQHA rules governing the event are discussed by AQHA judges Sonny Jim Orr and Billy Allen. Also available in Spanish. 23 minutes.

Working Cow Horse. Bobby Ingersoll, Don Dodge, and Al Dunning share their expertise on the working cow horse class. Dodge talks of the working cow horse's origin, while Ingersoll and Dunning explain and demonstrate basic training techniques for a prospective working cow horse. Several reining and cow-work performances are analyzed. Also available in Spanish. 25 minutes.

Western Horsemanship. Noted instructor Andy Moorman gives valuable pointers on proper Western horsemanship. Included is a series of exercises designed to build confidence in both horse and rider. Critiques of actual classes follow. This is an excellent film for youth and amateur competitors. 28 minutes.

Showmanship: The Basics. Pete and Tamra Kyle cover grooming and preparation of the horse and exhibitor for showmanship competition. Additionally, many dos and don'ts regarding class rules and routines are covered. 28 minutes.

Team Penning. AQHA-sanctioned team penning is a race against the clock to separate designated cattle from a herd and drive them into a holding pen. Al Dunning explains the basics of team penning, from arena and officials' setup to successful strategies for teamwork and winning runs. Examples of good and bad runs help illustrate right and wrong moves commonly made in the event. Dunning discusses proper team penning equipment and also outlines the qualities of a good team penning horse. 40 minutes.

Hunt Seat Equitation. AQHA judge Don Burt explains fundamentals of the event as well as maneuvers that adequately determine a contestant's riding ability. The desired position of the rider's body, hands, and legs is discussed, as well as attire and methods of performing specified maneuvers. 28 minutes.

In the English Tradition, Part I. The traditions of English riding are covered, with special emphasis on the hunter under saddle class. Traditions associated with English tack and apparel, plus selection of a horse to perform on the flat and what is expected of such horses, are discussed by judge Don Burt. Informative for beginners and experienced horsemen. Can be shown with or without Part II. 23 minutes.

In the English Tradition, Part II. Basic training techniques for a horse learning to jump fences (cavalettis) are covered. Don Burt explains class routine and gives pointers on showing and judging horses in hunter hack, working hunter, and jumping. Can be shown with or without Part I. 17 minutes.

Pleasure Driving. Tack and class procedures are discussed, and detailed demonstrations are critiqued by judge Don Burt. 10 minutes.

Horse Judging, Part I. This tape is designed to aid the formation of a horse judging team on a competitive level. Part I features halter and reining competition, with each class composed of four horses. Audiences have the opportunity to judge each class prior to the announcement of official placings. Explanations for the placings are then given by AQHA judge Jim Heird. One set of oral reasons follows each class. 46 minutes.

Horse Judging, Part II. Featuring the same format as *Horse Judging, Part I,* Part II includes Western pleasure and hunter under saddle competitions. 55 minutes.

Horse Judging, Part III. Featuring the same format as *Horse Judging, Part I,* Part III includes trail and Western riding classes discussed by AQHA judge Holly Hover of Parker, Colorado. 45 minutes.

Horse Judging, Part IV. Part IV features halter and reining competitions, with each class composed of four horses. Audiences have the opportunity to judge each class prior to the announcement of official placings. Explanations for the placings are then given by AQHA judge Don Topliff. One set of oral reasons follows each class. 46 minutes.

Judging Roping. This tape details judging of AQHA's approved roping events: dally team roping and heading, dally team roping and heeling, and calf roping. It includes criteria for each class, two actual classes with four horses each to judge, and an explanation of official placings. Pauses are implemented so the tape can be easily stopped for discussion. 33 minutes.

Judging Reining. A brief introduction to judging one of AQHA's most exciting events. Like the other judging tapes, this one includes two classes to judge plus official placings and explanations. 44 minutes.

Judging Working Hunter. Narrated by AQHA judge Don Burt, the presence and beauty of a good working hunter horse are presented. Viewers judge two classes and receive an explanation of the official placings. 30 minutes.

Selecting and Showing Western Pleasure Horses. The basic requirements of the Western pleasure horse, including the walk, jog, and lope, quietness, and ease of travel are featured. Trainers and judges Alex Ross and Mike Moser provide comments on several pleasure horses. An introduction to AQHA's most popular event. 55 minutes.

Reining Basics. World Champion trainer Craig Johnson discusses reining, the foundation for any performance competition and the keystone for general riding. He demonstrates individual and combined use of four types of communication cues to the horse by his rider: bridle and rein cues, leg cues, body cues, and voice or sound cues. 55 minutes.

Dally Team Roping. The more advanced team roper will appreciate AQHA and Professional Rodeo Cowboys Association (PRCA) World Champion John Miller's pointers on improving techniques and skill as a team roper. 28 minutes.

Training the Championship Trail Horse. Ken Garrett of Cave Creek, Arizona, discusses basic and advanced training methods for trail competition and illustrates the attributes of a good trail horse. He introduces various obstacles and ways to alter them to eliminate anticipation from the horse. 43 minutes.

Western Riding, a Competitive Edge. Noted trainer and exhibitor Pete Kyle explains basic techniques for success in the Western riding event. The riding pattern, scoring, and quality and preciseness of lead changes are demonstrated. 25 minutes.

Equitation Over Fences. Andy Moorman and Don Burt provide instruction for the equitation over fences class added to the youth and amateur divisions in 1993. The video outlines class procedures, critiques rounds, and provides classes for viewers to judge. 70 minutes.

Selecting and Showing Hunter Under Saddle Horses. Carla Wennberg and Leslie Lange show you what to look for in a hunter under saddle horse and how the event is judged. 48 minutes.

The following organizations offer information about their specific activities:

American Driving Society
P.O. Box 160
Metamora, MI 48455-0160
Phone: (810) 664-8666; fax: (810) 664-2405

American Horse Shows Association
220 E. 42 St.
New York, NY 10017-5876
Phone: (212) 972-2472; fax: (212) 983-7286

Intercollegiate Horse Show Association
P.O. Box 741
Stony Brook, NY 11790-0741
Phone: (516) 751-2803; fax: (516) 751-1157

National Barrel Horse Association
P.O. Box 1988
Augusta, GA 30901-1988
Phone: (706) 722-RACE; fax: (706) 722-9575

National Cutting Horse Association
4704 Hwy. 377 S.
Fort Worth, TX 76116-8805
Phone: (817) 244-6188; fax: (817) 244-2015

National Reining Horse Association
3000 N.W. 10 St.
Oklahoma City, OK 73107-5302
Phone: (405) 946-7400; fax: (405) 946-8410

National Snaffle Bit Association
1 Indiana Sq., #2540
Indianapolis, IN 46204-2014
Phone: (317) 632-6722; fax: (317) 637-9755

U.S. Team Penning Association
P.O. Box 161848
Fort Worth, TX 76161-1848
Phone: (800) 848-3882; fax: (817) 232-4771

United States Combined Training Association
525 Old Waterford Rd. NW
Leesburg, VA 20176
Phone: (703) 779-0440; fax: (703) 779-0550

United States Dressage Federation
P.O. Box 6669
Lincoln, NE 68506-0669
Phone: (402) 434-8550; fax: (402) 434-8570

American Quarter Horse Racing

In the year 1611, seventeen native English stallions and mares were imported to Virginia. Shortly after those first horses reached these shores, Governor Nicholson legalized horse racing, a sport that attained great popularity almost the moment the horses that made it possible arrived in America.

The blood of those English horses was crossed with horses of Spanish ancestry (primarily the Barb) to produce a compact and heavily muscled horse that could run short distances at incredible speeds. Colonists referred to these horses as Quarter Pathers (Pacers) or by the impressive title of "the Illustrious Colonial Quarter of a Mile Running Horse." These animals were the forerunners of today's American Quarter Horses.

By the beginning of the Revolutionary War, the colonists had grown very attached to Quarter Horse racing. The usual format was a match race between two horses running no more than a quarter of a mile. Such short sprints were particularly popular because they could be run down village streets or any suitably sized clearing.* In fact, any thoroughfare or unplanted field could serve as a racetrack, which may account for the dirt running surface that evolved in this country. This kind of sprint racing in the early colonies was the earliest-known example of American Quarter Horse racing in the United States.

The first recorded American Quarter Horse races were held at Enrico County, Virginia, in 1674. Reports show that large purses were offered by the end of that century, with large plantations often risked and won and lost on the outcome of one of those contests.

This type of racing continued to grow in popularity as the breed grew and as pioneers and early settlers moved into the Midwest, Southwest, and Western areas of the present United States. However, the sport remained on the informal basis of match races and weekend affairs at hundreds of small tracks that sprang up during the nineteenth century's westward expansion period.

Organized American Quarter Horse racing got its start in Tucson, Arizona, at a track called Hacienda Moltacqua. At that time, Hacienda Moltacqua boasted a card of races that included not only American Quarter Horses but Thoroughbreds, Standardbred trotters, and even steeplechasers. However, American Quarter Horse racing there soon outgrew its stage-sharing position with the other breeds. Popularity increased, and in 1943 a new racetrack in Tucson called Rillito Park was designed and built especially for American Quarter Horse racing.

Today, American Quarter Horse racing is conducted at more than 110 racetracks throughout North America, with total purses reaching some $50 million. The dream of many owners, trainers, and jockeys in American Quar-

---

*Longer races of a mile or more, for which the English Thoroughbred was bred, required far more cleared land, and that was always at a premium in colonial America.

ter Horse racing is to win the All American Futurity run each year on Labor Day at Ruidoso Downs in New Mexico.

In most respects, American Quarter Horse racing today is vastly different from the match races down village streets of colonial Virginia. Even the horse himself has changed: Today's American Quarter Horse is faster than ever, having been clocked at speeds in excess of fifty miles per hour to earn the reputation as "America's Fastest Athlete."

*The most famous American Quarter Horse race is the All American Futurity at Ruidoso Downs in New Mexico. Shown here is the 1995 winner, the gelding Winalota Cash, ridden by jockey Billy Peterson. (*The Quarter Racing Journal*/Gina Phipps)*

The AQHA Racing Department is the official record keeper for American Quarter Horse racing. Through the Racing Council, a ten-member steering committee that directs AQHA's involvement in the sport, the Racing Department provides an extensive marketing and promotional program to assist tracks where American Quarter Horses compete. Among the materials available to tracks, state racing associations, and racing fans are videos and written information about race handicapping and racehorse ownership.

The Challenge

The MBNA America Quarter Horse Racing Challenge is a program developed by AQHA to increase racing opportunities for older horses. Debuted in 1993, the Racing Challenge is a multimillion-dollar series of more than forty races run in ten regions at racetracks across the United States, Canada, and Mexico. Throughout the year, American Quarter Horses compete for starting positions in the final event, the MBNA America Quarter Horse Racing Challenge Championships run each November and known as "America's Fastest Day of Racing."

A one-time enrollment fee makes any American Quarter Horse eligible for lifetime participation in the Racing Challenge. The program has a competitive level for every caliber of athlete, and it increases racing opportunities for owners and their horses, especially older horses. Horses can run in any race in any region, as long as they meet the conditions of the race.

Within its first three years, the Challenge became the industry's premier program to date, having distributed millions of dollars in purses to owners and bonus awards to nominators and stallion owners. Of the program's total amount, less than 30 percent of the money comes from horsemen; the balance is provided by host racetracks and AQHA corporate sponsors.

Cutter and Chariot Racing

Most popular in intermountain Western states, chariot racing comes close to the original colonial Quarter Horse competitions of flat-out sprints along country roads. The difference here is that two horses work in tandem pulling a two-wheeled cart called a chariot.

At one end of the course is a starting gate. Four hundred forty yards away is the finish line. Each pair of horses loaded into the gate is helped by two assistants, called headers, who make sure the animals are standing square and facing straight ahead.

When the starter is satisfied that all entries are ready, the gate stalls spring open. Using their legendary American Quarter Horse ability to accelerate to top speed, the teams draw the chariots behind them quickly to speeds of up to forty miles per hour. Braced precariously on board, drivers urge their horses forward while trying to maintain a straight course; chariots that veer from their designated lanes can be moved down in the order of finish or even disqualified.

A pair of American Quarter Horses en route to a chariot race. (The Quarter Horse Journal)

At one time this type of racing used wheel-less sled-like vehicles called cutters (a word that continues to be applied to the sport's participants). Now the single-axle vehicles are fitted with wire wheels on sulky bike tires. Chariots weigh between fifty and sixty pounds, to which is added the weight of harness and the driver. Anything less than a total of 275 pounds requires weight to be added to assure equal competition among all the entries.

Parentage Verification and Tattooing

In a continuing effort to ensure the integrity of racing, every American Quarter Horse must be identified with a tattoo number prior to participating at an AQHA-recognized racetrack. An AQHA-authorized technician puts the number on the animal's upper lip, then the number is entered on the horse's registration certificate and filed with AQHA.

In order to be eligible for tattooing, the horse must undergo genetic (DNA) testing and parentage verification.

Buyers of any horses foaled before 1992 that have not had their parentage verified should be cautious. As the new owner, the buyer assumes the responsibility for genetic testing and parentage verification. If your horse's parentage cannot be verified due to an inability to genotype or blood-type a parent, you will, at the very least, encounter a delay in being able to race your horse. You might also have purchased a horse that cannot race.

For further information on genetic testing and parentage verification, contact AQHA.

Where Should Your Horse Run?

DETERMINING CLASS AND COMPETITIVE LEVEL

You've purchased and registered a horse, and had him genetically tested, parentage-verified, and tattooed. He's been in training with a professional whom you carefully selected and feel comfortable with. Now comes the day when the two of you sit down to discuss and decide the level at which your horse will compete.

The range of types of races allows each runner to compete with others of his own class. While everyone in racing hopes to own the next All American Futurity winner, the reality is that equine athletes are no different from human athletes: Some are simply more talented than others.

To help you and your trainer make decisions, racetracks print condition books that specify eligibility requirements. There are six basic types that a condition book might list. In some circles, this is known as the "class ladder." As you move up the ladder, you also move up in the level and quality of competition.

MAIDEN RACES

Maiden races are limited to horses that have never won a race. All American Quarter Horses are called maidens until they win their first race, although a maiden actually can run in races other than those restricted to maidens if the owner and trainer so choose.

CLAIMING RACES

Claiming races, which are the most popular type, constitute approximately 70 percent of all races run. Horses are entered for a specific price, and they can be claimed, or purchased, by any licensed owner at the track for that price. This procedure tends to equalize the class or competition, and it is within

The presence of another horse, called a lead pony, is a calming influence on the way from the paddock to the starting gate. (AQHA photo by Wyatt McSpadden)

the claiming ranks that many horses find their niche.

Claiming races might be written for horses worth anywhere from as little as $1,500 to as much as $50,000. Most American Quarter Horses can successfully compete somewhere between these two figures.

ALLOWANCE RACES

Allowance races, which are nonclaiming races for better-quality horses, generally offer higher purses than claiming races. Eligibility requirements and conditions are similar to those of claiming races, but the weight allowance assigned to each horse is based on money won and/or the number or type of victories within a specified time.

TRIAL RACES

Trials are designed to determine the qualifiers for finals in stakes races like futurities, derbies, and maturities. Eligibility to move on to such a stakes race is based on the fastest qualifying times or order of finish in the trial race.

STAKES RACES

Stakes races are showcases for horses of the highest racing caliber. Purses consist of nomination, entry, and starting fees, plus significant money added by the track or a sponsor. Graded stakes are the premier stakes races; the terms Grade One (G1), Grade Two (G2), and Grade Three (G3) indicate the class of horses participating, with Grade One (G1) the highest designation. The size of

Thick padding lines the insides of starting gate stalls. (AQHA photo by Wyatt McSpadden)

purse, amount of added monies, and historical significance of the race also are factors in determining the grade status.

HANDICAP RACES

Like stakes races, handicap races are written for the highest-quality horses. The track's racing secretary assigns weights in an attempt to equalize the winning chances of entries: Those horses that the racing secretary feels are of better quality in the race will carry more weight.

When a horse begins his racing career, his pedigree and purchase price or the value of his dam or sire help determine the level at which he will start. However, once a horse has a few races under his belt, regardless of how well he was bred, form becomes the major factor to consider when planning his next races.

While it might take a few races before you're able to determine the quality of your horse, many trainers and owners feel that letting a horse lose too many races before evaluating his program is not a good idea. Damaging the animal's confidence will only undo all the preparation you've invested in his early training. Your horse also may be most effective at a particular distance.

AQHA-approved distances range from 220 yards (an eighth of a mile, or one furlong) to 870 yards (10 yards shy of four furlongs, or a half mile), although American Quarter Horses are sometimes asked to challenge Thoroughbreds at distances up to 1,000 yards.

Down the stretch they run. Each entrant can be identified by the jockey's distinctive shirt and cap, known collectively as silks. (AQHA photo by Wyatt McSpadden)

As a general rule, breeders aim to produce horses that excel at 350, 400, or 440 yards, because races at these distances are the most lucrative. On the other hand, many horses that are not competitive at these routes flourish and become legends when they are "stretched out" to the 870-yard trip.

Another factor may be your horse's preference for running in a straight-away sprint versus "hook" races around one turn of a racetrack's oval. In American Quarter Horse racing, only the 870-yard race involves a turn.

As part of the process of determining a horse's class level, the animal's preference for distance and track conditions will become apparent after you and your trainer observe several workouts and a schooling race.

Locations of North American Quarter Horse Racetracks

Alameda County Fair
Pleasanton, California

Anthony Downs
Anthony, Kansas

Apache County Fair
St. Johns, Arizona

Arapahoe Park
Denver, Colorado

Arlington International Racecourse
Chicago, Illinois

Assiniboia Downs
Winnipeg, Manitoba

Beulah Park
Grove City, Ohio

Blue Ribbon Downs
Sallisaw, Oklahoma

Brown County Fair
Aberdeen, South Dakota

California State Fair
Sacramento, California

Canterbury Park
Shakopee, Minnesota

Cassia County Fair
Burley, Idaho

Central Wyoming Fair
Casper, Wyoming

Cochise County Fair
Douglas, Arizona

Coconino County Fair
Flagstaff, Arizona

Cow Capital Turf Club
Miles City, Montana

Dayton Days
Dayton, Washington

Delaware Park
Wilmington, Delaware

Delta Downs
Vinton, Louisiana

Desert Park Exhibition
Osoyoos, British Columbia

Dixie Downs
St. George, Utah

The Downs at Albuquerque
New Mexico State Fair
Albuquerque, New Mexico

The Downs at Santa Fe
Santa Fe, New Mexico

Eastern Idaho Fair
Blackfoot, Idaho

Eastern Oregon Livestock Show
Union, Oregon

Elko County Fairgrounds
Elko, Nevada

Emmett Racetrack
Emmett, Idaho

Energy Downs
Gillette, Wyoming

Eureka Downs
Eureka, Kansas

Evangeline Downs
Lafayette, Louisiana

Fair Grounds
New Orleans, Louisiana

Fair Meadows
Tulsa, Oklahoma

Fairmount Park
Collinsville, Illinois

Fairplex Park
Pomona, California

Flathead Fairgrounds
Kalispell, Montana

Fresno District Fair
Fresno, California

Gila County Fair
Globe, Arizona

Gillespie County Fair
Fredericksburg, Texas

Graham County Fair
Safford, Arizona

Grande Prairie
Grande Prairie, Alberta

Grays Harbor Park
Elma, Washington

Greenlee County Fair
Duncan, Arizona

Helena Downs
Helena, Montana

Hipodromo de las Americas
Mexico City, Mexico

Humboldt County Fair
Ferndale, California

Humboldt County Fair
Winnemucca, Nevada

Jerome County Fair
Jerome, Idaho

Kamloops Exhibition
Kamloops, British Columbia

Kin Park
Vernon, British Columbia

Laurel Brown Racetrack
South Jordan, Utah

Les Bois Park
Boise, Idaho

Lone Star Park at Grand Prairie
Grand Prairie, Texas

Los Alamitos
Los Alamitos, California

Louisiana Downs
Bossier City, Louisiana

Manor Downs
Manor, Texas

Marias Fair
Shelby, Montana

Marquis Downs
Saskatoon, Saskatchewan

MetraPark
Billings, Montana

Millarville Race Society
Millarville, Alberta

Minidoka County Fair
Rupert, Idaho

Mohave County Fair
Kingman, Arizona

Montana State Fair
Great Falls, Montana

Mt. Pleasant Meadows
Mt. Pleasant, Michigan

Navajo County Fair
Holbrook, Arizona

Oneida County Fair
Malad, Idaho

Oregon State Fair
Salem, Oregon

Picov Downs
Ajax, Ontario

Playfair
Spokane, Washington

Pocatello Downs
Pocatello, Idaho

Portland Meadows
Portland, Oregon

Prairie Meadows
Altoona, Iowa

Prescott Downs
Prescott, Arizona

Princeton Racing Days
Princeton, British Columbia

Prineville Turf Club
Prineville, Oregon

Ravalli County Fair
Hamilton, Montana

Remington Park
Oklahoma City, Oklahoma

Retama Park
San Antonio, Texas

Rillito Park
Tucson, Arizona

Rossburn Parkland Downs
Rossburn, Manitoba

Round-Up Park
Trinidad, Colorado

Ruidoso Downs
Ruidoso, New Mexico

Sam Houston Race Park
Houston, Texas

San Joaquin County Fair
Stockton, California

San Mateo County Fair
San Mateo, California

Santa Cruz County Fair
Sonoita, Arizona

Solano County Fair
Vallejo, California

Sonoma County Fair
Santa Rosa, California

Southern Oregon Race Assn.
Grants Pass, Oregon

Sun Downs
Kennewick, Washington

Sunland Park
Sunland Park, New Mexico

Teton Racing Association
Idaho Falls, Idaho

Tillamook County Fair
Tillamook, Oregon

Trinity Meadows
Willow Park, Texas

Trochu Downs
Trochu, Alberta

Turf Paradise
Phoenix, Arizona

Turtle Mountain Tribe
Belcourt, North Dakota

Verendrye Benevolent Assn.
Ft. Pierre, South Dakota

Waitsburg Racetrack
Waitsburg, Washington

Walla Walla Racetrack
Walla Walla, Washington

Weber Downs
Ogden, Utah

Wells County Downs
Fessenden, North Dakota

Will Rogers Downs
Claremore, Oklahoma

Western Montana Fair
Missoula, Montana

The Woodlands
Kansas City, Kansas

White Pine Raceway
Ely, Nevada

Wyoming Downs
Evanston, Wyoming

Whoop-Up Downs
Lethbridge, Alberta

Yuma County Fair
Yum a, Arizona

State & Provincial American Quarter Horse Racing Affiliates

When you're ready to buy an American Quarter Horse for racing or if you already have a horse and want to become involved in the sport, your state or provincial American Quarter Horse racing affiliate is your link to involvement. These affiliates support the growth of the breed by sponsoring AQHA-approved races and other programs.

For information, including the addresses and phone numbers of state and provincial racing affiliates, contact AQHA.

FOR FURTHER INFORMATION

For information about American Quarter Horse racetracks or to get the dates of major races, call AQHA at (800) 414-RIDE.

Other excellent sources of information include *The Quarter Racing Journal,* an award-winning monthly magazine, and *The Quarter Racing Journal EXTRA,* an industry newsletter published thirty-five times a year (for subscription information, phone 800-291-7323).

AQHA offers a free brochure, *A Guide to Owning Everyone's All-American— The Racing American Quarter Horse.*

AQHA also offers the following videos:

The Story of American Quarter Horse Racing. From the colonies of early America to the bright lights of Los Alamitos, the story of the racing American Quarter Horse explodes with excitement while owners, trainers, and jockeys describe their love of this thrilling sport.

Owning America's Fastest Athlete. A guide to what is involved in owning an American Quarter Horse racer, the tape includes the music video "Running Blood."

The Winner's Guide to Wagering. Produced by The Woodlands in 1990, this videotape on how to handicap horse racing features Rick Baedeker, whose family has been acknowledged as the leading West Coast handicappers for forty years. This first-class production has separate segments on Thoroughbred and American Quarter Horse racing and is an excellent tool for beginners and experts.

Racing Officials: Their Duties and Responsibilities. This tape details the duties and responsibilities of racing officials during the course of a race day at the Downs at Santa Fe. This tape is an excellent educational tool for racing officials, racetrack employees, and racing fans.

Appendix: A Guide for Buying Your American Quarter Horse

🐎 Understanding Your Needs

Horse ownership can be a rewarding experience, one enjoyed by persons of all ages through a wide variety of activities, including shows, rodeos, races, and recreational rides. The experience begins, naturally, with the purchase of your first horse. It is an important step, one that must be made with equal amounts of education and dedication, for your first purchase often sets the tone for your lifetime of horseback experiences.

The first step in horse ownership is asking yourself, "Why do I want a horse?" This question will help you form a goal, which in turn provides the framework for your buying decision. As a starting point, ask yourself the following:

- What is my goal?

- Do I want to become a better rider and increase my knowledge of horses?

- What types of activities do I want to do with this horse?

- How much can I afford to spend on the purchase of a horse, plus stall rental, feed, training, health care, and hauling?

- How much do I know about riding—am I a beginner; will I need additional riding instruction?

- Will I work with my horse on a daily, weekly, or monthly basis?

- How much time can I devote to feeding, care, lessons, shows, or trail rides?

Different goals require different types of horses and different skill levels of the rider. If you plan to show competitively, obviously, the type of horse will differ greatly—in level of training, and subsequently, price—from a recreational riding horse. Your overall goal as a horse owner is the foundation for your buying decision.

Just as you would research buying a car, you should also do your homework before purchasing a horse. The American Quarter Horse Association provides a toll-free number to help you locate others within your area who can aid your search for the perfect equine partner. Call (800)414-RIDE and AQHA can provide you with a referral to AQHA events in your area and other pertinent information to help you choose an area of interest to participate in.

Next, visit an AQHA event in your area in order to gain a perspective on available opportunities. At the event, watch the competition and try to determine how much work will be required to achieve your goal. Visit with others in attendance to get an idea of what it's like to compete in certain events, and evaluate your goals to see if they are realistic.

Once you've established a specific goal, the next step is evaluating your level of horseback skills. Would you categorize yourself as:

- beginning, with limited knowledge of horses and riding in general?

- intermediate, with a basic understanding of riding and knowledge of a chosen discipline?

- advanced, with considerable knowledge of horses and competitive at a chosen discipline?

AQHA INCENTIVE FUND

If you're planning to show your horse, look for a horse that is enrolled in the AQHA Incentive Fund. You can earn money for each point you earn in AQHA shows. The Incentive Fund has distributed more than $2 million to enrolled horse owners each year since 1990, averaging $28.04 per point. To be eligible for the Incentive Fund, the horse must have been sired by a stallion enrolled in the fund that year. The foals of these stallions can then be nominated into the Incentive Fund for life with a one-time fee. Call AQHA for details on the program and a list of Incentive Fund breeders.

Your skill level will indicate what kind of horse best fits your needs. For beginning or recreational riders, a broke, gentle gelding usually is the best bet. However, beginners with a competitive goal should locate a horse that has mastered requirements within the chosen activity, or is "seasoned." For example, if your goal is to one day become a competitive team roper, it's a good idea to find an older, yet sound gelding that has been roped upon extensively. Find a horse with enough experience to help you advance your riding skills first, while still allowing you to compete and hone your competitive talents.

Intermediate equestrians have a bit more freedom of choice than beginners in that their horse should demonstrate fundamental activity requirements, as evidenced by some level of past performance, but they may not necessarily require a horse with years of experience. However, the horse should at least be suitable for a desired discipline, or demonstrate adequate potential.

Advanced riders have the greatest latitude in buying a horse, as they may be able to take a young horse that lacks experience and train it for a chosen activity. While this may be a rewarding experience when accomplished effectively, it should only be considered by advanced horsemen with years of experience who have the time to work with the horse.

Where to Find a Horse for Purchase

It is important that you complete the following steps before you buy a horse:

- Decide what you want to do with your horse.
- Determine what level of rider you are.
- Arrange for or build a safe place to stable your horse.
- Decide who will feed and care for your horse.

Breeders

One of the beset sources for purchasing a horse is a breeder. Breeders normally have a large selection of horses on hand, representing an array of ages, levels of training, and dispositions. The main advantage of working with a breeder is that you can often gain credible insight about a horse. You have a chance to view other horses that have been bred by the owner; discuss pedigrees, performance, and race records; see the kind of environment in which the horse was raised and/or trained; and compare other horses of similar type. The breeder also can discuss the advantages of particular bloodlines, as well as provide additional information about his or her individual breeding program.

BREEDER REFERRAL PROGRAM
AQHA members and customers can call (800) 414-RIDE and receive a free referral to members of AQHA's Breeder Referral Program. This program matches buyers with reputable American Quarter Horse breeders who are guided by the Breeder Referral Program's strict code of ethics. Breeders belonging to the program are members in good standing with AQHA and have bred registered American Quarter Horses for at least three consecutive years.

Owners

Another way to purchase a horse is directly from the owner. The owner can provide the history of the horse's performance. Owners also may give helpful information regarding training and habits. Plus most owners will allow prospective buyers to "try" a horse several times before purchasing. This working one-on-one helps establish goodwill between buyer and seller. *The Quarter Horse Journal* and *The Quarter Racing Journal* are excellent resources, as they often advertise horse sales and horses for sale by owner.

Sales

Many beginners look to horse sales for finding a horse, since they are geographically widespread and offer horses of different ages, training levels, and prices. However, beginners must first understand that there are different types of sales, and not all may be the best place to purchase a horse. To get a better understanding of the types of sales available, take a look at the following.

PRODUCTION

A production sale often features horses produced by breeders. A variety of horses may be offered, including young horses, geldings, mares, and stallions. Horses in production sales are often bred similarly, or have similar purposes in mind, offering a basis for comparison. These are excellent opportunities to buy quality; however, horses with extensive training in a particular discipline may not be offered.

CONSIGNMENT

In consignment sales, a variety of horses have been consigned by their owners to be sold. The advantage of consignment sales is that they offer horses of different ages, sexes, and training. The disadvantage is that these horses are obtained from a variety of backgrounds, so you may not have access to information on disposition and training level. Since there is little time to view the horse once he is in the ring, it is a good idea to arrive prior to the sale. If you find a horse you are interested in purchasing, try locating the owner and discussing such characteristics as disposition of the horse, health, and past performance.

RACING

Unlike any other type of sale, racing sales feature horses specifically bred for racing. The most popular type of sale features yearlings—horses between twelve and twenty-four months of age—that are in training to be raced as two-year-olds. "Mixed sales" feature both racing stock and breeding stock, in addition to weanling prospects. Prices largely depend on market demand for certain bloodlines and the potential of each horse.

DISPERSAL

Dispersal sales may offer a unique opportunity to purchase a breeder's lifetime efforts. Like a production sale, a dispersal ordinarily features stock owned by one particular person or entity, with the age, sex, and training of the horses varying. Because this may be the first, or last, opportunity to purchase from a reputable entity, prices for these horses may be higher than at production or consignment sales.

Other locations for finding horses for sale include:

- Equine listings in newspapers
- "Trading posts" in feed and tack stores
- *The Quarter Horse Journal* and *The Quarter Racing Journal*
- Local equine veterinarians
- State or provincial American Quarter Horse affiliates

Professionals

Professionals, such as trainers, can serve as agents for prospective buyers, in addition to training horses and instructing clients. By discussing your needs in a horse and your skills, a trainer may help locate a horse that best fits your goals. Trainers usually charge a commission for helping you find a horse.

Professionals can help beginners select a horse. The need for a consultant is twofold. A consultant can help you locate, evaluate, and negotiate a prospective purchase. A consultant also can evaluate your skill as a rider and give you information on your chosen discipline.

You can find a professional in your area by calling AQHA at (800)414-RIDE and asking for a referral to the Association of Professional Horsemen.

MBNA AMERICA QUARTER HORSE RACING CHALLENGE
If you're looking for a horse to race, consider getting a horse enrolled in the MBNA America Quarter Horse Racing Challenge. The Challenge has forty races in ten regions where you can race for more than $1.5 million in added money. AQHA corporate sponsors and host racetracks add to the racing purses, making the Challenge the richest series of American Quarter Horse races in the world. Winners in each region receive a starting position at the Challenge Championships run each November. For more program details, call the Challenge Hotline at (800) 831-4447.

Beginners should try to find a professional who works well with beginners, or who has expertise in your chosen discipline.

Some helpful questions to ask a professional are:

- What experience do you have in the horse industry?

- What experience do you have in my chosen discipline?

- Whom else have you helped and what kind of success have they had under your guidance?

- How are your fees structured?

- What references do you have from other professionals?

When you retain a professional to aid you with your riding and competition, be sure to explain your goals thoroughly to your professional, and discuss candidly how much you can afford for purchasing a horse, feed, board, veterinary care, and other considerations.

Visiting a Breeder or Owner

Once you have found a prospective horse to buy, there are steps to follow that will aid you in purchasing a horse. If you are visiting the farm of a breeder, owner, or professional, it's a good idea to start by talking to the seller and establishing a good rapport.

Some excellent questions to ask the seller are:

- How much has the horse been ridden during the past year?

- Who has ridden the horse the most—trainer, amateur, youth?

- How easy is the horse to handle after being turned out for a while and not ridden?

- What kind of equipment has been used?

- How much training has the horse received and in what areas?

- Where has the horse been stalled?

- What type of feed and roughage does the horse eat and what is his feeding schedule?

- What kind of health (good, bad) has the horse had during the past year?

- Has the horse ever had any colic episodes?

- How often is the horse dewormed or shod?

- Does the horse have any vices?

- How often has the horse been away from home and what is his behavior in different surroundings?

- How does the horse react when being shod, clipped, or dewormed?

- And the best question—Why is the horse for sale?

The Evaluation Process

After you've identified a goal for yourself and located a prospective horse, the next step is an evaluation process whereby you determine if that horse will allow you to accomplish your goal—call it determining "suitability for purpose." While it's safe to say that any horse with acceptable past performance in your chosen endeavor is suitable for purpose, even beginners should have a basic understanding of the factors that influence a horse's abilities within a given activity, and utilize this information in the evaluation process. What are those factors? Generally, it can be said there are three: conformation, movement, and disposition.

Conformation

One of the most important criteria in selecting a horse for purchase is conformation, or his physical appearance. While it could be assumed that most horses with several years' seasoning and past performance have acceptable conformation, your goal in selection should always be to find the best-conformed horse possible, regardless of past performance. The reason? Horses with less-than-perfect conformation may encounter health problems as they mature or when stressed through competition.

Rating conformation depends upon objective evaluation of the following four traits: balance, structural correctness, degree of muscling, and breed and sex characteristics. Of the four, balance is the single most important, and refers to the structural and aesthetic blending of body parts. Balance is influenced almost entirely by skeletal structure.

AQHA'S PROFESSIONAL HORSEMEN

AQHA members and customers can call (800) 414-RIDE and receive a free referral to members of AQHA's Professional Horsemen. This program can give you a referral to professionals in your area who can help you with all your training needs. From training the horse to training the rider, AQHA's Pro Horsemen are respected members of the equine profession who have pledged to follow the program's strict code of ethics.

To gain a better understanding of ideal balance in an American Quarter Horse, there are several helpful ratios that you can draw in your mind's eye. Start by viewing a horse from its profile, and imagine a straight line determining length of back (the distance from point of withers to croup) and one along length of underline (point of elbow to stifle). Ideally, the length of back should be one-half that of the underline.

Next, draw an imaginary line down the top line of the neck (the distance from poll to withers) and the bottom line (the distance from throatlatch to neck-shoulder junction). Ideally, the top-line to bottom-line ratio of neck should be 2:1. Horses that deviate greatly from these two important ratios, becoming 1:1, are often deemed unbalanced.

What causes the deviations? Nothing is more critical to balance than slope of shoulder. When the shoulder becomes more vertically sloping, or "straighter," it shortens the top-line to bottom-line ratio of neck. The withers move forward as the shoulder becomes straighter, resulting in a longer back. Thus, the straight-shouldered horse has the appearance of being a tube.

Since a short top line and long underline are desirable, it is incorrect to compare shorter horses with taller horses, because horses of different sizes should not have the same length of body or underlines. The ratios are important in determining balance, and these are directly affected by the slope of shoulder. Moreover, when the shoulder is straight, other structural angles in a horse's body become straight, resulting in a horse with a short, steep croup, straight stifle, and straight pasterns. These latter traits are undesirable and contribute to a horse's lack of balance.

As balance is directly related to structure, the poorly balanced horse often lacks structural correctness and fundamental soundness. In general, the angle of the pasterns will correspond almost exactly with the angle of shoulder, so that a horse with too much slope to his shoulder also has weak, sloping pasterns. This condition, called "coon-footed," may be so severe as to allow the horse's fetlocks to hit the ground as he moves. The ideal slope of shoulder is approximately forty-five to fifty degrees; however, the angle may vary from ideal. You should not be overly influenced by demanding an exact degree of slope of shoulder. Instead, concentrate on balance and blending of structure.

Once you have evaluated a horse's overall balance, then structure, muscling, and breed and sex characteristics can be more definitively evaluated by examining individual body components, starting with the horse's head.

HEAD

A horse's head provides insight into his total conformation, as well as his behavior. In general, there is no physiological benefit to having a "pretty head" on a horse. However, most people don't like an ugly-headed horse, so selection is based upon beauty. What makes an attractive head? The set of ears, shape of eye, size of nostril, depth of mouth, and overall proportionality of the head are important considerations.

Another useful tip in evaluating a horse's head is to visually measure the distance from the horse's poll to an imaginary horizontal line between the eyes. Ideally, this distance is approximately one-half the distance from the horizontal line to the midpoint of the nostril. Thus, the eyes will be positioned one-third the distance from the horse's poll to muzzle. When the width across the orbit of the horse's skull is measured, that distance should be almost identical to the distance from the poll to the line between the eyes.

The ears should be proportional to the horse's head, and sit squarely on top of the head, pointing forward with an alert appearance. Any deviation in placement or carriage of the horse's ears detracts from the beauty of the head, and thus the horse's overall beauty. Since horses are proportional, length of head is the same percentage of height for both tall and short horses. Therefore, the term "long-headed" is somewhat a misnomer, as long heads are simply indicative of tall horses.

The head has qualities that are important when evaluating other factors, including behavior. Most notably, the eye provides insight into a horse's disposition. Large, quiet, soft eyes normally indicate a docile disposition, while small, "pig" eyes are associated with horses that are sullen and difficult to train. Look for a bright, tranquil eye with a soft, kind expression.

For American Quarter Horses, bulging, well-defined jaws are preferred, particularly in stallions, which are naturally deeper and bolder-jawed than mares. Pretty-headed horses will always have a well-defined muzzle, flaring into a refined chin and prominent jaw. For beauty's sake, look for large, flaring nostrils. Regarding depth of mouth, many horsemen feel that the shallower the mouth, the softer and more reactive the horse. Guard against horses that are thick-lipped and heavy across the bridge of the nose, for these are often less responsive to the bridle. Finally, make sure the horse is not parrot-mouthed (upper teeth in front of and over the lower teeth) or monkey-mouthed (lower teeth in front of the upper teeth).

NECK

After evaluating the horse's head, move on to the neck. The throatlatch should be trim and refined, with the depth being equal to one-half the length of the head. If the horse is thick in the throatlatch, flexion at the poll is restricted, and thus the horse may be prevented from carrying his head correctly during competition because of an inability to breathe correctly.

Some horsemen talk about "long, thin necks," when in reality, priority should be given to horses with an appropriate top-line to bottom-line neck ratio. Again, the top line of the neck to the bottom line should be 2:1 on a balanced horse. Invariably, horses with shorter necks are shorter-bodied, and since the horse is connected from his poll to tailset, a horse with a shorter neck may lack the flexion and suppleness desired for a more advanced training.

SHOULDER

In addition to overall balance, the slope of shoulder influences the length of stride. Thus, the straighter the shoulder, the shorter the stride. The angles of shoulder and pastern also serve to absorb shock when the horse moves. The straight-shouldered horse also will be shallow-hearted, as measured from top of withers to chest floor. Unlike the balanced horse, with legs that will measure approximately the same length as depth of heart, the straight-shouldered horse's legs will be longer than depth of heart. A straight-shouldered horse will always feel rough-riding compared with a horse with a desirably sloping shoulder.

WITHERS

The ideal withers are sharp, prominent, and slightly higher than the horse's hindquarters or croup. A balanced horse will appear to be sloping downhill from front to back. When the withers are higher than the croup, the hindquarters are properly positioned under the body and contribute to athletic ability. Strength of the top line over the back, loin, and croup, also is important in athletic ability and overall balance and soundness.

BARREL

As you view a horse from the front, always evaluate spring of rib and depth of heart, as they indicate athletic capacity. Select against horses that have a "pinched," flat-ribbed look, not a rounded, convex look to their rib cages.

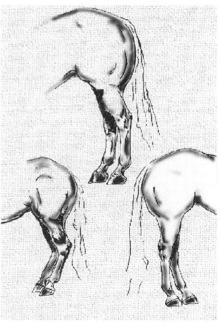

HINDQUARTERS

When viewed from the side, the hindquarters should appear square. How the corners of the square are filled in will depend on the breed, with American Quarter Horses being more desirably muscled when the hindquarters complete the square. The croup should not be too flat (resulting in too much vertical action in movement) or too steep (associated with a collected but very short, choppy stride).

The ideal American Quarter Horse has a hindquarter that is as full and as long from across the horizontal plane of the stifle as it is from point of hip to point of buttocks. Muscling is an important criterion in judging conformation of American Quarter Horse. It is important to realize that muscling is proportional (as one muscle in the body increases, total muscle mass increases). Horses visually appraised as heavily muscled generally have greater circumference of forearm, gaskin, and width of hindquarter than lightly muscled horses. The horse is a balanced athlete that is muscled uniformly throughout.

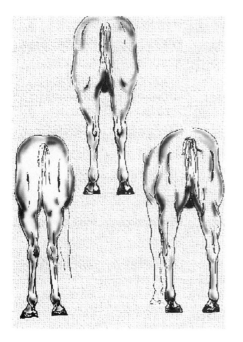

FEET AND LEGS

Structure of feet and legs are major considerations when evaluating a horse's conformation. When standing beside the horse, drop an imaginary line from the point of buttocks to the ground. Ideally, that line should touch the hocks, run parallel to the cannon bone, and be slightly behind the heel. The horse with too much angle to his hocks is **sickle-hocked,** and the horse that is straight in his hocks is **post-legged.**

Ideally, when viewed from the rear, any horse should be widest from stifle to stifle. Another imaginary line from the point of buttocks to the ground should bisect the gaskin, hock, and hoof. It is not critical that a horse be perfectly straight from the ankles down as viewed from the rear. In fact, most horses naturally stand with the cannons parallel and toe out slightly from the ankles down. This allows the horse's stifle to clear his rib cage in flight, resulting in a longer-striding, free-moving horse. However, when a horse is bowed inward at the hocks and the cannon bones are not parallel, he is **cow-hocked.** The horse that is cow-hocked has a tendency to be weak in the major movements that require work off the haunches such as stopping, turning, and sliding. Occasionally, there are horses that actually toe in behind and are **bow-legged,** most of which are very poor athletes.

The horse should stand on a straight column of bone with no deviation when viewed from the side. A horse that is "over at the knees" is **buck-kneed,** and the horse that is "back at the knees" is **calf-kneed.** Obviously, calf-kneed is the more serious condition, since the knee will have a tendency to hyperextend backward.

When the horse is viewed from the front, an imaginary line from the point of shoulder to the toe should bisect the knee, cannon bone, and hoof, with the hoof pointing straight ahead. When a horse **toes out,** he is **splay-footed** and will always **wing in** when traveling. When a horse **toes in,** he is **pigeon-toed** and will always **paddle out.** The more troublesome of these is the horse that wings in. If the cannon bone is off center to the outside, he is **bench-kneed.**

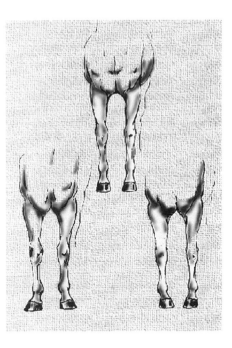

SOUNDNESS AND STRUCTURE

All horses should be serviceably sound. In young animals, there should be no indication of defects in conformation that may lead to unsoundness. An unsoundness is defined as any deviation in structure that interferes with the usefulness of an individual. Many horses will have blemishes—abnormalities that may detract from the appearance of the animal—but are sound. You should become familiar with all the common unsoundnesses and learn to recognize them.

Riding and Movement

After a basic evaluation of conformation, the next step is evaluating a horse's movement. Movement is an important criterion, particularly when selecting a horse for performance events, as most arena classes place some level of preference on movement.

For even a beginning recreational rider, a horse should at least walk, trot, lope, and accept leads in both directions. The horse should stop easily when asked "whoa" by the rider, and yield to leg aids. Ideally, horses should also demonstrate the following:

- The walk must be alert, with a stride of reasonable length in keeping with the size of the horse.

- The trot should be square, balanced, and with straight, forward movement of the feet.

- The lope should be a natural, three-beat stride and appear relaxed and smooth. Horses should accept both leads, and change with little difficulty.

In selecting a horse for arena performance, consider the following criteria:

WESTERN

The horse should have a free-flowing stride of reasonable length in keeping with conformation. The horse should cover a reasonable amount of ground with little effort and carry his head and neck in a relaxed, natural position, with the poll level with or slightly above the level of the withers. Ideally, the horse should have a balanced, flowing motion and be responsive to the rider's commands, yet smooth in transition of gaits and leads.

ENGLISH

The horse should move with long, low strides reaching forward with ease and smoothness; be able to lengthen stride; and cover ground with relaxed, free-flowing movement. Horses should be obedient, have a bright expression with alert ears, and respond willingly to the rider with light leg and hand contact. When asked to extend the trot or canter, the horse should move out with the same flowing motion. The poll should be level with or slightly above the withers. The head should be slightly in front of, or on, the vertical.

REINING OR SIMILAR ADVANCED DISCIPLINES

The horse should be willingly guided or controlled with little or no apparent resistance, and responsive to the rider's commands. Any movement on his own must be considered a lack, or temporary loss, of control. The horse should be smooth, demonstrating finesse, attitude, quickness, and authority in performing various maneuvers while using controlled speed.

Disposition

Probably the most important, and most abstract, aspect of the evaluation process is determining a horse's disposition. While American Quarter Horses have been selectively bred for generations for good disposition, and most often possess an inherently gentle nature, you must still place importance on this in the selection process. The reason? While a horse may be impeccably conformed and move like a champ, he still may not possess the correct frame of mind, which will allow both you and the horse to realize your true potential.

Evaluating disposition is particularly important for beginners. It can be frustrating to try to learn how to ride a horse that simply isn't cooperative. You may lose confidence and become afraid—the horse simply becomes confused. Often, both problems multiply if not corrected via professional help.

While evaluating some conformational traits may help determine disposition, the best method is seeing how a horse behaves when being groomed, saddled, ridden, and trailered. While the seller's opinions may be helpful, use your own eyes. Observe the horse being groomed, saddled, and trailered. Does the horse:

- Stand quietly when approached by the seller and yourself, or does he flinch or draw back?

- Halter or bridle without difficulty?

- Paw, set back, or lie down when tied?

- Accept the saddle?

- Stand patiently as a rider mounts?

- Load easily into a trailer?

Any signs of nervousness, pawing, bucking in place, biting, or refusal to comply during grooming, saddling, or trailering should be considered faults on the part of the horse. Since the horse may respond correctly with the owner, ask the owner if you may perform these tasks yourself, if you feel comfortable doing so.

Next, evaluate the horse's disposition during riding. Does the horse:

- Walk, trot, and lope, and accept these gaits willingly?

- Take both right and left leads easily?

- Respond and stop when asked to whoa, or when pressure is applied to the bit?

- Back without straining against the bit?

- Follow your commands, or act on his own?

The horse's disposition during riding is largely dependent upon the rider's skill. While beginning riders may experience varying levels of resistance or loss of control when performing the aforementioned tasks, at no time should the horse buck or act as if he is running off. Ideally, the horse should perform all requirements willingly, with little or no resistance on the bit. Any bracing or straining against the bit should be considered faults.

If you are a beginner, or even an intermediate horseman, it is always a good idea to have a professional with you if you choose to groom, saddle, or ride a horse. Ask the owner if your professional can ride the horse. As with any diagnostic process, you are always better off with a second opinion.

A good thing to keep in mind through the entire evaluation process is this: You are buying not only a horse, but a relationship with a horse. All horses have different personalities, and it's your goal to find a horse that best complements your personality. While conformation, behavior, and movement all play a role in the horse's suitability for purpose and personality, the final analysis often relies on one simple question: How am I getting along with this horse? The answer often is derived strictly from intuition.

Purchasing a Horse

Purchase Exam

If a horse seems like a good prospect, and meets your approval through the evaluation process, you may want to arrange to have a purchase examination performed by an experienced equine veterinarian. You can contact the American Association of Equine Practitioners at (800)GET-ADVM (800-438-2386) to find an experienced equine veterinarian in your area.

The purchase exam may involve X rays and a variety of diagnostic techniques, but all should include examinations of the following:

- Eyes and head
- Nose
- Mouth and teeth
- Ears
- Tail (for compliance with AQHA rules)

- Back and neck
- Legs
- Ankles and hooves
- Heart and lungs
- Hocks and knees

Although the veterinarian's findings may or may not affect your buying decision, it is always a good idea to have a purchase exam performed in order to have an experienced medical professional evaluate a potential purchase.

Laminitis (founder)—see page 135.

Navicular disease—see page 136.

Parrot-mouth—see page 129.

Ringbone—see page 134.

Cryptorchid—see page 129.

Hyperkalemic periodic paralysis (HYPP)—see page 129.

Price

All things considered, your goal is to purchase the most broke, seasoned horse you can afford with suitable conformation, disposition, and movement. Keep in mind, however, that a broke and unsound horse is likely less valuable than an unbroke and sound horse. Look for the horse that is the closest to ideal. Keep in mind that seasoned geldings are best suited for beginners, as they tend to be more gentle.

Also take into consideration pedigrees and past performance. Pedigrees and performance records may add value, but how do they relate to your intended use? For example, a racehorse that has won money on the track may not be suitable as a recreational riding horse. Always keep your ultimate goal close at hand when discussing purchase price with the owner. If the horse doesn't fit your objectives, don't invest your money.

As a rule, pricing is based upon the following factors, so a good understanding of their relationship to price is in order:

- Level of training—More training normally means a higher price.

- Pedigree—The closer and more often a horse has accomplished performers in his pedigree, the higher his price.

- Past performance—Greater levels of past performance normally mean higher prices.

- Sex—Stallions and mares are normally higher-priced, due to reproductive potential.

- Age—Young horses (one to four years of age), are often higher-priced due to their "potential," although horses above the age of ten may be more valuable due to seasoning or suitability for purpose.

In the end, the amount of money you will likely pay for a horse is directly related to the goals established at the beginning of the buying process.

After the Sale—AQHA Transfer Procedures

If a horse is registered with AQHA, any transaction regarding the sale or transfer of ownership should be recorded with the Association. It is the seller's responsibility to complete the written report to be sent to AQHA immediately following the transaction, whether the horse was sold through private treaty or an auction.

It is recommended that you purchase directly from the last recorded owner listed on the registration papers. If you do not purchase the horse from the last recorded owner, then you must have a transfer signed by the recorded owner as well as transfers signed by each owner between yourself and the recorded owner. Also, make sure that the horse you are buying matches the registration papers. Note age, sex, color, and all markings. The horse's registration papers and proper fees must be included when filing the transfer report. Payment of transfer fees can be negotiated between you and the seller.

If the horse being bought is not yet registered (however, always try to buy registered horses), then the name, registration numbers of the sire and dam, and other data should be included upon a registration application, to be completed by the breeder. Understand that registration fees double after a horse is seven months old and double again after twelve months. The registration fees are doubled or more each year after that until the horse is four years old. We point this out so that you will understand the high cost of registering older horses and avoid purchasing unregistered older horses.

Owner Responsibilities

As the owner of an American Quarter Horse, care and treatment of your horse is your responsibility. The care and humane treatment of American Quarter Horses is so important to AQHA that it is listed as a major commitment of the Association.

Every American Quarter Horse shall, at all times, be treated humanely and with dignity, respect, and compassion.

Stringent rules established and enforced by AQHA demand that American Quarter Horse breeders, owners, trainers, and exhibitors are continually responsible for the well-being and humane treatment of any American Quarter Horse entrusted to their care.

Above all, the American Quarter Horse's welfare is paramount to other considerations and the continual development of procedures which ensure humane treatment of the breed and fair competition supersedes all other concerns.

Neglect and outright abuse of American Quarter Horses should be reported to the local government authorities who are responsible for enforcing local animal welfare laws. Sometimes animals are abused out of ignorance by well-intentioned people who just don't know the proper dietary and care requirements of their animals. This is why it is important to know how to care for your horse before you purchase him.

Horse ownership is a continuous learning process. The more you learn, the more you and your horse will benefit. Some of the best resources for improving your knowledge are *The Quarter Horse Journal* and *The Quarter Racing Journal*. Each issue has regular columns on horse health care by equine veterinarians and articles on management, feeding, and training tips that will increase your knowledge of proper horse care.

You'll Always Remember the Ride

Having chosen an American Quarter Horse as your equine companion, you'll find that the American Quarter Horse Association offers an array of programs and services that will add to your enjoyment of your horse. The Association sanctions approximately 2,250 American Quarter Horse shows annually across the country, which are divided into the following categories: open (for all members, youth and adult, including professionals); amateur (nonprofessional riders of similar skill levels); youth (for riders ages eighteen and under); and novice (for both youths and amateurs who have not earned 10 AQHA performance points or 40 novice points).

Additionally, AQHA offers a Horseback Riding Program, whereby riders can earn awards for simply logging their hours spent riding or driving an American Quarter Horse. Also, American Quarter Horses are eligible for many awards and incentives when competing in non-AQHA competition, including the National Cutting Horse Association, United States Dressage Federation, Pro Rodeo Cowboys Association, National High School Rodeo Association, 4-H, and American Horse Shows Association.

What do these programs mean for you as an American Quarter Horse buyer? More opportunities, which translate to greater enjoyment of your horse. Plus, should you ever choose to sell your American Quarter Horse, the opportunities, incentives, and programs AQHA offers will likely translate to a higher resale value when compared with an unregistered horse.

It is the goal of the American Quarter Horse Association to provide you with this helpful buying information to aid you in your search for the perfect equine partner, and a lifetime of enjoyment. All in all, you'll find the American Quarter Horse to be the most popular, fun, safe, accessible, and affordable equine breed around, traits that have made the breed the world's most popular.

Remember, with the American Quarter Horse, you'll always remember the ride.

Glossary

action: a horse's way of going, especially with regard to knee and leg elevation.

added money: money added to a purse by the racing association (the track), sponsors, or another source in addition to monies from nominations and entry fees.

aged: a horse that is four years or older (also see *senior*).

aid: a signal from rider to horse (see *cue*).

alfalfa: a nutrient-rich legume widely used for hay.

allowance race: a race in which eligibility is based on amounts of money won or earned or number of races won over a specified time.

also eligible: a racehorse that is officially entered but not permitted to start unless the field is reduced by scratches at scratch time.

also-ran: a racehorse that did not finish in the money (that is, one that did not finish first, second, or third).

amateur: one who rides or drives horses without receiving compensation (as distinguished from a professional).

antibiotic: a medication intended to destroy bacteria.

antiseptic: free from germs. Also, a cleanser.

Appendix horse: one that has one AQHA numbered parent and one registered Thoroughbred parent, or one AQHA parent and one Appendix parent.

Appendix Registry: that portion of the AQHA registry for horses that are American Quarter Horse–Thoroughbred crossbreeds.

artificial insemination: the process of manually implanting a mare with semen that has been collected from a stallion, as opposed to a "live cover" breeding.

ascarid: a parasitic worm.

back cinch: the rear girth of a Western saddle.

back fence: in a cutting competition, the portion of the fence directly behind the herd; the cow being worked may not be allowed to reach any portion of the back fence.

backside: a familiar term for a racetrack's stable area.

backstretch: the far side of an oval racetrack; the side opposite the finish line.

bald face: a wide white marking that extends from forehead to nostrils.

barley: a cereal grain used as feed.

barrel: the midsection of a horse.

barrel racing: a timed horse show and rodeo event in which riders maneuver around three barrels in a cloverleaf pattern.

bars: 1. the space between the horse's incisor and molar teeth in which the bit rests in the mouth; 2. the portion of the hoof between the toe and heel.

bay: a body color ranging from tan through red to reddish brown, with a black mane and tail and usually black on the lower legs.

bedding: material such as wood shavings or straw used to cover the floor of a stall or trailer.

bell boot: a rubber boot worn on the front ankle to protect against overreaching.

bench-kneed: knees that are set to the outside of the cannon bones.

Bermuda grass: a grass used for hay.

billet: a strap on a saddle to which the girth or cinch is buckled.

bird's-foot trefoil: a legume grass used for hay.

bit: the mouthpiece portion of a bridle to which the reins are fastened.

black: a body color of true black, without any light areas; the mane and tail are also black.

blacksmith: a person who shoes horses; another word for farrier.

black type: Boldface type used in sale catalogs to distinguish horses that have won or placed in a stakes race. If a horse's name appears in uppercase boldface type, he has won at least one stakes race. If the name appears in upper/lowercase boldface type, he has placed in at least one stakes. Also, a method of distinguishing successful show horses in horse show programs, sale catalogs, and so on.

blaze: a broad white vertical marking extending the length of the face, of a relatively uniform width (narrower than a bald face).

blemish: any physical imperfection, such as a scar, that does not affect a horse's serviceability or soundness.

blister beetle: an insect often found in alfalfa; its body contains toxic substances.

bluegrass: a grass used as hay or roughage.

blue roan: a coat composed of white and black hairs, with black mane, legs, and tail.

bluestem: any of several forage grasses grown in the western United States.

body brush: a heavy brush used on a horse's body coat.

bog spavin: a swelling on the front of a hock due to a collection of fluid.

bolt: to run away, usually in an out-of-control fashion.

bone spavin: a bony growth on the inside of a hock.

book: the group of mares bred to a stallion in a given year.

bosal (pronounced "bo-SAL"): a braided rawhide hackamore that applies pressure to a horse's nose and chin.

bot fly: a parasitic insect.

bottom line: the maternal side of a horse's pedigree.

bowed tendon: an injury caused by the excessive stretching and tearing of the flexor tendon, usually in a front leg.

bow-legged: a conformation fault in which the hocks are too far apart.

boxing: the action of a working cow horse holding a cow along the rail at the end of the arena.

bradoon: the snaffle bit of an English double bridle.

bran: the husk of oats used in feed or in a mash as a laxative.

break: to train a horse to accept tack and then a rider or driver; despite the unfriendly connotations, the word is still used, although the term "start" is becoming more frequently heard.

breastcollar: a piece of tack that keeps a saddle from slipping back.

breed: 1. (n) any group of animals capable of passing along its distinctive characteristics; 2. (v) to mate a horse for purposes of reproduction.

breeder: the owner of a dam at the time she is bred. (Note: This definition applies to American Quarter Horses; the breeder of a Thoroughbred is the owner at the time the mare gives birth.)

bridle: a headpiece consisting of a bit, straps, and/or curb chain to keep the bit in place, and a set of reins.

bromegrass: a variety of hay grass.

bronc (or "broncho"): an uncontrolled horse, especially one used in certain rodeo events.

browband: the part of the bridle that connects the cheekpieces across the horse's forehead.

brown: a body color of brown or black with light areas at the muzzle, eyes, flank, and inside upper legs; the mane and tail are black.

buckskin: a dark yellow or gold coat with a black mane, lower legs, and tail (buckskins have no dorsal stripe).

bursa: a medical term for a sac or pouch.

butt bar: the restraining bar across the back of a trailer stall.

buy back: a horse that was put through a public auction but did not reach his reserve bid and was therefore kept by the consignor.

calf-kneed: a conformation fault in which the forelegs' carpal joints bend backward.

calf roping: a horse show class in which a horse is judged on how well he maintains proper position while the rider ropes a calf; in rodeo, a timed event.

cannon: the bone that extends from the knee or hock to the fetlock.

canter: a three-beat gait, a slow or collected gallop (known in Western riding as "lope").

cantle: the elevated rear portion of a saddle.

capped hock: an infected swelling at the point of hock.

cast (of a horse): lying down in a stall in such a position that the horse cannot get to his feet without assistance.

caveson: the noseband of an English bridle.

cecum: the portion of the digestive system where the large intestine begins.

center-rigged (also called center-fired): rigging in which the cinch is suspended under the center of the saddle's seat.

chaps (also pronounced "shaps"): leather leggings worn as protection against thorns, brush, and other sharp objects or for leg support. Chaps may be worn in certain Western horse show classes.

cheekpiece: the portion of a bridle that extends along the horse's cheek.

chestnut: 1. a dark red or brownish red coat, mane, and tail (sometimes confused with "sorrel"); 2. one of the hard knob-like growths on the insides of a horse's legs (also called "night eye").

chip: 1. (n) a fragment of bone in a joint; 2. (v) to add an extra half stride in front of a jump.

chronic (said of a disease or condition): existing over a substantial length of time.

cinch: the strap of a Western saddle that passes under the horse's belly to hold the saddle in place.

circuit: 1. several racetracks within a certain geographic area that have complementary racing dates; 2. a geographic division used with regard to horse show awards; 3. a consecutive series of AQHA horse shows held at the same facility over a number of days.

claimer: a horse that is consistently run in claiming races.

claiming price: the price for which a horse is running in a claiming race.

claiming race: a selling race in which each entry may be bought by a licensed owner at a stipulated price or range either directly or through a trainer. Claims are made up to immediately before the race; the claimed horse becomes the property of the new owner, with the purse (if the horse wins one) going to the previous owner. If a claimed horse is entered in another claiming race over the next thirty days, it must run for a 25 percent higher claiming price (see *jail*).

class: 1. an individual event within a horse show division; 2. a horse showing all the best qualities in breeding, conformation, ability, and stamina, as in the expression "the class of the race."

closing: the time after which nominations or entries will no longer be accepted for a race.

clover: a legume grass used for hay.

coffin bone: the terminal phalanx bone of the foot.

Coggins test: the test for the presence of equine infectious anemia.

colic: 1. (n) any irritation or blockage of the intestine; 2. (v) to show signs of pain from such intestinal distress.

collect: to "gather" or "package" a horse so that the animal's stride becomes more compact (see *extend*).

colon: the portion of the large intestine from cecum to rectum.

colostrum: the milk secreted by a mare right after giving birth.

colt: an ungelded male horse under the age of four.

combination: two or three jumps set a total of forty feet or less apart.

combined training: a sport in which horses and riders compete in dressage, cross-country, and stadium jumping. Also known as "eventing." Such competitions are called "horse trials" when they take place over one or two days, or "three-day events" if that long.

condition book: a booklet written by the racing secretary and published by the racing association usually every two weeks; it lists all races, conditions, and other information pertinent to the race meeting.

conditions: the qualifications or eligibility rules for a particular race, such as age, sex, or number of previous wins.

conformation: an individual horse's physical characteristics in relation to the standards of his particular breed or type.

contracted foot: an injury caused by a shortening of the flexor tendon and characterized by an inability to extend the fetlock.

contusion: an injury to the subsurface skin but with no break to the surface skin.

cooler: a lightweight blanket used after exercise to prevent the horse from catching a chill.

corn: 1. a cereal plant whose kernels are used for feed; 2. an injury caused by repeated pressure to the sole of the foot.

coronet: the portion of the foot to which the outer hoof wall is connected.

cottonseed meal: the crushed seed of the cotton plant, used as a laxative or source of protein.

coupled entry: two or more racehorses owned or trained by the same person and running as a single wagering unit.

coupling: the space between the last ribs and the loin; American Quarter Horse conformation calls for muscular short-coupled horses.

cover: a single breeding of a mare to a stallion.

cow: 1. the familiar term for any bovine, whether a cow, heifer, steer, or calf; 2. see *cow sense.*

cow-hocked: a conformation defect in which the hocks bow inward and the feet are widely separated.

cowpea: a forage plant prevalent in Southern states of the U.S.

cow sense: the inherited ability of a horse to work cattle. Also known as "cow."

crest: the upper portion of the neck from withers to poll.

cribbing: sucking air into the lungs while biting onto an object such as a feed bin; this bad habit (often a sign of boredom) can be discouraged by means of a cribbing strap buckled snugly around the horse's neck.

crop: 1. the group of foals sired by a stallion in a given season, or a group of foals of the same ownership; 2. a riding whip with a wrist loop at the handle end.

cross-canter: to canter on one lead with the forelegs and the other lead with the hind legs (also known as "cross-firing").

croup: the horse's rump from loin to dock.

crownpiece: that portion of a bridle that goes over the horse's head.

cue: a training term for a signal from rider to horse (see *aid*).

curb: 1. a hard swelling of the ligament, tendon, or skin below the point of hock on the cannon of a hind leg; 2. a bit with a port and cheek shanks, frequently worn by Western horses.

curb chain (or strap): a chain (or strap) worn with a curb bit under the horse's jaw.

curry: to clean a horse with a currycomb. Also, a general term for cleaning a horse's body, mane, and tail.

currycomb: a grooming implement used to remove body dirt.

cutter: 1. the rider in a cutting horse show event; 2. a participant in cutter and chariot racing.

cutting: a horse show class in which a horse separates (or "cuts") a cow from the herd and then prevents it from returning to the herd.

dally: to wrap a lariat rope around the saddle horn after a steer or calf has been roped; from the Spanish *dar la vuelta*, "to make a turn" (of the rope).

dally team roping: a horse show event in which the horse is judged on his ability to maintain position as the mount of either the header or the heeler in team roping; also, a timed event in rodeo referred to as team roping.

dam: the female parent, or broodmare.

dead heat: two or more horses crossing the finish line too close to tell which finished ahead of the other(s); all horses involved in a dead heat are deemed tied for that finishing position.

declaration: withdrawing an entered horse from a race before the closing of overnight entries.

diagonal: the sequence of footfalls at the trot. A rider who sits when the horse's right foreleg strikes the ground is said to be posting on the right diagonal when the horse is going counterclockwise.

direct rein: rein pressure exerted in a straight line from the rider's hand to the horse's mouth.

distaff: a racing designation for fillies and mares.

dock: the fleshy root of the tail.

double bridle: an English bridle that contains both a curb and a snaffle bit.

drag: 1. to bring up the rear while moving or driving a herd of cattle; 2. to prepare the surface of an arena for competition.

draw: the horse's position in a horse show event's order of go, determining the order in which it will perform.

dressage (pronounced "dreh-SAHZ"; French for "training"): the systematic schooling of a horse. Also, a competition in which horses and riders perform a prescribed sequence of movements.

D-ring: any of the D-shaped rings on a saddle to which the latigo or breastcollar is laced or buckled. Also, a variety of snaffle bit.

driving: 1. training a horse to pull a cart or another vehicle, or to accept the bit without being ridden; 2. winning a race with effort.

dropdown: a racehorse that is meeting a lower class of rivals than previously faced.

dry work: the familiar term for the initial reining work portion of a working cow horse class.

edema: a swelling caused by a gathering of fluid.

elbow: the joint at the upper end of the foreleg.

embryo: a foal in the initial stage of development inside the womb.

embryo transfer: the procedure in which an embryo is implanted into the womb of a second ("host") mare.

encephalomyelitis: an inflammation of the brain and spinal cord.

engagement: the degree to which a horse's hind end propels him forward and lightens his front end.

English: referring to a style of riding characterized by a flat, hornless saddle, as distinguished from Western riding. Also, the equipment used in this style.

enter: to enroll a horse in a race, horse show, rodeo, or other competition.

entry: 1. a horse that has been made eligible to run in a particular race; 2. two or more horses enrolled in the same race that have common ties of ownership, leasing, or training (see *coupled entry*); 3. a horse entered in a horse show.

entry fee: money paid to enroll a horse in a race.

equine infectious anemia: A circulatory disease, also known as swamp fever, caused by bacteria and detected by the Coggins test; frequently referred to as "EIA."

equitation: another word for horsemanship.

equitation over fences: a horse show class in which amateur or youth riders are judged on their form and control over a course of jumps.

ergot: a small callus at the back of the fetlock joint.

esophagus: the tube that connects the mouth and the stomach.

estrus: the period during which a mare is sexually receptive; at that time the mare is said to be "in season" or "in heat."

extend: to encourage a horse to open his stride (see *collect*).

farrier: a person who shoes horses (also known as a "horseshoer" or "blacksmith").

fault: a penalty in jumper classes for knocking down or refusing to jump an obstacle, or for exceeding the time limit.

fence work: the familiar term for the second portion of the working cow horse class, in which the horse works the cow.

fender: the wide panel between the seat and stirrup of a Western saddle.

fescue: a variety of hay grass.

fetlock: the joint between the pastern and the cannon bones.

fiador (sometimes pronounced "Theodore"): a part of the hackamore that goes over the horse's poll and knots behind the jaw to keep the bosal in place.

filly: a female horse under the age of four and that has not had a foal.

fistula: one of a variety of inflammations characterized by the formation of passages that lead up to the skin.

fistulous withers: a swelling of bursa at the withers.

fit: in peak condition.

flake: a section of baled hay.

float: to file down the sharp edges of teeth.

flying change of lead: a switch of leads at the canter or lope without the horse's breaking stride to the trot or walk.

foal: a colt or filly that has not yet been weaned.

forearm: the portion of foreleg from the elbow to the knee.

forging: interference in which the hind feet strike the forefeet; also known as "overreaching."

form: an assessment of a racehorse's ability based on past performance and current workouts. A horse that is considered competitively fit is said to be "in good form."

forward-rigged: rigging in which the cinch is suspended from any point ahead of the center of the saddle.

forward seat: the jumping position in which the rider's weight stays over the horse's center of gravity.

foul: an act by a racehorse or jockey that interferes with another horse during the running of a race and results in disqualification.

founder (also known as "laminitis"): an inflammation and separation of the laminae, the walls of the foot, that often leads to rotation of the coffin bone.

fresh: 1. (said of cattle) not previously used for cutting or team penning; 2. frisky, such as a horse that's "feeling his oats."

frog: the V-shaped soft portion of the bottom of the foot.

full board: a full-service boarding arrangement that includes grooming and turnout exercise (see *rough board*).

full brothers/sisters: horses that have the same sire and dam.

full-forward (also known as front-fired): rigging in which the cinch is suspended below the pommel of the saddle.

full-rigging (also known as double-rigging or rim-fire): rigging in which roping saddle's two cinch straps are attached to the saddle, each to its own ring.

futurity: a stakes race for two-year-olds or horse show event for three-year-olds for which owners pay a nominating and further sustaining fees.

gait: one of the distinctive movements of a horse in motion. The American Quarter Horse moves at the walk, the jog or trot, the lope or canter, and the gallop.

gallop: the horse's natural running gait.

galloping boot: routinely worn by racehorses, a device that protects the ankle, shin, and tendons against abrasion by the racetrack surface.

THE AMERICAN QUARTER HORSE

Galwayne's groove: the groove in the upper incisor teeth that grows with age.

gaskin: the portion of the hind leg between the stifle and the hock.

gelding: a castrated male horse.

gestation: the period between conception and birth, approximately eleven months for a horse.

get: the offspring of a stallion.

girth: 1. the circumference of a horse's body behind his elbow; 2. a strap that passes under a horse's belly to secure the saddle in place.

girth mark: a scar usually signified by white hair behind the foreleg.

grade: a horse of no specific breed; an unregistrable horse.

graded race: one of a ranking of races according to quality of horses and/or purse sizes, with Grade 1 (G1) as the highest, Grade 2 (G2) the next highest, and so on.

granddam: the mother of a horse's dam (also known as the "second dam").

grandsire: the father of the horse's sire.

gray: a mixture of white with any other-colored hairs. Gray horses are often born solid-colored or almost solid-colored and grow lighter with age as more white hairs appear.

grazing bit: a curb bit with rear-curving shanks.

green: untrained or just beginning training.

green working hunter: a horse show class for horses in their first year of showing over fences or those that have not yet earned more than 10 points in working hunter or jumping classes.

grullo: a smoky or mouse-colored body color (not a mixture of black and white hairs, but each hair mouse-colored) with black mane and tail and usually a black dorsal stripe and black on the lower legs.

gullet: the arched open portion of a Western saddle below the horn or pommel.

hack: a pleasure ride.

hackamore: a bitless bridle that controls the horse by pressure on his nose. A hackamore can be either of the bosal or the mechanical variety.

half pass: a lateral maneuver in which the horse simultaneously moves sideways and forward.

halt: the position of a horse that is standing still.

halter: 1. the bridle-like apparatus worn to facilitate leading or restraining the horse; 2. another term for a horse show conformation or breeding class.

hand: the unit by which horses are measured from their withers to the ground; one hand equals four inches.

handicap: a race in which weights are assigned according to the horses' past performance and present form. The racing secretary assigns the weights to create a theoretical dead heat among all horses in the race.

handicapper: the racetrack official, usually the racing secretary, who assigns weights.

handicapping: assessing the relative merits of the horses in a race in order to predict the winner.

handily: winning a race easily.

handle: the aggregate amount of money passing through the pari-mutuel machines for a given period (one race, the entire day's racing, and so on).

hay: dried grass used as to feed livestock as a source of roughage.

hay grass: any of various species of grass rich in carbohydrate (see *legume*).

head: 1. (n) a margin between racehorses equal to the length of a head; 2. (v) to place a horse in front of a cow to stop or to force the cow to change directions.

header: 1. in team roping, the contestant who ropes the steer's horns; 2. in chariot racing, the assistant who makes sure the horses are facing straight ahead at the start of the race.

headstall: the part of the Western bridle that fits over the horse's head and to which the bit is attached.

heat: 1. the condition of a mare that is ready to be bred; ovulating or in estrus; 2. one of a series of qualifying horse races.

heaves: a disease, similar to asthma in humans, characterized by difficulty in breathing. A horse that suffers from it is often referred to as being "heavy" (pronounced "HEE-vee").

heel: the rear portion of the foot.

heeler: in team roping, the contestant who ropes the steer's hind legs.

hinging: a horse's movement from side to side in anticipation of a cow's next move.

hitch: 1. (n) the device on the back of the towing vehicle to which the trailer is attached; 2. (v) to secure (a horse) to a cart or another driving vehicle.

hitching: braided horsehair decoration on a Western bridle.

hobble: a restraint strap attached to a horse's legs to prevent the animal from wandering away.

hock: the joint of the hind leg between the gaskin and the cannon bones; the equivalent of a human elbow or knee.

homebred: a horse bred by his owner or in the breeder's home state.

hoof: the hard inclusive portion of the horse's foot.

hook: a sharp protrusion on a cheek tooth, routinely filed away by floating the tooth.

horn: the upright projection on the front of a Western saddle, especially designed to dally a rope (see *dally*).

horsemanship: the skill of a rider in terms of form and control.

hunter: a horse show division in which horses are judged on their style of moving and jumping ability suitable for the foxhunting field.

hunter clip: a pattern of clipping a coat in which all the body hair is trimmed except for a patch below the saddle and the lower legs.

hunter hack: a horse show class in which horses are first judged over two low fences and then at the walk, trot, and canter.

hunter under saddle: a horse show class in which horses are judged on their ability to move at the walk, trot, and canter as a hunter-type horse.

hunt seat equitation: a horse show class in which riders are judged on their English-style horsemanship form and control.

identification: a system of recognition of several types of markings noted on a horse's certificate of registration and including coat color, lip tattoos, markings, scars, and brands.

in-and-out: a combination of two horse show fences set one stride apart.

indirect rein: rein pressure exerted toward the rider's opposite hand.

influenza: a highly contagious viral disease.

inquiry: a stewards' investigation to see whether a foul occurred during the running of a race.

intramuscular: an injection administered into a muscle.

intravenous: an injection administered into a vein.

invitational: a race or horse show open only to those entries that are asked to take part.

irons: a term for stirrups on an English or racing saddle.

jail: the thirty-day period after a racehorse has been claimed, in which it must run for a claiming price 25 percent higher than the price for which it was claimed.

jockey: 1. (n) a professional race rider; 2. (v) to maneuver a horse during a race.

jockey agent: a person employed by a jockey to secure mounts.

jog: the Western term for trot, especially a slow, collected trot.

jumper: a horse show division in which horses are scored on their ability to jump fences without regard to form or style.

jump-off: an additional, tie-breaking round in a jumping competition.

junior: in AQHA show competition, a horse that is five years old or younger.

juvenile: a two-year-old, the youngest age at which an American Quarter Horse is eligible to race.

keeper: 1. a notched leather strap by which a billet is held in place; 2. a leather loop that secures the end of a strap.

knee: the joint in the foreleg between the forearm and cannon bone.

laceration: any cut or puncture of the flesh.

laminae: the parts of the foot that attach the wall of the hoof to the coffin bone.

laminitis: see *founder*.

latigo: the strap that fastens the cinch on a Western saddle.

layup: a period of time in which a horse is sent away for rest or recuperation.

lead: the foreleg that precedes the other at the lope (or canter) and gallop. A loping/cantering horse is described as being on either his right or left lead.

leather: the strap by which the stirrup of an English saddle is attached to the saddle.

legume: any of the nitrogen-rich grasses used for hay.

leg wraps: protective material on a horse's front legs to prevent injuries.

leg yield: any lateral or sideways movement, such as a side pass.

lespedeza: a legume grass used for hay.

linseed meal: a meal made from flaxseeds, used as a laxative or a source of protein.

lockjaw: see *tetanus*.

loin: the portion of the back between the back and the croup.

longe (pronounced and sometimes spelled "lunge"): to exercise a horse by urging him to circle around his handler at the end of a rope or canvas or leather "longe line" attached to the halter or bridle.

lope: a three-beat gait; a slow or collected gallop (called "canter" in English riding).

maiden: a horse of either sex that has never won a race.

mare: a female horse of four years or older, or female horse of any age that has given birth.

markings: the pattern of marks, usually white, on a horse's head and legs that help in identification.

martingale: a strap between the horse's forelegs and attached from the girth to either the caveson (standing martingale) or the reins (running martingale); its purpose is to control excess head movement.

match race: a challenge race between two horses.

maternal grandsire: the sire of a horse's dam.

mecate: the portion of a hackamore that ties to the back of the bosal and acts as reins.

medication list: a list kept by the racetrack veterinarian and posted at the track showing which horses have been treated with legally permitted medication.

mites: tiny parasitic insects.

mixed sale: a sale consisting of more than one type of horses, such as yearlings, broodmares, horses in training, and so on.

monkey mouth: an undershot upper jaw (see *parrot-mouth*).

mount fee: the flat fee earned by a jockey who has not ridden any of the top three finishers in a race (where he might earn a percentage of the purse).

muck out: to clean a stall of manure and soiled bedding.

mustang: the wild horse native to the Western United States.

mutton-withered: a horse with poorly defined, flat withers.

muzzle: the portion of a horse's face between the nostrils and the upper lip.

navicular: a tiny bone in the coffin joint of the foot. Also, an inflammatory condition of that bone.

near side: the left side of a horse.

neck: the portion of the body connecting the horse's head to his shoulders. Also, a margin between racehorses equal to the length of a neck.

neck (or bearing) rein: to apply outside rein pressure against the horse's neck in the direction of the turn.

neck rope: in calf roping, a circle of rope around a horse's neck, through which the roper's rope passes from the saddle horn to the roper's hands. The system prevents a horse from running off after the roper dismounts.

night eye: another name for *chestnut* (definition 2).

nose: the front portion of the head below the nostrils. Also, the distance between racehorses equal to the length of a nose.

oats: a cereal grain widely used as feed.

objection: a claim of foul lodged by a horse's jockey, trainer, or owner before the race has been declared official.

off side: the right side of a horse.

opening (or leading) rein: to apply rein pressure by moving the rein hand out to the side (see *neck rein*).

orchard grass: a type of hay grass.

osslets: bony growths on the ankle.

overnight: a race for which entries close seventy-two hours or less before the post time for the first race on the day that race is to be run.

overreaching: see *forging*.

oxbow: a Western stirrup with a rounded bottom.

oxer: an obstacle in a hunter or jumper class composed of two or more elements that give the obstacle width.

pace: a two-beat lateral gait (for example, the right foreleg and the right hind leg move simultaneously).

paddle out: a movement defect in which at least one foot swings to the outside in a paddle-like motion.

palomino: a golden yellow coat with white mane and tail.

papers: common term for a horse's AQHA certificate of registration.

park gait: in pleasure driving, a stylishly elegant medium trot.

parrot-mouth: an overshot upper jaw that AQHA considers an undesirable trait.

parturition: the act of giving birth.

pastern: the portion of the lower leg between the fetlock and the foot.

past performances: 1. information published by the *Daily Racing Form* or the racetrack that gives complete information on a horse's most recent races and workouts for handicapping purposes; 2. in horse showing, the record of a horse's AQHA points and awards.

patrol judge: an official stationed at a point around the track who observes the running of the race and reports any possible infractions to the stewards.

Pelham: a one-piece combination curb and snaffle bit.

penning: see *team penning*.

pigeon-toed: a conformation defect in which the toes of both forelegs angle in toward each other.

pig-eyed: a conformation defect in which small, round eyes are set too close together.

pinworm: a small worm that infests the intestines and the rectum.

pivot: in reining work, a 90-degree turn with one stationary foot acting as a pivot.

placenta: the organ formed in the uterus that provides for the nourishment of the fetus.

placing judge: the racetrack official in charge of determining the order of finish.

pleasure driving: a horse show class in which horses harnessed to a two-wheel cart are judged on their movement and manners.

point: 1. the widest part of a body feature, such as point of hip, point of shoulder, or point of hock; 2. a sharp edge on a cheek tooth, routinely filed away by floating.

points: the mane, leg, and tail colors when different from body color.

pole bending: a timed horse show event in which horses and riders slalom down and back between six poles.

poll: the highest portion of a horse's head behind its ears.

poll evil: a bacterial infection of the bursa in the poll area.

pommel: the elevated front portion of an English or Western saddle.

port: the arched portion of the mouthpiece of a curb or Pelham bit.

post: 1. (n) the starting line of a race; 2. (v) to rise out of and sink back into the saddle at the trot to counteract that gait's impact on the rider.

post-legged: a conformation fault characterized by overly straight angulation between the gaskin and cannon, with a correspondingly straight hock joint.

post parade: the prerace procedure when horses come on the racetrack and pass in front of the grandstands for review by the spectators.

post position: the order of racehorses in the starting gate, indicated by numbers that begin with the stall at the rail and then go outward.

prairie grass: a variety of hay grass.

preference list: a system in which horses with the longest time since their last race or chance to race are given the higher preference for the next race entered; the system is intended to ensure fairness.

progeny: the offspring of a male or a female horse.

program: 1. a publication that includes all vital information on the day's racing card, including race number, conditions, distance, types of betting, horses' names, numbers, jockeys, and weights; 2. a listing of horse show entries usually available at large shows.

protest: a written complaint signed by the protester against any horse that has started in a race, and made to the stewards within forty-eight hours of the running of the race.

public trainer: a trainer whose services are available to the public and who trains horses owned by more than one owner.

pulley rein: an "emergency brake" stopping technique in which the rider braces one hand against the horse's withers while pulling back and up with the rein in the other hand.

purse: the prize monies offered in a competition. In racing, purses are generally made up of the added money based on handle and/or sponsor's contribution, and any nomination, sustaining, or entry fees.

qualifying points: the number of points that must be accumulated in each event over the year to become eligible for the AQHA or AQHYA World Championship Shows.

quarter crack: a crack in the hoof extending downward from the coronet toward the sole (also known as "sand crack").

quartering (of a roping horse): pivoting on one hind leg to pull a steer ninety degrees from the direction the steer had been moving.

racing board/commission: a state-appointed body in charge of regulating and supervising the conduct of racing in that state or province.

racing secretary: the official responsible for establishing the conditions of races and general administrative duties.

rate: in working cow horse and roping classes, the ability of a horse to maintain relative speed and position on a cow by speeding up or slowing down as necessary.

rectum: the end of the intestine that ends in the anus.

red dun: a form of dun with a yellowish or flesh-colored body color; a mane and tail that are red or reddish, flaxen, white, or mixed; a red or reddish dorsal stripe and usually red or reddish zebra stripes on the legs; and a transverse stripe over the withers.

red roan: a more or less uniform mixture of white with red hairs on a large portion of the body, but usually darker on the head and lower legs. A red roan can have a red, black, or flaxen mane and/or tail.

reed canary grass: a hay grass.

registration certificate: a document issued by the AQHA registry that certifies a horse is a duly registered; the document also includes the birthdate and all identification markings of that animal, registration number, owner, breeder, and the state in which the horse was foaled.

reining: a horse show class in which horses are judged on their ability to execute a prearranged pattern of such maneuvers as rundowns, sliding stops, rollbacks, circles, and spins.

reins: the straps extending from the bridle to the rider's hands, used to guide the horse's head.

restricted stakes: a stakes race in which conditions limit the participants based upon certain criteria such as state-bred horses or horses purchased through or consigned to a certain sale.

rhinopneumonitis: a contagious upper respiratory condition.

rigging: the manner by which one or more cinches are attached to a Western saddle.

ringbone: a bony growth on one or both sides of the pastern.

road gait: in pleasure driving, an extended trot.

rollback: a reining pattern movement in which the horse halts, turns 180 degrees while pivoting on the inside hind leg, and then moves off to continue the pattern.

romal (pronounced "roh-MAHL"): a type of rein in which the straps coming from the bit join into one rein at the point where the rider holds them. Also, the style of riding in which the rider uses such a rein.

rough board: a boarding arrangement in which the horse is fed and watered and his stall mucked out, with all other chores the responsibility of the horse's owner (see *full board*).

rowel: the pointed wheel of a spur.

rug: an old British term for a horse blanket.

rundown: 1. a reining pattern movement in which the horse lopes or gallops from one end of the arena to the other; 2. a type of protective bandage.

rye: a cereal used as feed.

rye grass: a hay grass also used as straw.

saddle: the piece of tack in which a rider sits.

saddle mark: a scar with white hairs behind the withers.

scotching (of a horse): anticipating a stop before the rider gives the cue for one.

scratch: the act of withdrawing an entered horse from a race or horse show after the close of entries.

scratch time: the deadline established by the racing office for horses to be scratched prior to the printing of the official program. Generally, scratch time is twenty-four hours before race day; for stakes races, scratch time can be up to fifteen minutes before post time.

scurf: scaly or encrusted skin (also known as "scarf").

seat: 1. the rider's position in the saddle; 2. a specific style of riding, such as Western stock seat or English hunt seat.

seedy toe: a separation of the wall of the hoof from the laminae.

senior: a horse that is six years or older according to AQHA standards.

settle: 1. to allow a horse to relax at the halt; 2. to cause a herd of cattle to become accustomed to the arena.

sex allowance: the practice of allowing fillies and mares to carry less weight when racing against male horses.

shadow roll: a piece of sheepskin placed across a racehorse's nose to block the sight of distracting shadows on the ground.

shank: 1. the long lever-like pieces of a curb bit to which the reins are attached; 2. the rope or strap by which a haltered horse is led (also known as "lead shank").

shed row: the racetrack stable area with barns and walkways under a roof.

shoulder: the part of the body between the neck and barrel to which the forelegs are attached.

showmanship: a horse show class for youth and amateur exhibitors in which the halter class skills of the exhibitors are judged.

sickle-hocked: a conformation fault in which the hind legs from the hocks down stand under the body.

sidebone: a hardening of the cartilages of (usually) the forefeet.

side pass: a maneuver in which the horse moves to the side with no forward or backward motion.

silks: the jockey's distinctive racing shirt and cap that identify an owner's colors or a horse's post position.

skid boots: protective devices worn on hind-leg pasterns and fetlocks. Also known as "sliding boots" (for the protection they give against the abrasion of sliding stops).

skirt: the portion of a saddle under a Western saddle's cantle or over the stirrup bars of an English saddle.

snaffle: a bit with a straight or jointed mouthpiece and no port.

snip: a white marking near the nostrils.

sock: a white marking that extends from the coronet halfway up the cannon bone, or halfway to the knee on the foreleg, or halfway to the hock on the hind leg.

sole: the bottom or undersection of the foot, surrounded by the hoof.

sophomore: 1. a three-year-old racehorse; 2. a horse in his second season of competition.

sorrel: a reddish or copper-red body color; the mane and tail are usually the same color as the body, although they may be flaxen. The predominant color of American Quarter Horses, sorrel is often considered a Western term for "chestnut."

sound: in healthy condition and free from lameness.

soybeans: a legume plant used as feed.

spavin: an enlargement of the hock (see *bog spavin* and *bone spavin*).

speculum: an apparatus used to keep a horse's mouth open, especially during dental work.

spin: a reining maneuver in which the horse makes one or more 360-degree turns while pivoting around an inside hind foot.

splay-footed: a conformation fault in which the toes point outward and away from each other.

splint: a bony growth on the sides of the cannon bone of a front leg.

split reins: separated, unjoined reins.

stacked (said of pant legs): having several accordion-like folds between the knees and cuffs when the wearer is standing. Many Western riders favor this style because the pants are long enough to cover the entire length of the wearer's legs when on horseback.

stakes: a race in which the owners of entered horses post a nominating and starting fee, which is added to the purse; stakes races usually attract higher-caliber horses.

stakes-placed: finishing second or third in a stakes race.

stakes producer: a mare that has produced at least one foal that finished first, second, or third in a stakes race.

stakes winner: a horse that has won a stakes race.

stallion: an ungelded male horse of three years or older.

star: a white marking on the forehead.

star-gazing (of a horse): carrying his head too high.

starter: the race official in charge of assuring a fair start.

starter's allowance: an allowance or handicap race restricted to horses that have started for a specific claiming price.

state-bred: a horse bred and/or foaled in a U.S. state in a manner that meets the criteria to be eligible to compete in special races or purse supplements.

steward: one of three officials who preside over a race meeting. Stewards rule on claims of foul, conduct inquiries, and enforce other regulations.

stifle: the joint between the thigh and the gaskin.

stirrups: metal or wooden devices in which the rider places his or her feet.

stocking: a white marking extending from fetlock to knee or hock.

stomach: the organ for storing and digesting food.

stop: in reining and working cow horse classes, a halt from the gallop in which the horse shifts his weight to his haunches and slides to a complete stop.

strangles: contagious abscess of the lymph nodes or other parts of the body (also known as "distemper").

strawberry roan: a nickname for a red roan.

stretch: the straight portion of the racetrack leading to the finish line.

stretch call: the position of the horses at designated pole markers, depending upon the length of the race.

stride: the full length of step at a particular gait.

stringhalt: exaggerated involuntary flexing of the hock joint in motion.

strip: a narrow marking extending vertically between the forehead and nostrils.

strongyles: a parasitic disease transmitted by bloodworms and causing anemia.

subcutaneous: located below the skin.

Sudan grass: a variety of hay grass.

surcingle: a strap that fastens around the girth to hold a blanket in place or as extra security for a racing saddle.

swamp fever: see *equine infectious anemia*.

tack: a collective term for saddles, bridles, and other horsewear.

tapadero: a leather protection over the front of a Western stirrup.

tapeworm: a flat parasitic worm.

tattoo: a form of identification placed under a horse's upper lip. The tattoo's letter/number combination is also entered on the animal's AQHA registration certificate.

team penning: a horse show event in which a team of three riders sorts three specific cows from a herd and then drives them into an enclosure (the pen) at the opposite end of the arena.

tetanus: a severe infection characterized by muscular rigidity; also called "lockjaw."

thoroughpin: an abnormal swelling above the hock joint that causes lameness.

throatlatch: 1. the portion of the body between the neck and the lower jawbone; 2. the bridle strap that buckles under a horse's throat.

thrush: an infection of the frog of the foot.

tie-down: Western tack's standing martingale.

timothy: a type of hay.

toe: the front portion of the foot.

toed-in: see *pigeon-toed*.

toed-out: see *splay-footed*.

tongue strap: a strap or tape bandage used to tie down a racehorse's tongue as a prevention against choking.

trace clip: a pattern of clipping in which just the belly, girth, and chest areas are trimmed.

trail: a horse show class in which horses are judged on their ability to deal with the sort of obstacles encountered during a trail ride.

trainer: the person who conditions and prepares horses for racing or showing, or who starts a horse in training.

tree: the wooden, metal, or plastic skeletal frame of a saddle.

trial: 1. a race in which eligible horses compete to determine the finalists in a nomination race; 2. a combined training competition that takes place over one or two days (also called "horse trial"); 3. any dressage competition.

trot: the two-beat gait in which the horse's feet move in diagonal pairs (also known as "jog").

tush: a canine tooth.

twitch: a restraining device that exerts a distracting pressure on the animal's lip; particularly used in conjunction with medical examination or treatment.

unsoundness: an imperfection or a condition, such as lameness, that prevents a horse from being usable.

valet: an attendant who takes care of a jockey's equipment.

vertical: any type of jump composed of a single element of width (see *oxer*).

Vetrap: the brand name of a type of elastic bandage used for medical treatment and also to wrap legs for support.

Visalia: a Western bell-shaped stirrup with an inch-wide tread.

wall: the hard supportive structure of the hoof.

warm-up: 1. a prerace slow gallop or canter to the starting gate; 2. any preliminary exercise to loosen a horse up for further physical activity.

washy (said of a horse): broken out in a nervous sweat before a race.

weanling: a young horse that has been recently separated from his mother. The term applies until the animal becomes a yearling on January 1 of the following year.

weigh-in: the postrace procedure in which the clerk of scales makes certain that all jockeys carried their correct assigned weight.

weigh-out: the prerace procedure in which the clerk of scales makes certain that all jockeys will carry their correct assigned weight.

weight-for-age: a fixed scale of weights to be carried by horses according to age, sex, distance of race, and season of year.

weight pad: the pad worn under a racehorse's saddle that contains slots for the lead bars that make up any difference between the jockey's actual weight and the weight the horse has been assigned to carry.

Western horsemanship: a horse show class in which the rider's form and control are judged.

Western pleasure: a horse show class in which the horse's performance as an enjoyable mount is judged.

Western riding: a horse show class in which the horse is judged on the quality of gaits and especially on precise lead changes.

Weymouth: the curb bit of an English double bridle.

wheat: a cereal, the stalks of which are used as straw.

wind galls: swellings on the side of the tendon just above the fetlock (also known as "wind puffs").

wing-in: a movement fault in splay-footed horses that causes the legs to interfere with each other (see *paddle-footed*).

winner's circle: the enclosure adjacent to the race oval where a winning horse is brought for a ceremonial photo with the owner, trainer, and their friends.

withers: the highest part of the back, where it meets the base of the neck.

wolf tooth: a premolar that is unnecessary for chewing and is routinely removed before a horse begins training.

working cow horse: a horse show class in which horses are judged first on their reining ability and then on how they control a cow.

working hunter: a horse show class in which the horse's jumping style over fences is judged.

wrap: a leg bandage that furnishes support and/or protection.

yearling: a horse between the ages of one and two.

Index

DATE DUE

SEP 9 1999	
SEP 1 4 1999	
SEP 8 2000	
OCT 6 2000	
OCT 3 0 2001	
FEB 1 1 2003 LC	
OCT 1 8 2004	
JAN 2 4 2006	
OCT 1 2 REC'D	